Teacher's Annotated Edit

Grade **2**

Scott Foresman

The Grammar & Writing Book

ISBN: 0–328–20485–4

5 6 7 8 9 10 V000 12 11 10 09 08 07

PEARSON
Scott
Foresman

Editorial Offices: Glenview, Illinois • Parsippany, New Jersey • New York, New York
Sales Offices: Boston, Massachusetts • Duluth, Georgia • Glenview, Illinois
Coppell, Texas • Sacramento, California • Mesa, Arizona

Table of Contents

Test Tips

Overview

The Grammar and Writing Book is designed to support and enhance the grammar and writing strand in *Reading Street*. The book includes weekly grammar and writing lessons, a Writer's Guide, writing-for-tests lessons, and a Grammar Patrol handbook.

Writer's Guide

- The Writer's Guide gives students strategies and models for effective writing.

- There is a lesson for each of the following writing traits: Focus/Ideas, Organization/Paragraphs, Voice, Word Choice, Sentences, and Conventions.

- Each lesson has leveled exercises to reinforce the skill.

- There are rubrics for each of the four major modes of writing: Narrative, Descriptive, Persuasive, and Expository.

- 4-, 3-, 2-, and 1-point models for each mode are provided with customized rubrics.

Weekly Grammar and Writing Lessons

PAGE 1	PAGE 2	PAGE 3	PAGE 4	PAGE 5	PAGE 6
Grammar Instruction and Leveled Exercise A	**Grammar** Leveled Exercises B and C	**Grammar** Test Preparation	**Grammar** Review	**Writer's Craft**	**Writing Model**

- Thirty 6-page lessons correspond to the grammar and writing lessons in the Teacher's Edition of *Reading Street*.

- Leveled exercises reflect the topics and themes in the corresponding reading lessons.

- Review and assessment are provided in the standardized test format.

- The writing pages provide support for the end-of-unit process writing lesson in the Teacher's Edition of *Reading Street*. Leveled exercises culminate in a brief writing assignment that relates to the end-of-unit product. For Grade 2, the writing products are as follows:

  Unit 1—Personal Narrative (Story About Me)
  Unit 2—How-to Report
  Unit 3—Compare/Contrast Paragraph
  Unit 4—Descriptive Paragraph
  Unit 5—Persuasive Letter
  Unit 6—Research Report

Writing for Tests

- Lessons teach test-taking strategies for developing skills such as understanding a prompt, finding a topic, organizing ideas, developing and elaborating ideas, and writing a strong beginning and ending.

- Lessons support the end-of-unit process writing lessons in the Teacher's Edition of *Reading Street*.

- Five prompts duplicate the prompts in the end-of-unit process writing lesson.

- A student model illustrates an exemplary piece of writing.

- Following the model is an explanation of why it merits a top score.

Grammar Patrol

- This handbook includes sections on grammar, capitalization, punctuation, spelling, and handwriting.

Instructional Planner

	Day 1	Day 2
2-3 minutes **Daily Fix-Its**	Use the Daily Fix-Its on pp. TR1–TR10 or the Daily Fix-It Transparencies.	Use the Daily Fix-Its on pp. TR1–TR10 or the Daily Fix-It Transparencies.
15-20 minutes **Grammar and Writing**	Introduce the Grammar Skill. • Guided Practice • Leveled, Independent Practice	Test Preparation • Grammar Practice • Standardized Test Format

The Grammar and Writing Book and *The Grammar and Writing Book Teacher's Annotated Edition* provide many other resources for language arts instruction.

Additional Grammar Practice
Extra Practice for Differentiated Instruction, pp. TR11–TR16

Day 3	Day 4	Day 5
Use the Daily Fix-Its on pp. TR1–TR10 or the Daily Fix-It Transparencies.	Use the Daily Fix-Its on pp. TR1–TR10 or the Daily Fix-It Transparencies.	Use the Daily Fix-Its on pp. TR1–TR10 or the Daily Fix-It Transparencies.
Review the Grammar Skill.	Writer's Craft Lesson • Improve Writing Skills	Examine a Writing Model. • Key features of different types of writing

Additional Writing Resources in the Student Book
• Writing Traits in the Writer's Guide, pp. 2–25
• Rubrics and Models for Narrative, Descriptive, Persuasive, and Expository Writing, pp. 26–45
• Check Your Writing, pp. 46–48
• Writing for Tests, pp. 231–243

Additional Writing Resources in the Teacher's Annotated Edition
• Writing Traits and Writing Features, pp. VIII–IX
• Strategies and Activities, pp. TR17–TR19
• Prompts for Each Writing Mode, pp. TR20–TR21
• Alternative Rubrics, pp. TR22–TR25
• Self-Evaluation Guides, pp. TR26–TR27

Writing Traits

Traits

- Focus/Ideas
- Organization/ Paragraphs
- Voice
- Word Choice
- Sentences
- Conventions

Focus/Ideas refers to the main purpose for writing and the details that make the subject clear and interesting. It includes development of ideas through support and elaboration.

Organization/Paragraphs refers to the overall structure that guides readers through a piece of writing. Within that structure, transitions show how ideas, sentences, and paragraphs are connected.

Voice shows the writer's unique personality and establishes a connection between writer and reader. Voice, which contributes to style, should be suited to the audience and the purpose for writing.

Word Choice is the use of precise, vivid words to communicate effectively and naturally. It helps create style through the use of specific nouns, lively verbs and adjectives, and accurate, well-placed modifiers.

Sentences covers strong, well-built sentences that vary in length and type. Skillfully written sentences have pleasing rhythms and flow fluently.

Conventions refers to mechanical correctness and includes grammar, usage, spelling, punctuation, capitalization, and paragraphing.

Writing Features

The features below combine to make a writing task successful.
The diagram to the left shows how 6-trait writing used in
Scott Foresman Reading Street correlates to these features.

Traits

- **Focus/Ideas**
- **Organization/ Paragraphs**
- **Voice**
- **Word Choice**
- **Sentences**
- **Conventions**

Focus is the topic/subject of a piece of writing in response to a prompt. It is determined by the purpose, audience, and context of a written work. Writers must establish a focus that responds to each writing task. The topic/subject should be clear, although it need not be stated explicitly.

Organization is the movement and relatedness of ideas. In a well-organized composition, ideas are complete and developed. There is a consistency of purpose shown in features that contribute toward a beginning, middle, and end. The progression of ideas is clear and smooth, often with connectors that show relationships. There are no gaps that leave readers confused.

Support and Elaboration is the use of specific details that develop the topic/subject and make it clear to readers. Key concepts are related ideas and sufficient supporting details. This means that supporting details must be related to the subject matter and sufficiently developed to present it fully. Effective elaboration excludes details that are off the topic, vague, underdeveloped, or repetitive.

Style is the effective use of language as seen through word choice and sentence fluency. Such language is compatible with the purpose, audience, and context of the writing task. Precise words, along with their arrangement and sound, contribute to an effective style. A variety of sentence types and lengths adds interest and rhythms to writing and helps convey ideas.

Conventions covers correct grammar, usage, mechanics, and sentence formation. Good writers show reasonable control over specific areas such as agreement, tense, capitalization, punctuation, and spelling, and write in complete sentences.

Writer's Guide

Focus/Ideas

My class and I talk about an amusement park we know or have read about. We list all the areas of the park and vote on the one we like best. We write that name in the center of a web. Then we write details about it around the center. Children quickly see how this helps them focus on a topic and organize their ideas as a preparation for writing.

Focus/Ideas

Good writers **focus** on a **main idea.** They give details about this idea. They also keep in mind their **purpose.** The purpose may be to persuade someone, teach something, or make the reader laugh.

A thank-you note has a main idea and a purpose.

Dear Aunt Ani,

Thank you so much for my great birthday present. The set of markers is terrific! I'll draw a picture just for you.

Jamie

Main Idea   To say that you liked a present

Purpose   To thank your aunt for the present

Details   Details add information. Be sure all details focus on your main idea.

Strategies for Focus and Ideas

• Choose a topic you can support with details.

• Keep focused on your topic.

A **Match** the number of each topic with the purpose that it fits best.

   A   Make someone laugh

   B   Persuade

   C   Give information

B **1.** Why people should help with the park clean-up

A **2.** A silly trick my brother played

C **3.** What birds do in winter

B **Read** the main-idea sentence. Then **write** the numbers of any details that do not focus on the main idea.

Main Idea   The zoo has many interesting animals.

4. The zebra looks like a black and white horse.

5. The monkeys chatter happily.

6. Cows are useful farm animals.

7. The elephant has a long trunk.

8. My town has many interesting sights.

6, 8

Improving Focus/Ideas

Original

> Tigers are in the cat family. They are much larger than pet cats. A tiger might weigh 400 pounds. It can be 9 feet long. Tigers are my favorite animals. They have interesting striped coats. Wild tigers live in India and other places in Asia. Tigers hunt at night. They can leap very far to catch their prey. Tigers could die out. That would be a shame! Find out how tigers are different from lions. Tigers are so beautiful.

Revising Tips

Add a main-idea sentence that gets readers' attention.   (*Have you ever seen a 400-pound cat?*)

Use only details that focus on the main idea.   (*Tigers are my favorite animals* tells about the writer. It doesn't tell about tigers.)

Use lively, interesting words.   (*They have brown or orange coats with black stripes* paints a clear picture.)

Keep your purpose in mind.   Take out the sentence that begins *Find out...* because it doesn't inform.

Improved

Have you ever seen a 400-pound cat? If you have seen a tiger, you have. Tigers are in the cat family. But they are much larger than pet cats. They can be 9 feet long. Tigers are beautiful because they have interesting colors. They have brown or orange coats with black stripes. Wild tigers live in India and in other places in Asia. Tigers hunt at night. They can leap very far to catch their prey. Tigers could die out because people hunt them. That would be a shame! Tigers are strong and beautiful animals.

Writer's Corner

Your main idea sentence is like a camera lens. Use it to focus your paper. If any detail does not make the main idea clearer, take it out.

Writer's Guide **5**

Organization/Paragraphs

The class and I talk about ways in which we bring order to our lives every day. I write children's ideas on the board:

- My mom writes doctors' appointments on our calendar.

- I write my homework assignments in a notebook and then check them off when I'm done.

- There's a list on the refrigerator of things we need from the grocery store. Everybody in the family adds to it.

Then we talk about order in our writing. The goal is to get children to see that planning will help them to tell someone the steps for making or doing something or to write a story with a beginning, middle, and end.

Organization/Paragraphs

A good writer tells what happens in the right order. Your **organization** holds your writing together.

Here are some ways to organize your writing.

- A story with a beginning, middle, and end
- A paragraph that compares and contrasts
- A description
- A how-to explanation

Before you begin, think about how you will arrange your writing. For example, to write about your favorite and least favorite sports, comparison and contrast would be best. If you write about your winter vacation, a story form would work.

Once you decide, choose the details you want to use. Arrange your details from beginning to end.

Strategies for Organizing Ideas

- Begin a paragraph with a topic sentence that tells the main idea.
- Start or finish with the most important detail.
- Use order words such as *first*, *later*, *last*, and *next*.

A **Match** the number of the topic with the letter of the kind of organization that works best.

A   Comparison-Contrast

B   Description

C   Story

D   How-to Explanation

D **1.** How to Make a Clay Pot

C **2.** A Funny Event at the School Fair

B **3.** My Garden in Spring

A **4.** Hockey or Soccer: Which Is Better?

B **Write** the sentences about learning to ride a bike. **Put** them in correct order to tell what happened.

5. Second, David gave me a push.

6. Finally, David let go and I rode by myself.

7. Next, David held the seat while I pedaled.

8. First, David held the bike while I got on.
Sentence order: 8, 5, 7, 6

C **Tell** how to do an outdoor activity. **Use** order words such as *first*, *then*, and *next* to organize the details.
Possible answer is on page TR33.

Writer's Guide **7**

Improving Organization

Original

My teacher held me so I floated. I put all the actions together. I moved my arms in long strokes. I kicked my legs up and down. I practiced moving my head to one side. I learned to take a breath each time I moved my head. I swam all the way across the pool.

Revising Tips

Include a topic sentence that tells your main idea. (Start with *Last summer I learned how to swim.*)

Organize details in the correct order. When you tell how you did something, put events in time order. (*I put all the actions together* should come later.)

Use order words such as *first, then,* and *next* to make the steps clear. (*First, my teacher held me so I floated.*)

Tie ideas together in your conclusion. (*Before long, I had reached an important goal* tells why the event was important to the writer.)

Improved

Last summer I learned how to swim. First, my teacher held me so I floated. Soon I could float all by myself. Next, I moved my arms in long strokes. I kicked my legs up and down with all my strength. Then the teacher showed me how to move my head to one side. I learned to take a breath each time I moved my head. Finally, I put all the actions together. Before long, I had reached an important goal. I could swim all the way across the pool!

Writer's Corner

Include vivid details. For example, don't just say *kicked up and down*. If you say *kicked up and down with all my strength*, your story comes alive.

Writer's Guide **9**

Voice

> Your writing style shows your **voice**. It tells how you feel and think about your topic. Your writer's voice shows that you know and care about your topic. It lets you speak directly to the reader.

- When I saw my new kitten, I was happy. (weak voice)
- I squealed with delight when I saw that furry little face. (strong voice)

Strategies for Developing a Writer's Voice

- Think about your readers and your reason for writing. Use a playful voice to write about a funny event. Use a more serious voice in a book report.

- Choose words that match your voice. In a letter to a friend, contractions or funny words would sound like your everyday voice. A letter to your principal would have a more serious voice.

- Your writing voice is a way that you can speak directly to your readers. Let readers know how you feel about a subject.

A **Match** each opening sentence with the letter of the reader it fits best.

A   My cousin Louis

B   The mayor of my town

C   Students in my school

c **1.** Support me for class president! You won't be sorry.

b **2.** Thank you for letting us help plan the parade.

a **3.** I played the coolest game last weekend.

B **Write** *S* for the sentence that shows a strong voice. **Write** *W* for the sentence that shows a weak voice.

s **4.** I never knew ice skating could be so much fun!

w **5.** I can ice skate.

C **Complete** one of these opening sentences. **Add** sentences to write a paragraph about that topic. **Use** a voice that fits your topic.
Possible answer is on page TR33.

• When I do chores, I ___.

• The best thing I ever ate was ___.

• Here are some simple steps for ___.

Writer's Guide **11**

Improving Voice

Original

Dear Ms. Jenkins,

We want to have a special Presidents' Day program. It would be awesome! We could sing that song about the presidents. You said we sang it great. I'll work on it before the program. Each person could tell about one president. Our parents could come and everything. We could serve refreshments. Remember the fruit salad James brought last time? Please, could we?

Tara Roberts

Revising Tips

Think about your reader and your reason for writing. When you write a persuasive letter to a teacher or principal, use a serious voice. (*It would be awesome* would be better in a letter to a friend.)

Use words that match your purpose. (Replace contractions such as *I'll* and unclear expressions such as *could come and everything.*)

Make your voice strong and clear. (*Please, could we?* sounds like begging instead of being persuasive.)

Improved

Dear Ms. Jenkins,

Our class would like to have a special Presidents' Day program. We could sing the song about the presidents that we learned. Each person could tell something about a president. Some people might even dress up like George Washington or Abraham Lincoln. We could invite our parents and serve refreshments. This would be a great way to learn. We could have fun at the same time. I hope we can plan this special program.

Tara Roberts

Writer's Corner

Read your paper out loud to yourself. Does it sound like you? Change the places where the voice does not sound natural.

Word Choice

Most children do a good job of using descriptive words to tell about something they see. However, they are often at a loss to tell about images acquired through the senses of hearing and smell. I bring in music and objects to help children develop vocabulary for describing these senses. Some of the words children have used to tell about the music from *Peter and the Wolf* are *scary, thundering,* and *clomping.* Feta cheese was described as smelling *lemony, sharp,* and *sour.* We have even had tasting sessions and recorded words such as *buttery, salty,* and *sugary.* The class posts lists of words for each sense on the bulletin board. When we find good "sense words" in our reading, we add them to our lists.

Word Choice

Choose your **words** carefully to add style to your writing. Use exact nouns, strong verbs, and exciting adjectives. They will make your work interesting, clear, and lively.

- The pet of my friend is nice. (wordy and dull)
- My friend's Siamese cat plopped onto my lap. (lively and exact)

Strategies for Choosing the Right Words

- Choose exact nouns. (*sandal* instead of *shoe*)
- Use strong verbs. (*clattered* instead of *made a noise*)
- Replace dull words such as *nice, bad,* and *thing* with clear words. (*My head felt achy and hot* instead of *My head felt bad*)
- Include words that give readers pictures. (*The lemonade made my mouth pucker* instead of *The lemonade was sour*)
- Don't be wordy. (*because* instead of *the reason was because*)

A **Choose** the more exact word in ( ) to complete each sentence. **Write** each sentence.

(1) The boys and girls (walk, <u>stroll</u>) in the park. (2) The trees are full of (<u>robins</u>, birds). (3) They (<u>chirp</u>, call) in the bright sunshine. (4) (Flowers, <u>Daisies</u>) grow in the field. (5) They look (nice, <u>cheerful</u>).

B **Choose** a word from the box to replace each underlined word. **Write** the sentences.

8 golden	9 shouted	10 cast
6 pond	7 leaped	

6. Tom and Dan put their boat on the <u>water</u>.

7. A fish suddenly <u>came</u> out.

8. The fish looked <u>bright</u>.

9. Tom <u>spoke</u>.

10. Dan <u>put</u> his fishing line in to catch the fish.

C **Write** a description of a flower or tree that you like. **Use** strong, exact words to make your writing come alive.

Possible answer is on page TR33.

Improving Word Choice

Original

Our town had a big bicycle race. The riders were all ages. They went through town. Then they raced on two country roads that went through the countryside. My family and I watched the people go down Main Street. They wore bright shirts. They went fast. I liked the way the racers looked in a big group. Everybody in town liked the race.

Revising Tips

Choose exact nouns.   (*racers* instead of *people*)

Use strong verbs.   (*zip* instead of *go*)

Replace dull words with clear ones.   (*They looked like a big swarm of colorful bees* instead of *I liked the way the racers looked in a big group.*)

Include words that use our senses.   (*Each racer wore a bright shirt of red, yellow, or blue.*)

Don't be wordy.   Rewrite sentences that contain words you don't need. (Make the fourth sentence clearer and more specific.)

Improved

Our town had an exciting bicycle race. Young and old bicycle riders raced through town. Then they raced uphill, downhill, and curved around two country roads. My family and I watched the racers zip down Main Street. Each racer wore a bright shirt of red, yellow, or blue. The racers whooshed by. They looked like a big swarm of colorful bees. The crowds on the sidewalk clapped and cheered for the racers.

Writer's Corner

Take time to pick the best words. As you write, close your eyes and picture in your mind what you are describing. What words can bring the object or event to life?

Writer's Guide **17**

Sentences

To get at the idea of using different kinds of sentences to make their writing more interesting, I write the following on the board:

Cats are nice. Dogs are nice. Fish are nice.

I ask children to tell me how we can combine these three short sentences into one longer sentence. They are usually able to do it. (Dogs, cats, and fish are nice.) Then I ask them to replace the word *nice* in the combined sentence. They offer replacements such as *frisky, good pets, fun to own,* and so on. Finally, I ask children to continue writing about these animals, this time asking a question. Soon children begin to see how using different kinds and lengths of sentences helps make their writing more interesting.

Sentences

Good writers use different kinds of **sentences**. This gives the writing rhythm and style. A mix of short and longer sentences lets your writing flow.

Here are some ways to improve your sentences.

- Use questions, exclamations, and commands.
- Don't use only short, choppy sentences. Longer sentences can help your writing sound smooth.
- Use different beginnings. Too many sentences that begin with *I, she, the,* or *a* can be boring.
- Combine short sentences with connecting words such as *and, or,* or *but* to make them flow better.

Strategies for Improving Your Sentences

Use a checklist as you edit your writing:

- Circle sentences that begin with *I, the, he,* or *a.*
- Underline short, choppy sentences.
- List the different kinds of sentences you used.
- Now look at your sentences. Make changes to improve your sentences.

A Use the connecting word in ( ) to join the two sentences. **Add** a comma and change a capital letter. **Write** the sentences.

Example   I can skate. I cannot swim. (but)
I can skate, but I cannot swim.

1. I take the bus to school. I ride my bike. (or)
I take the bus to school, or I ride my bike.
2. Dad drove to the lake. We rode on a boat. (and)
Dad drove to the lake, and we rode on a boat.
3. I like trains. I have never ridden on one. (but)
I like trains, but I have never ridden on one.

B Rearrange the words in each sentence so that it begins with the underlined words. **Write** the sentences.
Possible answer is on page TR33.

Example   We drove to Milwaukee <u>last summer</u>.
Last summer we drove to Milwaukee.

(4) The family goes to the beach <u>each year</u>.
(5) The seashore gets very crowded <u>in June</u>.
(6) The dog will come too <u>this summer</u>.

C Describe a place you visited and how you got there. **Use** different kinds of sentences. **Begin** each sentence with a different word.
Possible answer is on page TR33.

Improving Sentences

Original

> I went bowling last Saturday. It was my first time. I used the lightest ball. It still felt heavy. I rolled the ball down the alley. It went into the gutter. I rolled it again. It went into the gutter too. I finally started to get the hang of the game. I rolled the ball again. I knocked down five pins. I rolled the ball right down the center of the alley next time. I knocked down all ten pins. I scored a strike.

Revising Tips

Combine choppy sentences with connecting words. (*I used the lightest ball, but it still felt heavy.*)

Use different beginnings. Don't always start with the subject of the sentence. (*Last Saturday I went bowling* instead of *I went bowling last Saturday*)

Use questions, exclamations, and commands as well as statements. (*I scored my first strike!*)

Use both short and longer sentences.

Improved

Last Saturday I went bowling for the first time. I used the lightest ball, but it still felt heavy. I rolled the ball down the alley, and it went into the gutter. The next time I rolled the ball, it went into the gutter again. Finally, I started to get the hang of the game. I rolled the ball again. Would you believe I knocked down five pins? Next time, I rolled the ball right down the center of the alley. All ten pins toppled over. I scored my first strike!

Writer's Corner

Here is a good way to get your readers interested. Start your paper with a question. People will keep reading to find out the answer!

Conventions

Children love a chance to play newspaper editor. I laminate 3 x 5 cards on which I have copied the major proofreading marks and bring in visors for children to wear while they check each other's work. They are very serious about their work. Sometimes they even suggest replacing a word with a more colorful one.

Conventions

Conventions are the rules for writing.

- jack plast the babe roben bak in the nest (weak)
- Jack placed the baby robin back in the nest. (strong)

Strategies for Conventions in Writing

- Start each sentence with a capital letter. End sentences with an end punctuation mark.
- Each sentence should tell a complete idea. Use the correct verbs to go with singular and plural nouns.
- Use correct verb tenses.
- Follow the rules for punctuation marks.
- Spell all words correctly.
- Use pronouns correctly.

Proofreading Marks

¶	New paragraph
≡	Capital letter
/	Lowercase letter
○	Correct the spelling.
∧	Add something.
ℒ	Remove something.

A **Choose** the correct word in ( ) to complete each sentence. **Write** the sentences.

1. (Me, <u>I</u>) kicked the soccer ball all morning.

2. Mike (<u>saw</u>, seen) me score a goal.

3. Mike (say, <u>says</u>) that I am a good player.

4. I will play on a team next (<u>year</u>, yeer).

B Each sentence has one mistake. **Correct** the mistake and **write** the paragraph.

   (5) It was time for the soccer game? **(6)** the teams stood on the field in their bright shirts. **(7)** One player kicks the ball. **(8)** My friend peter blocked the kick.

5. It was time for the soccer game. 6. The teams stood on the field in their bright shirts. 7. One player kicked the ball. 8. My friend Peter blocked the kick.

C **Write** three sentences about one of the topics below. **Follow** the rules for capitalization, punctuation, grammar, and spelling. **Trade** papers with a partner. Proofread each other's work.

Possible answer is on page TR34.

- My favorite outdoor game

- A person who is good at a sport

- An activity for a rainy day

Improving Conventions

Original

Do you have any pets. Then you might know my Neighbor, dr. Mason. She is an animal docter. She cares for pets. She takes care of dogs and cats. Sometimes takes care of hamsters. When we got a new cat, we took her to dr Mason. She cheks to make sure fluffy was healthy. Then she gives her some shots. I woud like to be a animal docter like dr Mason when I grow up.

Revising Tips

Check for correct capitalization. Do not capitalize common nouns. (*neighbor* instead of *Neighbor*, *Dr.* instead of *dr.*, *Fluffy* instead of *fluffy*)

Make sure each sentence has a subject and a verb. (*Sometimes <u>she</u> takes care of hamsters.*)

Use verb tenses correctly. (*She <u>checked</u> to make sure Fluffy was healthy. Then she <u>gave</u> her some shots.*)

Use correct end punctuation. (*Do you have any pets?* instead of *Do you have any pets.*)

Check spelling. (*docter, cheks, woud*)

Improved

Do you have any pets? Then you might know my neighbor, Dr. Mason. She is an animal doctor. She cares for people's pets. She takes care of dogs and cats. Sometimes she takes care of hamsters. When we got a new cat, we took her to Dr. Mason. She checked to make sure Fluffy was healthy. Then she gave her some shots. I would like to be an animal doctor like Dr. Mason when I grow up.

Writer's Corner

When you proofread, look for one mistake at a time. For example, look for correct capital letters first. Then look for correct punctuation. Then look for spelling errors.

Rubrics and Models

Narrative Writing *Scoring Rubric*

A scoring **rubric** can be used to judge a piece of writing. A rubric is a checklist of traits, or writing skills, to look for. See pages 2–25 for a discussion of these traits. Rubrics give a number score for each trait.

Score	4	3	2	1
Focus/Ideas	Detailed ideas on topic; beginning, middle, and end	Good story; details mostly about topic	Unfocused story with some details not on topic	Unclear story with many details not on topic
Organization/ Paragraphs	Ideas easy to follow, with order words	Details given in some order	Details not in clear order	No order
Voice	Lively and shows writer's feelings	Mostly lively and shows writer's feelings	Not lively; little or no feelings	Careless with no feelings
Word Choice	Vivid, clear word pictures	Good word picture	No word pictures	Incorrect, dull, or overused words
Sentences	Smooth sentences; different kinds	Most sentences smooth; some different kinds	Many stringy or choppy sentences	Hard to understand, not complete, or choppy
Conventions	Few or no errors	No serious errors	Many errors	Too many errors

Following are four models that respond to a prompt. Each model has been given a score, based on the rubric.

Writing Prompt   Write a story about a surprise that a character has. The character may be a person or an animal.

Narrative Writing Model *Score 4*

> Robbie was a rabbit. Robbie's mother gave Robbie two carrots each day. He ate lettuce and peppers too. Robbie liked carrots best. One day Robbie headed home. He had hopped in the fields all day. He was hungry for a snack. Robbie walked into his little rabbit home. Then seven rabbits jumped out. They said, "Surprise!" It was Robbie's birthday! Can you guess what Robbie's friends gave him for a present? Carrots! It was the best surprise ever!

Focus/Ideas Focused on the event; many details

Organization/Paragraphs Order words show time order (*One day, Then*)

Voice Shows writer's imagination and personality

Word Choice Exact word choice and word pictures (*hopped, little rabbit home*)

Sentences Different sentence kinds and lengths

Conventions Excellent spelling, grammar, and punctuation

Narrative Writing Model *Score 3*

> One day Rosa walked home from school. She liked looking at flowers. She forgot her lunchbox. Rosa hurried back to school. No lunchbox! Poor Rosa was sad. She went home and told her mom. Rosa's mom said she wood get Rosa a new lunchbox. The next day her mom gave her a big paper bag. Rosa looks inside. It's a new lunchbox. Just like her old lunchbox! Rosa wood never forget her lunchbox again.

Focus/Ideas   Focused on character's experience; one sentence off topic *(She liked looking at flowers.)*

Organization/Paragraphs   Details in time order

Voice   Writer's feelings revealed *(Poor Rosa was sad.)*

Word Choice   Uses some vivid words *(forgot, hurried, big paper bag)*

Sentences   Many sentences begin with *Rosa* or *she*.

Conventions   Errors in verb forms and tense *(her mom gived; Rosa looks; It's)*; spelling error *(wood)*; fragments

Narrative Writing Model *Score 2*

Tommy's surprise was he got to go to the city. He never went there before. All his freinds had went. Tommy saw big bildings buses and peple. He ate lunch there he saw anemels at the zoo. A lion a tiger a monkey were some of the anemels. Tommy had a good surprise.

Focus/Ideas Focused on the experience; one sentence off topic (*All his freinds had went.*)

Organization/Paragraphs No clear beginning, middle, and end

Voice Few feelings expressed

Word Choice Includes specific nouns (*lion, tiger, monkey*); needs vivid adjectives

Sentences Needs some different lengths; could use a question or an exclamation

Conventions Many misspellings (*freinds, bildings, peple, anemels*); errors in verb forms (*freinds had went*); run-on sentence; commas missing in series

Narrative Writing Model *Score 1*

> James was a boy he got a new bike. His mom and dad give it to him for his brithday. Its blue my bikes red. He go fast on the bike. I like suprises.

Focus/Ideas   Topic not presented clearly; few details

Organization/Paragraphs   Unclear order; no beginning, middle, and end

Voice   Little sense of writer's personality

Word Choice   Limited, dull word choice

Sentences   No variety of length or type

Conventions   Subject-verb agreement errors (*He go*); verb tense shifts (*got a new bike; His mom and dad give; Its blue*); misspellings (*brithday, Its, bikes, suprises*); run-on sentences

Descriptive Writing *Scoring Rubric*

Score	4	3	2	1
Focus/Ideas	Focused ideas on topic; excellent description	Good description; details mostly focused on topic	Description not focused, with some details not on topic	Ideas not clear or on descriptive topic; few details
Organization/ Paragraphs	Ideas easy to follow and in some order	Details given in some order	Little order	No order
Voice	Lively writing; shows writer's feelings	Mostly lively; shows writer's feelings	Not lively; little or no feeling	Careless with no feeling
Word Choice	Vivid, clear word pictures that appeal to senses	Good word pictures; some appeal to senses	Dull word pictures	Incorrect, dull, or overused words
Sentences	Smooth sentences; some different kinds	Most sentences smooth; some different kinds	Many stringy or choppy sentences	Hard to understand, not complete, or choppy
Conventions	Few or no errors	No serious errors	Many errors	Too many errors

Following are four models that respond to a prompt. Each model has been given a score, based on the rubric.

Writing Prompt Describe your favorite kind of weather. Use precise nouns and vivid adjectives to help your reader see, hear, and feel the weather.

Descriptive Writing Model *Score 4*

Snowy days are my favorite weather. The sky is a pale gray, and the whole world looks white. The air feels as cold as a freezer. Snowflakes float slowly through the air. Soon they cover the ground. It is quiet because the snow doesn't make any noise. The only sounds are when I walk across the snowy ground. My boots squeak in the snow. I love snowy days.

Focus/Ideas   Strong focus on the weather with many supporting details

Organization/Paragraphs   Clear introduction and conclusion; logical order of details

Voice   Shows love of season

Word Choice   Vivid words and phrases that appeal to senses (*pale gray, as cold as a freezer, squeak*)

Sentences   Clear sentences of different lengths; however, several beginning with *the*

Conventions   Excellent grammar, spelling, and punctuation

Descriptive Writing Model *Score 3*

Windy weather makes things move. You can feel the wind blow across your face. It blows your hair all around. You can see the wind blow the tree brachs. It can blow trash and other things around too. People should pick up the litter. You can fly a kite in the wind or you can take a walk. You feel like the wind might blow you over. Its fun to go outside on a windy day.

Focus/Ideas   Many details about topic; one sentence off topic (*People should pick up the litter.*)

Organization/Paragraphs Good introduction and ending

Voice   Sense of writer's personality

Word Choice   Some word pictures (*fly a kite in the wind*); some words not exact (*other things*); some repetition (*blow, blows, you can*)

Sentences   Needs different lengths and kinds; too many sentences beginning with *You*

Conventions   A few mistakes; some spelling errors (*brachs, Its*)

Descriptive Writing Model *Score 2*

Sunny wether is the best wether you can go to the beach. The sun feel nice and hot. And the sky is kind of brit. Sometimes you get real hot, but its still nice. You could cool of in the warter. The warter in the oshun tastes like salt. Be careful in the waves.

Focus/Ideas Some details on topic; last two sentences off the topic

Organization/Paragraphs Good beginning; needs conclusion that sums up topic

Voice Shows some feelings about sunny weather

Word Choice Some word pictures (*tastes like salt*); some dull words (*nice*); sometimes general (*kind of*)

Sentences Some differences in length

Conventions Many misspellings (*wether, brit, its, of, warter, oshun*); error in subject-verb agreement (*The sun feel*); run-on sentence

Descriptive Writing Model *Score 1*

> Rain is good some times. Everything get wet and you have stay inside and play vidio games and some you could play a bord game with Mom and Dad. What is your faverit. Theres pudels in the yard thats why you have to play in side. I dont like rain all the time but rain is good and it maks trees grow and thats why rain is good.

Focus/Ideas   Paragraph not a clear description of the weather; sentence off the topic (*What is your faverit.*)

Organization/Paragraphs   No clear sense of order

Voice   Doesn't show writer's personality

Word Choice   Dull word choice (*good, is*); no word pictures; repetition (*Rain is good.*)

Sentences   Too many *ands*

Conventions   Many misspellings; some words left out (*you have stay inside; some you could*); incorrect end punctuation; error in subject-verb agreement (*Everything get*); run-on sentence

Persuasive Writing *Scoring Rubric*

Score	4	3	2	1
Focus/Ideas	Clear opinion; good reasons used to persuade	Clear opinion; reasons help persuade	Opinion not always clear or on persuasive topic; few reasons	Ideas not clear or on persuasive topic; no reasons
Organization/ Paragraphs	Good introduction and conclusion	Facts given in some order	Order not clear	No order
Voice	Lively writing; shows writer's feelings	Mostly lively; shows writer's feelings	Not lively; little or no feeling	Careless with no feeling
Word Choice	Good use of persuasive words	Some use of persuasive words	Few persuasive words	Dull word choice; no persuasive words
Sentences	Smooth sentences of different lengths and kinds	Most sentences smooth; some different lengths and kinds	Many stringy or choppy sentences	Hard to understand, not complete, or choppy
Conventions	Few or no errors	No serious errors	Many errors	Too many errors

Following are four models that respond to a prompt. Each model has been given a score, based on the rubric.

Writing Prompt   Think about a special activity for the students in your class. Write a letter to your teacher. Persuade him or her to have the activity.

Persuasive Writing Model *Score 4*

Dear Ms. Murray,

    Our class should have an arts and crafts fair. Some people could draw pictures. Some people could make clay bowls, and some could make kites or birds out of paper. Then we can display all the art and crafts around our classroom. We can invite the other students to come look. Maybe we could have prizes. Everyone would have fun. I think everyone would love an arts and crafts fair.

Yours truly,

Mark Shaw

Focus/Ideas   Clear opinion; many persuasive details

Organization/Paragraphs   Strong introduction and conclusion help persuade

Voice   Shows writer's feelings about topic

Word Choice   Uses persuasive words (*should, fun*)

Sentences   Clear sentences of different lengths

Conventions   Excellent grammar, spelling, and punctuation

Persuasive Writing Model *Score 3*

Dear Mr. Ochoa,

   May we have a school game day? The students at Roosevelt school could run in short and long races. We could also have relay races for teams. Each team with three or four people. We could have jumping and thowing to see who could jump the highest and thow the longest. A game day would really help school spirit! It would help everyone get in shape too.

Yours truly,

Alicia Adams

Focus/Ideas   Clear request; many persuasive details

Organization/Paragraphs   Order of importance of reasons not always clear

Voice   Shows some excitement; needs personality

Word Choice   Some persuasive words (*help*)

Sentences   Includes question and exclamation

Conventions   Capitalization error; spelling errors (*thowing, thow*); fragment

Persuasive Writing Model *Score 2*

Dear Mrs. Kaufman

   We should have a inter national day. That's when evryone brings food from another contry. Or something else. You could choose france or Mexico then you put it all around. Evryone gets to look at the stuff and learn.

Your friend,

Toby Rice

Focus/Ideas   Focused on the request; needs more focused reasons

Organization/Paragraphs Details need clear order; no clear ending

Voice   No clear writer's voice

Word Choice   Unclear (*or something else, put it all around, stuff*); some persuasive words

Sentences   Choppy and stringy sentences

Conventions   Several misspellings; capitalization error (*france*); incorrect word (*a inter national*); no comma after greeting; fragment; run-on sentence

Persuasive Writing Model *Score 1*

Dear Mr. Line

Cold we go to the water park before schools out because its real fun. Well, my grandma lives near the water park and one time she took us their then we spent the night their then we got up. Slideing on the slides. And, other things. we shold go to the water park because its fun.

Jenny Fong

Focus/Ideas Includes many details not about topic

Organization/Paragraphs No clear order

Voice No clear writer's voice

Word Choice Unclear words (*And, other things*); repeated words (*fun*)

Sentences Stringy sentence

Conventions Misspellings; apostrophe errors; capitalization error; run-on; no comma after greeting; no closing; fragments

Expository Writing *Scoring Rubric*

Score	4	3	2	1
Focus/Ideas	Clear topic with many facts; excellent explanation	Good explanation; clear ideas with some facts	Explanation not always clear or on topic; few facts	Explanation not clear or on topic; few or no facts
Organization/ Paragraphs	Ideas easy to follow	Facts given in some order	Unclear order	No order
Voice	Shows writer's feelings, but serious	Mostly serious; shows writer's feelings	Not lively; little or no feeling	Careless with no feeling
Word Choice	Clear, well-chosen words	Words mostly well chosen	Words sometimes not fitting topic	Words often not fitting topic
Sentences	Smooth sentences of different lengths and kinds	Most sentences smooth; some different lengths and kinds	Many stringy or choppy sentences	Hard to understand, not complete, or choppy
Conventions	Few or no errors	No serious errors	Many errors	Too many errors

Following are four models that respond to a prompt. Each model has been given a score, based on the rubric.

Writing Prompt   Write about a holiday that Americans celebrate. Support your main idea with facts about the holiday.

Expository Writing Model *Score 4*

The Fourth of July is an important holiday for us. It started in 1776. That's when America became free from England. On the Fourth of July, there are many parades. People from the Army and Navy march in the parade. Bands play American music. Flags are everywhere. People have picnics and cook outside with their friends and families. At night, they watch beautiful fireworks. They remind Americans of their freedom.

Focus/Ideas   Main idea clearly presented; supported with many facts and details

Organization/Paragraphs   Clear order of details; good beginning and ending

Voice   Friendly but serious voice

Word Choice   Specific word choice (*People from the Army and Navy, beautiful fireworks*)

Sentences   Clear sentences of different lengths and varied beginnings

Conventions   Excellent grammar, spelling, and punctuation

Expository Writing Model *Score 3*

Americans celebrate Thanksgiving to show we love our country. The holiday reminds people of the Pilgrims. They came from england in the 1600s. Their boat was the <u>Mayflower</u>. They settled in Masatchusets. They had a hard time, but the Indians helped them. They learned to grow food. They had a big feast because they were happy. Today Americans have Thanksgiving each november. We eat turkey, potatoes, and pumpkin pie. We are thankful for our country. We remember the Pilgrims and Indians.

Focus/Ideas Clear main idea in first sentence; many supporting details, some off topic (*the <u>Mayflower</u>*)

Organization/Paragraphs Needs order words

Voice Serious voice; could show more feelings

Word Choice Exact, clear nouns (*feast, turkey*)

Sentences Many choppy and begin with *They* or *We*

Conventions Some capitalization and spelling errors (*england, Masatchusets, november*)

Expository Writing Model *Score 2*

Do you like to selbrate Presidents day. Presidents day is a American holiday. I like it because it is selbrateing some presidents Washington Lincoln and others and they all helped our country. We put flags on our house sometimes so we rember our great presidents. We get a day off school.

Focus/Ideas   Main idea clear; focus unclear at end; needs more details about holiday

Organization/Paragraphs   Good introduction; details need better order; stronger conclusion needed

Voice   Writer shows personality

Word Choice   Unclear words (*and others*)

Sentences   One stringy sentence; some different sentence kinds and lengths

Conventions   Misspellings (*selbrate, rember*); missing commas in series; error in end punctuation; capitalization and apostrophe errors (*Presidents day*); incorrect word (*a American*)

Expository Writing Model *Score 1*

My best holiday is fun. Gess what it is. Its in febuary you allways have a school party and then you take you valentines home and then you show them to your mom. And you can make your own decratons at home too. Everyone give valentines to there friends and eat treats and have valentines parties. Decrate with harts and have a party. It is fun.

Focus/Ideas   Main idea not presented clearly

Organization/Paragraphs   No clear order; needs strong conclusion

Voice   Strong voice

Word Choice   Repeated words (*fun*); dull; few specific words

Sentences   Long, stringy sentences; hard to understand

Conventions   Many misspellings; subject-verb agreement error; error in end punctuation; errors with apostrophes and capitalization; wrong pronoun; fragment and run-on sentence

Check Your Writing

Check your writing by reading it over carefully. Try the following strategies.

Read your work aloud.

- If it sounds choppy, combine short sentences.
- Rewrite a long, stringy sentence as several sentences.
- Sentences should not all begin with *the* or *I*.
- Do ideas seem connected? If not, add words such as *then, next,* or *but.*

Check your style. It should match your audience and purpose. You might begin an e-mail to a friend, "Hey, you won't believe the cool thing that happened." For a test, the following would be a better beginning: "An unusual thing happened today."

Be sure you have answered the prompt.

- Look for key words in the writing prompt.

    <u>Compare</u> a <u>bike</u> and a <u>car</u>. Tell <u>two ways they</u>
    <u>are alike and two ways they are different.</u>

    Topic: bike and car
    What you need to do: Compare
    What to include: Two likenesses and two differences

Make sure your writing is focused. Take out sentences that are off the subject.

Check that there is enough support.

- Use details to give readers pictures.
- Support your opinion with reasons.
- Explain a main idea with good details.

Do you have a strong beginning? Does a question, a surprising fact, or an interesting detail get a reader's interest?

Is your ending good? A conclusion may say the main idea in a new way, tell what you have learned, or ask a question.

Check that you have used good words—and not too many of them.

- Strong verbs, precise nouns, and vivid adjectives make your writing clear and lively.
- Replace wordy phrases such as *blue in color* with *blue* and *in a careful way* with *carefully*.

Checklist

- [ ] My writing sounds smooth and easy to read.
- [ ] I have used a good style for my audience and purpose.
- [ ] My writing answers the prompt or assignment.
- [ ] My writing is focused.
- [ ] I have used enough support.
- [ ] I have a strong beginning.
- [ ] I have a satisfying conclusion.
- [ ] I have used good words and avoided wordiness.

Grammar and Writing Lessons

Sentences

- Recognize sentences.
- Use sentences correctly in writing.
- Become familiar with sentences on standardized tests.

TEACH

Read aloud the definition, instruction, and examples in the box on p. 50. Then say:

To be a sentence, a group of words must do four things:

- It must tell a complete idea.
- The words must be in an order that makes sense.
- It must begin with a capital letter.
- It must end with a punctuation mark, such as a period.

Write the first sentence from the box (*I play with my ball.*) on the board. Point to it.

Think Aloud **Model** As I look at this group of words, I know that it is a sentence because it tells a complete idea, the words are in an order that makes sense, and it begins with a capital letter and ends with a period.

Sentences

A **sentence** is a group of words that tells a complete idea. The words are in an order that makes sense. A sentence begins with a capital letter. Many sentences end with a period **(.)**.

I play with my ball.

This is a complete sentence.

with my ball

This is not a complete sentence.

A **Find** the sentence. **Write** the sentence.

1. the ball   I throw the ball.
2. Walter catches it.   catches it
3. My friend has a pony.   a pony
4. rides the pony   He rides the pony.
5. Walter is my friend.   my friend

50 Grammar

RESOURCES

Daily Fix-It Lesson 1
    See p. TR1.
    See also Daily Fix-It Transparency 1.
Grammar Transparency 1

B **Put** each group of words in order to make a sentence. **Write** the sentences.

1. are blooming. The roses
   The roses are blooming.
2. birds Some are singing.
   Some birds are singing.
3. is tall. The tree
   The tree is tall.
4. at night. Stars shine
   Stars shine at night.
5. fast. The pony runs
   The pony runs fast.
6. was fun. The farm
   The farm was fun.

C **Add** a word or words from the box to make each group of words a sentence. **Write** the sentences.

is in a tree	Squirrels	brings games with her
The house	climb up a ladder	Dad

7. The little house ___.
   The little house is in a tree.
8. ___ is made of wood.
   The house is made of wood.
9. Iris and I ___.
   Iris and I climb up a ladder.
10. ___ run by.
    Squirrels run by.
11. Iris ___.
    Iris brings games with her.
12. ___ makes us lunch.
    Dad makes us lunch.

Grammar **51**

Guided Practice Ⓐ

Go through the exercise with children. Ask them to tell how they chose the sentence each time. Write the incorrect models on the board and invite volunteers to correct them.

TEACHING TIP

Help children understand that a group of words cannot be a sentence unless the words are in an order that makes sense.

- Rearrange the words of a simple sentence and write them on the board.
- Ask children to help you arrange the words in an order that makes sense.
- Have volunteers begin the sentence with a capital letter and end it with a period.

Independent Practice Ⓑ and Ⓒ

Have children complete the exercises. For Differentiated Instruction and Extra Practice, see p. TR11.

Differentiated Instruction

Strategic Intervention

Write sentences on the board putting the beginning capital letters and end punctuation in the wrong places. For example:

we went to. my house

Let volunteers correct the sentences.

We went to my house.

Advanced

Have children write on slips of paper two sentences telling about themselves, such as *I have red shoes. I am tall.* Collect the slips, mix them, read the two sentences on a slip, and invite children to guess who wrote them.

ⒺⓁⓁ

Have children finish this sentence: *My friend and I ___.* Ask them to tell about something they do with a friend. Write their sentences on the board. Have children come to the board and highlight the beginning capital letter and the ending period.

Monitor Progress

Check Grammar

If... children have difficulty identifying sentences,	**then...** write incomplete and complete sentences on the board. Help children choose the complete sentences by pointing out what is missing in the incomplete sentences.

Test Preparation

☑ **Write** the letter of the sentence.

1. ⊗ **A** Grandpa milks the cows.
   ○ **B** Milk from the cows.
   ○ **C** Grandpa with the cows.

2. ○ **A** Walter for a visit.
   ⊗ **B** Walter comes for a visit.
   ○ **C** Walter and the visit.

3. ○ **A** Rides the pony.
   ⊗ **B** Barb rides the pony.
   ○ **C** The fast pony.

4. ○ **A** Grandma the corn.
   ○ **B** Corn on the cob.
   ⊗ **C** Grandma picks corn.

5. ⊗ **A** Pete counts the stars.
   ○ **B** Counts the stars.
   ○ **C** The stars for Pete.

6. ○ **A** Ann with skates.
   ○ **B** The new skates.
   ⊗ **C** Ann has new skates.

52　Grammar

Review

✔ **Write** the group of words that is a sentence.

1. The birds in the house.
   <u>We look at the birds.</u>

2. <u>Zack runs fast.</u>
   Zack on a ladder.

3. The spider in the web.
   <u>The spider spins a web.</u>

4. Matt in the park.
   <u>Matt explores the park.</u>

✔ **Choose** the word that makes the group of words a sentence. **Write** each sentence.

5. Alex ___ on the door.
   Sue   <u>knocks</u>   friends

6. A ___ lives in the woods.
   climb   stop   <u>bear</u>

7. Mom ___ at the joke.
   <u>smiles</u>   horse   Dru

8. The ___ pet the pony.
   stays   <u>children</u>   jump

Grammar **53**

Summarize

Ask children to tell four important things they remember about identifying and writing sentences.

- Tell a complete idea.
- Put words in an order that makes sense.
- Begin with a capital letter.
- End with a punctuation mark, such as a period.

Grammar-Writing Connection

Ask children to think of something they like and write a sentence about it, for example, *I like my dog. I like football.* Have them write the sentence at the bottom of a sheet of paper and then draw a picture of what they like above the sentence. Remind children that their sentences must tell complete ideas.

Voice

OBJECTIVES

- Identify characteristics of a description.
- Write a description using words that show how you feel.
- Develop criteria for judging a piece of writing.

TEACH

Read aloud the first two sentences in the box at the top of p. 54. Then say: *Listen as I read two sentences.*

Think Aloud *I ate all my dinner.* Does this sentence tell us anything about how the writer feels? No, it tells us only that the writer ate his or her dinner. It doesn't tell us anything about how the writer feels about the dinner. *I gobbled up every tasty bite.* Does this sentence tell us anything about how the writer feels? Yes, the words *gobbled* and *tasty* tell how the writer feels about the dinner. The sentence shows the writer's voice.

Guided Writing

Read both sentences in item 1 with children. Ask them which sentence shows how the writer feels. *(The red dress is my favorite.)* Have volunteers tell which words in the sentence help show this. *(my favorite)* Continue with items 2–5.

Independent Writing

Read aloud the directions for Exercise 2. Ask children about times when they have been scared. Discuss what they did and how they felt. When they have finished writing, ask children to share what they have written.

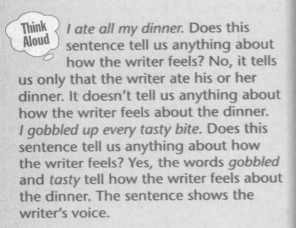

Voice

> **Voice** is the <u>you</u> in your writing. It shows how you feel.
>
> | | |
> |---|---|
> | **Weak Voice** | I ate all my dinner. |
> | **Strong Voice** | I gobbled up every tasty bite. |

 Which sentence in each pair tells how the writer feels? **Write** the sentence.

1. I got a red dress yesterday.
   <u>This red dress is my favorite.</u>

2. <u>Exercise makes me feel good.</u>
   I exercise every morning before school.

3. Our family has a kitten.
   <u>I love this playful kitten.</u>

4. <u>Tears poured down my face after the movie.</u>
   The movie was sad.

5. <u>I shook with fear inside the dark cave.</u>
   I went inside the dark cave.

 Write about a time when you were scared. **Use** words that show readers how you felt and acted.
Possible answer is on page TR34.

54   Writing

RESOURCES

Writing Transparency 1

Describe a Special Place

> **Writing Prompt** Write about your special place. Tell what you see and do there.

Aunt Maya's Kitchen

My special place is Aunt Maya's kitchen. It is bright yellow with many plants in baskets. I go there on Saturdays after soccer practice. For lunch I always sit at the round wooden table. Sometimes we water the plants or make gingerbread cookies. This place is special because it is just for Aunt Maya and me.

Details help readers "see" the kitchen.

Writer tells what they do.

Ending tells why the place is special for the writer.

Writing **55**

Describe a Special Place

ANALYZE THE MODEL

Read aloud the model and the callouts to the left of it. Then prepare children to write their own descriptions.

PROMPT

Think about a place that is special to you. First tell what the place looks like. Then tell what you do there and why it is special.

Getting Started Children can do any of the following.

- Use an organizer (pp. TR28–TR32).
- Talk about special places with a friend.
- Picture the place in their minds.

Editing/Revising Checklist

☑ Do my sentences tell complete ideas?

☑ Did I use words that show how I feel?

☑ Did I put capital letters and periods in my sentences?

Self-Evaluation Distribute copies of p. TR26 for children to fill out.

Scoring Rubric — Description

Rubric 4 3 2 1	4	3	2	1
Focus/Ideas	Excellent description of place; focused on topic	Good description of place; mostly focused on topic	Fair description of place; some details not on topic	Ideas not clear or on topic; few details
Organization/ Paragraphs	Ideas easy to follow; in order that makes sense	Ideas in some order	Ideas in little order	No order to ideas
Voice	Lively writing; shows writer's feelings	Mostly lively; shows writer's feelings	Not lively; shows few or none of writer's feelings	Does not show writer's feelings at all
Word Choice	Vivid, clear word picture of place	Good word picture of place	Dull word picture	No word picture
Sentences	Complete sentences	Most sentences complete	Some incomplete sentences	Many incomplete sentences
Conventions	Few or no errors	No serious errors	Many errors	Too many errors

Subjects

- Recognize subjects.
- Use subjects correctly in writing.
- Become familiar with subjects on standardized tests.

TEACH

Read aloud the definition and examples in the box on p. 56. Then say:

To find the subject of a sentence, we look for who or what does something in the sentence.

Write on the board the first sentence from the box. (*Neil Armstrong walked on the moon.*) Point to it.

Think Aloud

Model We know that the subject of a sentence tells who or what does something. This sentence says *Neil Armstrong walked on the moon*. If I ask *Who or what walked on the moon?*, I see that *Neil Armstrong* is the answer to that question, so *Neil Armstrong* is the subject of this sentence.

LESSON 2

Subjects

The **subject** of a sentence tells who or what does something.

Neil Armstrong walked on the moon.
The moon goes around the Earth.

A **Write** each sentence. **Underline** the subject.

1. <u>Ann</u> traveled in an airplane.
2. <u>The airplane</u> flew very high.
3. <u>The girl</u> loved the ride.
4. <u>She</u> will be an astronaut one day.
5. <u>Astronauts</u> study space.
6. <u>One spaceship</u> went to the moon.
7. <u>Men</u> flew in the spaceship.
8. <u>Men and women</u> will go to Mars someday.

56 Grammar

RESOURCES

Daily Fix-It Lesson 2
   See p. TR1.
   See also Daily Fix-It Transparency 2.
Grammar Transparency 2

B Choose a subject from the box to complete each sentence. **Write** the sentences.

| The moon | Their homes | Tools |
| Windows | Some astronauts | |

1. ___ fly to a space station.
Some astronauts fly to a space station.

2. ___ help them work.
Tools help them work.

3. ___ let them see outside.
Windows let them see outside.

4. ___ shines outside their windows.
The moon shines outside their windows.

5. ___ are far away.
Their homes are far away.

C Write a subject to complete each sentence.

Check that your sentences make sense.
Possible answers:

6. ___ likes planets.
Mary likes planets.

7. ___ will be an explorer.
Miguel will be an explorer.

8. ___ might fly into space.
He might fly into space.

9. ___ reads many books.
My brother reads many books.

10. ___ learns new things.
He learns new things.

Grammar **57**

Guided Practice A

Go through the exercise with children. Remind them to ask themselves *Who or what ___?* *(traveled in an airplane, flew very high,* and so on) after they read each sentence to help them find the subject of the sentence.

TEACHING TIP

Help children become familiar with *who* and *what.*

• Say sentences with a variety of subjects and after each sentence, use *who* or *what,* as appropriate, to ask about the subject of the sentence.

    Kyle watches the stars. Who watches the stars?

    The dogs ran away. What ran away?

• Continue with other sentences.

Independent Practice B and C

Have children complete the exercises. For Differentiated Instruction and Extra Practice, see p. TR11.

Differentiated Instruction

Strategic Intervention

Write this sentence on the board:

    Jim likes spaceships.

Who likes spaceships? (Jim) Jim *is the subject of the sentence.* Circle the words *likes spaceships. Is this the subject of the sentence? (no)* Have a volunteer circle the correct subject. *(Jim)* Continue with other sentences.

Advanced

Ask children to think of a planet or other object in space they would like to visit. Have them write several sentences naming and explaining their choice. Ask volunteers to read aloud their sentences one at a time, and have the others identify the subject in each sentence.

ELL

Extend the lesson concept by writing the subjects *Planes, Jeff,* and *The stars* on index cards. Write these sentences on the board:

    ___ *burn brightly.*

    ___ *is a pilot.*

    ___ *carry people.*

Have children match the subjects with their sentences.

Monitor Progress

Check Grammar

If... children have difficulty identifying the subjects in sentences,	then... write additional sentences on the board and have children answer *who* or *what* to identify the subjects.

Test Preparation

✓ **Write** the letter of the correct answer.

1. ___ went to the Space Museum.
   - ○ **A** Fly
   - ⊗ **B** David and Stu
   - ○ **C** Let

2. ___ were everywhere.
   - ○ **A** Play
   - ○ **B** Drive
   - ⊗ **C** Airplanes

3. ___ learned about the planets.
   - ⊗ **A** They
   - ○ **B** Far
   - ○ **C** Big

4. ___ is as big as Earth.
   - ○ **A** Soft
   - ○ **B** Blue
   - ⊗ **C** Venus

5. ___ were in the museum.
   - ⊗ **A** Some children
   - ○ **B** Eat
   - ○ **C** Stay

6. ___ talked to David.
   - ○ **A** Good
   - ⊗ **B** One girl
   - ○ **C** Little

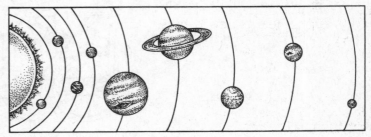

58 Grammar

Review

✓ **Write** each sentence. **Underline** the subject.

1. <u>Mark</u> studied about plants in school.
2. <u>The class</u> had a little garden.
3. <u>Plants</u> are interesting.
4. <u>The seeds</u> grow fast.
5. <u>The space station</u> has some plants.
6. <u>Sunlight</u> comes through the windows.

✓ **Choose** the correct subject in ( ). **Write** the sentences. Student answers should have these subjects:

7. ___ shows things far away. (<u>A telescope</u>, Many)
8. ___ study the sky. (<u>Two men</u>, Fly)
9. ___ is the time for stars. (Sixty, <u>Night</u>)
10. ___ are tiny spots in the sky. (<u>Planets</u>, Pull)
11. ___ looks very close. (See, <u>The moon</u>)
12. ___ is far away. (<u>It</u>, Go)

Grammar **59**

REVIEW

Summarize

Ask children what important thing they remember about identifying the subject in a sentence.

• The subject of a sentence tells who or what does something.

Grammar-Writing Connection

Ask children to think of a trip they have taken to a new place. Have them write several sentences about the trip, encouraging them to use a different subject in each sentence. After they have finished writing, ask them to circle the subject of each sentence and see how many different subjects they used.

Use Descriptive Words in Subjects

OBJECTIVES

- Identify characteristics of a list.
- Write a list using descriptive words in the subjects.
- Develop criteria for judging a piece of writing.

TEACH

Read aloud the information in the box at the top of the page. Then say: *Listen as I read two sentences. Pay particular attention to the subjects of the sentences.*

 Think Aloud *The rocket was ready.* What is the subject of this sentence? *(the rocket)* Does the sentence tell us very much about the rocket? No, it tells us only that the rocket was ready. *The huge silver rocket was ready.* Does this sentence tell us very much about the rocket? Yes, the words *huge* and *silver* are describing words, and they give a clearer picture of the subject, the rocket.

 ## Guided Writing

Read the two sentences in each item in Exercise 1 with children. Ask them to identify the subjects of the sentences before they choose the sentence that gives a clearer picture of the subject. What word has been added to the subject?

Independent Writing

Read aloud the directions for Exercise 2. Discuss words children might use to describe what they see or hear in the sky at night. When they have finished writing, ask volunteers to read what they have written.

60 Writing

 WRITER'S CRAFT

Use Descriptive Words in Subjects

> **Use descriptive words in subjects.** These words can give readers a clear picture of your subjects.
>
> **No Descriptive Words**   The rocket was ready.
>
> **Descriptive Words**   The <u>huge silver</u> rocket was ready.

 Which sentence in each pair gives a clearer picture of the subject? **Write** the sentence.

1. The astronauts walk in space.
   <u>The brave astronauts walk in space.</u>

2. <u>Their bulky spacesuits keep them warm.</u>
   Their spacesuits keep them warm.

3. <u>The happy crew comes home.</u>
   The crew comes home.

4. <u>The proud captain lands the spaceship.</u>
   The captain lands the spaceship.

5. The trip is over.
   <u>The long trip into space is over.</u>

 Write some sentences about the sky at night. **Use** descriptive words in your subjects to give a clear picture. Possible answer is on page TR34.

60 Writing

RESOURCES

Writing Transparency 2

Make a List

Writing Prompt An astronaut is going on a trip to the moon. Make a list of things she needs for the trip. Tell why she needs those things.

Things an Astronaut Needs

List uses bullets to organize items.

- A fast spaceship takes astronauts. The moon is far away.

Descriptive words give readers a clear picture of subjects.

- A thick spacesuit keeps her warm. The moon is a cold place.

- A hard helmet protects her head. The moon is a dangerous place.

Writer explains why the spaceship, spacesuit, and helmet are necessary.

- Air, water, and food are very important. People need these things to live.

- Other astronauts must go on the trip. There are many jobs to do.

Writing **61**

Make a List
ANALYZE THE MODEL

Read aloud the model and the callouts to the left of it. Then prepare children to write their own lists.

PROMPT

Now make your own list of things you think an astronaut might need. Remember to tell why she needs those things.

Getting Started Children can do any of the following.

- Use an organizer (pp. TR28–TR32).
- List things they take on a trip.
- Think about what astronauts do in space.

Editing/Revising Checklist

☑ Did I include subjects in my sentences?

☑ Did I use describing words in my subjects?

☑ Did I support my ideas with reasons?

Self-Evaluation Distribute copies of p. TR26 for children to fill out.

Scoring Rubric — Make a List

Rubric 4 3 2 1	4	3	2	1
Focus/Ideas	Excellent list; focused ideas on topic	Good list; mostly focused ideas on topic	Fair list; some details not on topic	Ideas in list not clear; few details
Organization/ Paragraphs	Ideas easy to follow; organized in list	Ideas in some order; attempts list	Ideas in little order; no list	No order to ideas; no list
Voice	Lively writing; shows writer's feelings	Mostly lively; shows writer's feelings	Not lively; shows few or no feelings	Does not show writer's feelings
Word Choice	Many describing words in subjects	Some describing words in subjects	Few describing words in subjects	No describing words in subjects
Sentences	Complete sentences	Most sentences complete	Some sentences incomplete	Few complete sentences
Conventions	Few or no errors	No serious errors	Many errors	Too many errors

Predicates

OBJECTIVES

- Recognize predicates.
- Use predicates correctly in writing.
- Become familiar with predicates on standardized tests.

TEACH

Read aloud the definition and examples in the box on p. 62. Then say:

We know that the subject of a sentence tells who or what does or is something. The predicate of a sentence tells what the subject does or is.

Write the first sentence from the box *(My family goes on hikes.)* on the board. Point to it.

Think Aloud **Model** As I look at this sentence, I know that the subject of the sentence is *my family.* I ask myself, *Who or what does something?* and the answer is *my family.* To find the predicate of this sentence, I look for the words that tell me what the subject does or is. What does the subject *my family* do? The words *goes on hikes* answer that question. So *goes on hikes* is the predicate of this sentence.

Predicates

The **predicate** tells what the subject of a sentence does or is.

My family **goes on hikes**.
A hike **is fun**.

A **Write** each sentence. **Underline** the predicate.

1. Our family <u>hiked up a mountain</u>.
2. The trail <u>was hard</u>.
3. Dad and I <u>climbed very high</u>.
4. I <u>got very tired</u>.
5. My dad <u>helped me a little</u>.
6. He <u>gave me some water</u>.
7. The view <u>was great</u>.
8. The ground <u>looked far away</u>.
9. Everyone <u>climbed down slowly</u>.
10. The whole family <u>sits and rests</u>.

RESOURCES

Daily Fix-It Lesson 3
    See p. TR1.
    See also Daily Fix-It Transparency 3.
Grammar Transparency 3

B **Choose** the predicate that completes each sentence. **Write** the sentence.

1. Lucy (<u>has a backpack</u>, a heavy load).

2. The backpack (to school, <u>is red</u>).

3. Two books (on the bottom, <u>sit inside</u>).

4. One book (<u>tells about a hike</u>, a picture on the cover).

5. Lucy and Mom (a long trip, <u>hike and camp</u>).

C **Choose** a predicate from the box to complete each sentence. **Write** the sentences.

chattered and ran past us
walked in the woods
grew everywhere
was long
sang in the trees

6. Our family ___.
Our family walked in the woods.

7. Tall trees ___.
Tall trees grew everywhere.

8. A squirrel ___.
A squirrel chattered and ran past us.

9. Birds ___.
Birds sang in the trees.

10. Our walk ___.
Our walk was long.

Grammar **63**

Guided Practice **A**

Go through the exercise with children. Ask volunteers to identify the subject in each sentence first. Review the difference between the subject and the predicate in each sentence.

TEACHING TIP

Show children that every sentence must have a subject and predicate.

- Write a paragraph from a story on the board. Read each sentence, circling the subject and underlining the predicate.

- Ask children what would happen if a sentence did not have either a subject or a predicate. (It would not be a complete sentence and it wouldn't make sense.)

Independent Practice **B** and **C**

Have children complete the exercises. For Differentiated Instruction and Extra Practice, see p. TR11.

Differentiated Instruction

Strategic Intervention

Write this sentence on the board: *The cup is red.* Tell children that the subject of the sentence is *The cup.* Ask them what the predicate is. Underline the predicate. Write this sentence: *The cup breaks into pieces.* Again tell the subject and ask children to tell the predicate. Continue to make up sentences with *The cup* as the subject, each with a different predicate.

Advanced

Have children think of an outdoor activity they like to do and write several sentences about it. Then invite volunteers to act out their activities and let others guess what they are doing. Then have volunteers read aloud their sentences and call on others to identify the predicates of the sentences.

ELL

Provide scaffolding to English learners. Write predicates on the board that will help children complete Exercise C: *cooked on an open fire, hiked and camped, built a nest,* and so on. Ask children to share these phrases in their home languages. Then emphasize the phrases in English and help children add subjects to form new sentences. Have them circle the predicates in the sentences.

Test Preparation

✓ **Write** the letter of the correct answer.

1. A fawn ____.
   - ○ **A** and its mother
   - ○ **B** with spots
   - ⊗ **C** is a baby deer

2. The fawn ____.
   - ○ **A** long legs
   - ⊗ **B** hides in the grass
   - ○ **C** small and brown

3. A baby bear ____.
   - ⊗ **A** is a cub
   - ○ **B** with fur
   - ○ **C** up a tree

4. Cubs ____.
   - ○ **A** brown or black
   - ○ **B** sharp teeth
   - ⊗ **C** climb trees and swim

5. A baby fox ____.
   - ○ **A** fast
   - ⊗ **B** is a kit
   - ○ **C** with red fur

6. A kit ____.
   - ⊗ **A** sleeps in a den
   - ○ **B** long nose
   - ○ **C** and its mother

Review

✓ **Write** each sentence. **Underline** the predicate.

1. I <u>saw a rainbow</u>.
2. It <u>was in the sky</u>.
3. We <u>stopped and counted the colors</u>.
4. The rainbow <u>had seven colors</u>.
5. Dana <u>liked orange best</u>.
6. The rainbow <u>lasted a long time</u>.

✓ **Choose** the predicate that completes each sentence. **Write** the sentences.

7. Pedro (<u>has a pet dog</u>, a great pet).
8. Spot (a cute name, <u>is the dog's name</u>).
9. This pet (<u>has brown fur</u>, Pedro's friend).
10. The dog (<u>shakes hands</u>, a trick).
11. He (good dog, <u>rolls over too</u>).
12. Pedro and Spot (friends, <u>play together</u>).

Grammar **65**

Summarize

Ask children what important thing they remember about identifying the predicate in a sentence.

- The predicate of a sentence tells what the subject of the sentence does or is.

Grammar-Writing Connection

Display a picture of an animal doing an action, such as a frog jumping. Ask children to write sentences about the picture. If necessary, prompt them with questions: *What is the animal? What does it look like? What is it doing? What else can it do?* Remind them that their sentences must have subjects and predicates.

Use Descriptive Words in Predicates

OBJECTIVES

- Identify characteristics of an outdoor story.
- Write an outdoor story using descriptive words in predicates.
- Develop criteria for judging a piece of writing.

TEACH

Read aloud the information in the box at the top of the page. Then say: *Listen as I read two sentences. Pay particular attention to the predicates of the sentences.*

 Think Aloud *Mudge has a toy.* What is the predicate of this sentence? *(has a toy)* Does the predicate tell us very much about what happens? No, it tells us only that Mudge has a toy. *Mudge has a chewy toy in his mouth.* Does the predicate in this sentence tell us more about what happens? Yes, the words *chewy* and *in his mouth* give a clearer picture of the toy and what Mudge is doing with it.

Guided Writing

Read the two sentences in each item in Exercise 1 with children. Ask them to identify the predicates of the sentences before they choose the sentence that tells more about what happens. What words have been added to the predicate?

 ### Independent Writing

Read aloud the directions for Exercise 2. Discuss with children things they do outdoors and words they might use to describe these things. When they have completed their writing, call on volunteers to read what they have written.

Use Descriptive Words in Predicates

> **Use descriptive words in predicates.** These words can tell more about what happened.
>
> **No Descriptive Words**   Mudge has a toy.
>
> **Descriptive Words**   Mudge has a <u>chewy</u> toy <u>in his mouth</u>.

 Which sentence in each pair tells more about what happened? **Write** the sentence.

1. Henry swam.
   <u>Henry swam in the lake.</u>
2. <u>They made a huge fire on the sand.</u>
   They made a fire.
3. Dad cooked dinner.
   <u>Dad cooked fish and potatoes for dinner.</u>
4. <u>Mom set up our new tent under a tree.</u>
   Mom set up our tent.
5. <u>Henry gathered chunks of dry wood.</u>
   Henry gathered wood.

 Write about something you do outdoors. **Use** descriptive words to show readers what happened.
Possible answer is on page TR34.

RESOURCES

Writing Transparency 3

Write an Outdoor Story

Writing Prompt Write a story about an outdoor place that you like. Tell about something that happened there.

Opening sentence tells who, what, when, and where.

Story has a beginning, middle, and end.

Descriptive words tell readers exactly what happened.

Saturday in the Park with Mom

Last Saturday my mom and I went to Thompson Park for a picnic. We sat under a shady oak tree. We put our fruit and sandwiches out on an old wool blanket. Then a squirrel ran over and started looking at our food. We gave him a few ripe cherries. Soon there were six gray squirrels begging for food! Our picnic basket was empty when we went home.

Writing **67**

Outdoor Story
ANALYZE THE MODEL

Read aloud the model and the callouts to the left of it. Then prepare children to write their own outdoor stories.

PROMPT

Think of an outdoor place that you like. Then think of something that happened there that will make a good story. Now write your own story.

Getting Started Children can do any of the following.

- Use an organizer (pp. TR28–TR32).
- Put in order events that happened.
- Make a list of descriptive words to use.

Editing/Revising Checklist

☑ Did I include predicates in my sentences?

☑ Did I use describing words in my predicates?

☑ Does my story have a beginning, middle, and end?

Self-Evaluation Distribute copies of p. TR26 for children to fill out.

Scoring Rubric — Outdoor Story

Rubric 4 3 2 1	4	3	2	1
Focus/Ideas	Strong story; detailed ideas on topic	Good story; details mostly on topic	Unfocused story; some details not on topic	Unclear story; many details not on topic
Organization/ Paragraphs	Events told in order; clear beginning, middle, and end	Events somewhat in order; beginning, middle, and end	Events not in clear order; no beginning, middle, and end	No order; no story organization
Voice	Lively; shows writer's feelings	Mostly lively; shows writer's feelings	Not lively; few or no feelings	No attempt to show feelings
Word Choice	Vivid, clear word picture; many describing words	Good word picture; some describing words	No word picture; few describing words	Incorrect, dull, or overused words
Sentences	Complete sentences; reads smoothly	Most sentences complete; reads fairly smoothly	Many stringy or choppy sentences	Incomplete, choppy, or hard to understand sentences
Conventions	Few or no errors	No serious errors	Many errors	Too many errors

Statements and Questions

- Recognize statements and questions.
- Use statements and questions correctly in writing.
- Become familiar with statements and questions on standardized tests.

TEACH

Read aloud the definitions, instruction, and examples in the box on p. 68. Then say:

We know that sentences that are statements and questions both begin with capital letters. The difference between them is that a statement tells something and ends with a period, while a question asks something and ends with a question mark.

From the box on the board, write the two sentences: *Some places are very dry. Is a desert a dry place?* Point to each as you talk.

Think Aloud **Model** When I look at the first sentence, I know that it is a statement because it tells me something—that some places are very dry. I can also tell that it is a statement because it has a capital letter at the beginning and a period at the end. When I look at the second sentence, I know that it is a question because it asks something—Is a desert a dry place? I look at the beginning and the end of the sentence too. It begins with a capital letter and ends with a question mark. The question mark is a good clue. Only questions have question marks at the end.

Statements and Questions

A **statement** is a sentence that tells something. A statement ends with a **period (.)**.

Some places are very dry.

A **question** is a sentence that asks something. A question ends with a **question mark (?)**.

Is a desert a dry place?

All statements and questions begin with capital letters.

A **Read** each sentence. **Write** *S* if the sentence is a statement. **Write** *Q* if the sentence is a question.

1. Can an oak tree live in a desert? Q
2. An oak tree needs plenty of water. S
3. It cannot live in a very dry place. S
4. Are there any trees in the desert? Q
5. Where does a cactus grow? Q
6. A cactus can grow in the desert. S
7. Does a cactus have spines? Q
6. A cactus has waxy skin. S

RESOURCES

Daily Fix-It Lesson 4
  See p. TR2.
  See also Daily Fix-It Transparency 4.
Grammar Transparency 4

B **Write** the correct statement or question in each pair.

1. Rattlesnakes live in the desert.

   rattlesnakes live in the desert

2. I have never seen a rattlesnake?

   I have never seen a rattlesnake.

3. Are they dangerous?

   are they dangerous?

4. What other animals are in the desert.

   What other animals are in the desert?

5. it is too hot for most animals

   It is too hot for most animals.

C **Write** the sentences. **Use** a capital letter and the correct end mark.

6. many countries have deserts
   Many countries have deserts.

7. are the deserts large or small
   Are the deserts large or small?

8. some are very large
   Some are very large.

9. they are hundreds of miles wide
   They are hundreds of miles wide.

10. would you like to visit a desert
    Would you like to visit a desert?

Guided Practice **A**

Go through the exercise with children. Ask volunteers to tell how they decided whether each sentence was a statement or a question.

TEACHING TiP

Show children another important clue that end punctuation gives when identifying statements and questions.

- Write several statements and questions on the board.

- Read them aloud and point out how your voice goes up a little at the end of the questions but not at the end of the statements.

- Have children say the statements and questions. Ask them how the questions sound different from the statements. (Our voices go up a little at the end of the questions.)

Independent Practice **B** and **C**

Have children complete the exercises. For Differentiated Instruction and Extra Practice, see p. TR11.

Differentiated Instruction

Strategic Intervention

On the board, write pairs of sentences, such as these: *Jack is walking to school. Is Jack walking to school?* Read the sentences aloud and ask children to tell you which one tells something *(the statement)* and which one asks something. *(the question)* Continue with other pairs of sentences.

Advanced

Write a number of statements and questions on the board. Challenge children to change the statements into questions and the questions into statements. For example:

We are going to the zoo.

Are we going to the zoo?

Will he come with us?

He will come with us.

Remind children to use correct end punctuation.

ELL

Write several statements and questions on the board without punctuation. Pair English language learners with children who have mastered the concept. Have the partners work together to choose the correct end marks for the sentences.

You may wish to point out to children that in Spanish, the question mark appears at the beginning of a question, written as ¿, and at the end of the question, written as ?.

Monitor Progress

Check Grammar

If... children have difficulty identifying statements and questions,	**then...** write a paragraph from a familiar book on the board and help them identify statements and questions.

Test Preparation

✓ **Write** the letter of the correct answer.

1. ○ **A** is a cactus a plant or an animal
   ○ **B** is a cactus a plant or an animal?
   ⊗ **C** Is a cactus a plant or an animal?

2. ⊗ **A** A cactus is a plant.
   ○ **B** a cactus is a plant
   ○ **C** A cactus is a plant

3. ○ **A** Do cactuses grow tall
   ⊗ **B** Do cactuses grow tall?
   ○ **C** do cactuses grow tall

4. ○ **A** Some cactuses are very big
   ⊗ **B** Some cactuses are very big.
   ○ **C** Some cactuses are very big?

5. ○ **A** Does a cactus have leaves.
   ○ **B** does a cactus have leaves?
   ⊗ **C** Does a cactus have leaves?

6. ⊗ **A** A cactus has spines.
   ○ **B** A cactus has spines
   ○ **C** A cactus has spines?

Review

✓ **Write** the sentences. **Circle** each statement. **Underline** each question.

1. Did you go to the desert?
2. We went for a visit.
3. I rode a mule.
4. Did you see a lizard?
5. We saw one lizard.
6. Will you go back?

✓ **Write** each sentence correctly. **Use** a capital letter and the correct end mark.

7. some birds live in the desert
   Some birds live in the desert.
8. which birds live there
   Which birds live there?
9. you can find woodpeckers in deserts
   You can find woodpeckers in deserts.
10. hawks also live in the desert
    Hawks also live in the desert.
11. some birds build nests in cactuses
    Some birds build nests in cactuses.
12. what kinds of birds do that
    What kinds of birds do that?

Grammar **71**

Summarize

Ask children what they remember about identifying statements and questions.

- A statement tells something. It begins with a capital letter and ends with a period.
- A question asks something. It begins with a capital letter and ends with a question mark.

Grammar-Writing Connection

Use statements and questions to make your writing more interesting.

I went to the store. I wanted to buy some milk. When I got there, I saw my friend Leah. We talked for a while.

This paragraph has only statements. Change at least one statement to a question. This will make readers read on to answer the question.

I went to the store. I wanted to buy some milk. Who did I see when I got there? I saw my friend Leah. We talked for a while.

Words That Show Feelings

- Identify characteristics of an expository paragraph.
- Write an expository paragraph about your neighborhood using words that show feelings.
- Develop criteria for judging a piece of writing.

TEACH

Read aloud the instruction in the box at the top of the page. Then say: *As I read the following paragraph, listen carefully for words that show the writer's feelings.*

Think Aloud My sisters and I went to the ocean for the first time, and we loved it. We splashed each other and laughed and laughed. We built big, beautiful sand castles and watched the waves knock them down. We had fun.

Review with children the words they heard that told them how the writer feels about her day at the beach. Write the words on the board. *(loved, laughed, beautiful, fun)*

Guided Writing

Read items 1–5 in Exercise 1 with children. Have them tell which word from the Word Bank they would use to complete each sentence. Then call on volunteers to read each completed pair of sentences.

Independent Writing

Read aloud the directions for Exercise 2. List things that children have done for the first time and words they might use to tell how they felt at the time. Ask volunteers to read their sentences aloud.

 WRITER'S CRAFT

Words That Show Feelings

Good writers tell how they feel. They use **words that show their feelings**.

 Write a word from the box to tell how the writer feels. **Use** each word one time.

happy	mad	tired	sad	scared

1. We feel ___. sad
Our dog is lost.

2. The boy is ___. scared
He sees a tornado.

3. Sara is ___. happy
She won first prize.

4. I am ___. mad
Linda took the last apple.

5. Juan feels ___. tired
He just ran eight miles.

Write about something you did for the first time. **Use** words that show how you felt. Possible answer: I was scared the first time I rode on the big roller coaster. My stomach hurt, and my mouth was dry. I was also excited. I couldn't stand still as we waited in line.

72 Writing

RESOURCES

Writing Transparency 4

Tell About Your Neighborhood

Writing Prompt Write about your neighborhood. Tell what happens there and how you feel about it.

Writer begins with main idea about her neighborhood.

Details support the main idea and help readers "see" and "hear" the place.

Writer tells how she feels about topic.

A Busy Neighborhood

My neighborhood is a busy place. Cars, trucks, and buses rush up and down. Horns honk and sirens scream. Big machines fix holes in the streets. People hurry in and out of the stores and buildings. They talk and laugh and shout. My neighborhood is busy, but it is also exciting. I love it because something is always going on there.

Writing **73**

Tell About Your Neighborhood

ANALYZE THE MODEL

Read aloud the model and the callouts to the left of it. Then prepare children to write their own paragraphs.

PROMPT

Think about your neighborhood. What happens there and how do you feel about it? Write a paragraph about your neighborhood.

Getting Started Children can do any of the following.

- Use an organizer (pp. TR28–TR32).
- Close their eyes and picture their neighborhood on a typical day.
- Tell their ideas to a partner.

Editing/Revising Checklist

☑ Did I use words that show my feelings?

☑ Did I give details that support my main idea?

☑ Did I use correct end marks?

Self-Evaluation Distribute copies of p. TR26 for children to fill out.

Scoring Rubric
Paragraph About Neighborhood

Rubric 4 3 2 1	4	3	2	1
Focus/Ideas	Clearly stated main idea; strong supporting details	Good main idea; good supporting details	Main idea not clear; few supporting details	Main idea unclear; few or no supporting details
Organization/ Paragraphs	Main idea and details in clear order	Main idea and details in order	Unclear order	No order
Voice	Clearly shows writer's feelings	Mostly shows writer's feelings	Shows few feelings	Shows no feelings at all
Word Choice	Clear, well-chosen words	Words mostly well chosen	Words sometimes off topic	Words often off topic
Sentences	Complete sentences; includes statements and questions	Most sentences complete; includes at least one question	Some incomplete sentences; no variety	Many incomplete sentences; no variety
Conventions	Few or no errors	No serious errors	Many errors	Too many errors

Commands and Exclamations

OBJECTIVES

- Recognize commands and exclamations.
- Use commands and exclamations correctly in writing.
- Become familiar with commands and exclamations on standardized tests.

TEACH

Read aloud the definitions and examples in the box on p. 74. Then say:

We know that sentences that are commands and exclamations both begin with capital letters. The difference between them is that a command tells someone to do something and ends with a period, while an exclamation shows surprise or strong feelings and ends with an exclamation mark.

Write the first and third examples from the box (*Pack your suitcase. What a great trip this will be!*) on the board. Point to them as you talk.

Think Aloud **Model** When I read the first sentence, I see that it is telling someone to do something. Also it ends with a period, and the subject is *you* although *you* does not appear in the sentence. I know that this sentence is a command. When I read the second sentence, I see that it shows strong feelings about a trip. Also it ends with an exclamation mark. I know that this sentence is an exclamation.

Commands and Exclamations

A **command** is a sentence that tells someone to do something. It ends with a **period (.)**. The subject of a command is *you*, but *you* is usually not shown.

Pack your suitcase.   Please come with me.

An **exclamation** is a sentence that shows surprise or strong feelings. It ends with an **exclamation mark (!)**.

What a great trip this will be!   I am so happy!

All commands and exclamations begin with capital letters.

A **Write** each sentence. **Write** *C* if the sentence is a command. **Write** *E* if it is an exclamation.

1. Bring your camera.
   C
2. Put your jacket on.
   C
3. Oh dear, we are so late!
   E
4. Please get in the car.
   C
5. Hooray, we're on our way!
   E

74 Grammar

RESOURCES

Daily Fix-It Lesson 5
   See p. TR2.
   See also Daily Fix-It Transparency 5.
Grammar Transparency 5

B **Write** the correct command or exclamation in each pair.

1. <u>My, what a lot of snow there is!</u>
   My, what a lot of snow there is.

2. play in the snow with me.
   <u>Play in the snow with me.</u>

3. Please put on your mittens?
   <u>Please put on your mittens.</u>

4. here comes the sun?
   <u>Here comes the sun!</u>

5. Oh no, the snow is gone?
   <u>Oh no, the snow is gone!</u>

C **Complete** each command or exclamation. **Put** a period at the end if the sentence is a command. **Put** an exclamation mark at the end if the sentence is an exclamation. Possible answers:

6. Look at this ____
   Look at this sunset.

7. Wow, it ____
   Wow, it is so red!

8. How beautiful ____
   How beautiful the sky is!

9. Take a ____
   Take a picture of it.

10. Show everyone ____
    Show everyone your picture.

Guided Practice Ⓐ

Go through the exercise with children. Read the sentences aloud together. This will help children hear the differences between the commands and the exclamations. Then ask volunteers to tell why they chose each answer.

TEACHING TIP

Help children better understand the subject of a command, even though it is not shown in the sentence.

- Write the sentence *Shut the door* on the board. Ask children who or what is doing something in this sentence. (you)

- Point out that what the sentence is really saying is *(You) shut the door.* Write this sentence on the board. Explain that *You* is not stated in the command; it is "understood," that is, readers understand that *you* is the subject of the command.

Independent Practice
Ⓑ and Ⓒ

Have children complete the exercises. For Differentiated Instruction and Extra Practice, see p. TR11.

Differentiated Instruction

Strategic Intervention

Write these exclamations on the board, but end each with a period:

What a day I have had.

I am so excited.

I can't wait.

Read aloud the sentences to children with the appropriate expression. Ask them what is wrong with the way the sentences are written. Have volunteers add exclamation marks to the sentences and then read the sentences aloud together.

Advanced

Display a picture of an animal doing something amazing, such as a cheetah running or a whale breaching. Ask children to write several sentences about the animal. Tell them to include at least one exclamation and one command. Check to see that they punctuated their sentences correctly. Ask volunteers to read their sentences to the group.

ELL

Have each child write a large exclamation mark and a large period on two index cards. Then say an exclamation or a command using the appropriate expression. Have children hold up the correct end mark for the sentence. Then say the sentence together.

Monitor Progress

Check Grammar

If... children have difficulty identifying commands and exclamations,	**then...** read aloud commands and exclamations from magazine ads and let children identify the kind of sentence each is.

Test Preparation

✔ **Write** the letter of the correct answer.

1. ○ **A** pick up this rock
   ⊗ **B** Pick up this rock.
   ○ **C** Pick up this rock

2. ⊗ **A** It is so heavy!
   ○ **B** it is so heavy.
   ○ **C** It is so heavy

3. ○ **A** please be careful?
   ○ **B** Please be careful
   ⊗ **C** Please be careful.

4. ⊗ **A** I have a great idea!
   ○ **B** i have a great idea!
   ○ **C** I have a great idea

5. ○ **A** Stand over there
   ⊗ **B** Stand over there.
   ○ **C** stand over there!

6. ○ **A** hurray, we did it
   ○ **B** hurray, we did it.
   ⊗ **C** Hurray, we did it!

76   Grammar

Review

✓ **Write** the sentences. **Circle** each command. **Underline** each exclamation.

1. (Please help me)
2. (Choose the strongest animal.)
3. Gosh, that is hard!
4. (Tell me your answer.)
5. I just don't know!
6. (Make your best guess.)

✓ **Write** each sentence correctly. **Use** a capital letter and the correct end mark.

7. look at this ant
   Look at this ant.
8. wow, it is so tiny
   Wow, it is so tiny!
9. what a huge crumb it has
   What a huge crumb it has!
10. pick up your lunch
    Pick up your lunch.
11. ants are on my sandwich
    Ants are on my sandwich!
12. throw it away
    Throw it away.

Grammar **77**

Summarize

Ask children what they know about commands and exclamations.

- A command tells someone to do something. It begins with a capital letter and ends with a period. The subject of a command is *you*, but the word *you* usually does not appear in the sentence.
- An exclamation shows surprise or strong feelings. It begins with a capital letter and ends with an exclamation mark.

Grammar-Writing Connection

Explain to children they should not write too many exclamations. Read this paragraph aloud.

> *I can't believe my luck! I found the coolest rock! It's covered in shiny stones that look like diamonds! I bet it's worth millions! I can't wait to show my friends!*

Point out that reading this paragraph is tiring because every sentence shows surprise or strong feelings. Remind children that good writers use different kinds of sentences in their writing to make it interesting. Read this paragraph aloud.

> *I found the coolest rock! Look at it. It's covered in shiny stones that look like diamonds. Is it worth millions? I can't wait to show my friends!*

Use Commands and Exclamations

- Identify characteristics of a tale about an animal.
- Write a tale about an animal using commands and exclamations to add variety.
- Develop criteria for judging a piece of writing.

TEACH

Read aloud the instruction in the box at the top of p. 78. Then say: *As I read this paragraph, listen to the kinds of sentences I use.*

Think Aloud *Look at that big anthill. The ants built it in one day. That is amazing! How did they do it?*

Ask children to identify the kinds of sentences. (*command, statement, exclamation, question*) Ask them how they recognized each sentence.

Guided Writing

Read items 1–5 in Exercise 1 with children. Have them tell which sentence in each pair shows strong feelings and what clues they used to decide.

Independent Writing

Read aloud the directions for Exercise 2. Ask children to tell about exciting things that have happened to them. After they have finished their writing, ask volunteers to share what they have written.

 WRITER'S CRAFT

Use Commands and Exclamations

> **Use commands and exclamations** to add variety to your sentences. They also let your readers know your feelings.
>
> Look at those ants. How tiny they are!

 Which sentence in each pair shows strong feelings? **Write** the sentence.

1. We saw many ants.
   <u>We had never seen so many ants!</u>

2. <u>That ant bit me!</u>
   Do ants bite?

3. <u>Don't step on the ants.</u>
   The ants are on the steps.

4. The ants are moving slowly.
   <u>Watch the ants carry those big crumbs.</u>

5. <u>I think ants are amazing!</u>
   Do you like ants?

 Write about something exciting that happened to you. **Use** a command and an exclamation.

Possible answer: Once fire ants bit me. I had 30 bites on my legs! They really hurt. Don't mess with fire ants.

78 Writing

RESOURCES

Writing Transparency 5

Tell a Tale About an Animal

Writing Prompt Imagine that you have discovered an amazing animal. Tell what the animal is and why it is amazing. Also tell how you feel about the discovery.

Writer mixes real and make-believe details.

Writer shows his feelings.

Writer ends with a command.

A Talking Rabbit!

Yesterday I was walking home from school. As I passed by the woods near the highway, I heard someone say hello. I looked around, but no one was there. Then I saw a rabbit. It told me its name was Roger. I had found a talking rabbit! I was so excited! I asked Roger to come with me. Look for us tonight on the news.

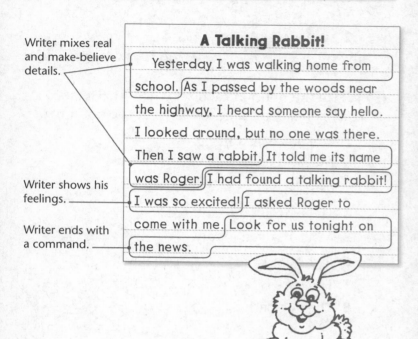

Writing 79

Tell a Tale About an Animal

ANALYZE THE MODEL

Read aloud the model and the callouts to the left of it. Then prepare children to write their own tales about an animal.

PROMPT

Think of an animal that can do something amazing. Write a story about the animal. Use commands and exclamations to show your feelings.

Getting Started Children can do any of the following.

- Use an organizer (pp. TR28–TR32).
- Look through a book of animals to get ideas.
- Talk about their ideas with a partner.

Editing/Revising Checklist

☑ Did I explain why my animal is amazing?

☑ Did I use commands and exclamations?

☑ Did I put the correct marks at the ends of my sentences?

Self-Evaluation Distribute copies of p. TR26 for children to fill out.

Scoring Rubric — Tale About an Animal

Rubric 4 3 2 1	4	3	2	1
Focus/Ideas	Strong story; all details on topic	Good story; most details on topic	Unfocused story; some details not on topic	Unclear story; many details not on topic
Organization/ Paragraphs	Clear beginning, middle, end; easy to follow	Details mostly in order	Details not in clear order	No order
Voice	Imaginative, lively; shows writer's feelings	Fairly imaginative and lively; shows some feelings	Not very imaginative or lively; shows few feelings	Careless; shows no feelings
Word Choice	Vivid; clear word pictures	Good word pictures	Vague word pictures	Dull word choices; no word pictures
Sentences	Complete sentences; good variety	Most sentences complete; some variety	Some incomplete sentences; little variety	Many incomplete sentences; no variety
Conventions	Few or no errors	No serious errors	Many errors	Too many errors

Nouns

TEACH

Read aloud the definition and examples in the box on p. 80. Then say:

When I see a word that names a person, place, animal, or thing, I know that the word is a noun. A noun is a word that names a person, place, animal, or thing.

Write the nouns from the box (*man, lake, dog, ice*) on the board. Point to them.

Think Aloud **Model** The word *man* names a person, so *man* is a noun. The word *lake* names a place, so *lake* is a noun too. Words that name an animal or a thing are also nouns, so *dog* is a noun, and *ice* is a noun. *Dog* names an animal, and *ice* names a thing.

LESSON 6

Nouns

A **noun** names a person, place, animal, or thing.

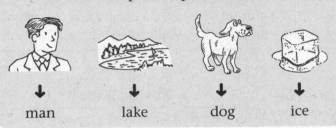

man   lake   dog   ice

A **Write** the noun in each sentence. **Write** *person, place, animal,* or *thing* to tell what the noun names.

1. The boy was waiting.
   boy; person
2. His farm is nearby.
   farm; place
3. Chickens cluck noisily.
   chickens; animal
4. The barn is large and red.
   barn; thing
5. A bus honked loudly.
   bus; thing
6. A child waved.
   child; person
7. The park is far.
   park; place
8. The dog barks.
   dog; animal

80 Grammar

RESOURCES

Daily Fix-It Lesson 6
    See p. TR2.
    See also Daily Fix-It Transparency 6.
Grammar Transparency 6

B There are three nouns in each sentence. One noun is underlined. **Write** the other two nouns.

1. The pond was covered with <u>ice</u> and snow.
   pond, snow
2. The ducks and <u>geese</u> had no food.
   ducks, food
3. Two <u>children</u> lived in a house across the street.
   house, street
4. The girl and boy brought <u>bread</u>.
   girl, boy
5. With many loud <u>honks</u>, the birds ate the crumbs.
   birds, crumbs

C **Complete** each sentence with a noun. **Write** the sentences. Possible answers:

6. My dog and I play in the ___.
   My dog and I play in the park.
7. I toss him a ___.
   I toss him a ball.
8. My dog may chase a ___.
   My dog may chase a squirrel.
9. My ___ comes too.
   My friend comes too.
10. The dog runs on the ___.
    The dog runs on the grass.

Grammar **81**

PRACTICE

Guided Practice Ⓐ

Go through the exercise with children. Remind them to look for the word in each sentence that names a person, place, animal, or thing. Ask volunteers to tell how they identified the noun in each sentence.

TEACHING TIP

Help children distinguish nouns from other words.

- Write the words *hat*, *sit*, and *book* on the board.
- Challenge children to choose the word that is *not* a noun.
- Continue with other sets of words, such as *build, chair, woman; bicycle, shoe, eat; cat, wear, bracelet.*

Independent Practice
Ⓑ and Ⓒ

Have children complete the exercises. For Differentiated Instruction and Extra Practice, see p. TR12.

Differentiated Instruction

Strategic Intervention

On the board, draw four columns and label them *Person, Place, Animal,* and *Thing.* Ask volunteers to think of nouns that name people. Write children's suggested words in the first column. Then continue with the other categories.

Advanced

Ask children to write sentences about a place they like to visit. Tell them to use at least two nouns in each sentence and to leave space between their sentences. After they have written their sentences, have them underline the nouns and identify each as naming a *person, place, animal,* or *thing.*

ELL

Show children detailed illustrations or photographs from books or magazines. Ask them to name as many persons, places, animals, or things in the pictures as they can. Write their responses on the board and read the words together. Point out that all these words are nouns. Invite children to share words in their home languages for the people, places, animals, and things.

Monitor Progress

Check Grammar

If... children have difficulty identifying nouns,	**then...** give them a copy of a page from a familiar story and have them circle all the nouns.

Test Preparation

☑ **Write** the letter of the correct answer.

1. Dogs are our ___.
- ○ **A** happy
- ⊗ **B** friends
- ○ **C** soft

2. They can have important ___.
- ○ **A** run
- ○ **B** swim
- ⊗ **C** jobs

3. Some dogs are ___ for people.
- ○ **A** few
- ○ **B** bark
- ⊗ **C** helpers

4. Some dogs find people in the ___.
- ⊗ **A** woods
- ○ **B** look
- ○ **C** right

5. Strong dogs can pull ___.
- ⊗ **A** sleds
- ○ **B** find
- ○ **C** like

6. A dog may watch a ___.
- ○ **A** have
- ⊗ **B** house
- ○ **C** new

82 Grammar

Review

✓ **Choose** the noun in ( ) to complete each sentence.
Write the sentences.

1. There are all kinds of (<u>dogs</u>, says).

2. Some dogs have short (very, <u>tails</u>).

3. Many dogs have long (sing, <u>hair</u>).

4. Most dogs have sharp (keep, <u>teeth</u>).

5. Some dogs swim in (old, <u>lakes</u>).

6. Many (know, <u>people</u>) like dogs.

✓ **Choose** a noun from the box to replace each
underlined word. **Write** the sentences.

| food | vet | dish | yard | dog | tub |

7. A pet <u>animal</u> needs care.
   A pet dog needs care.
8. Feed it good <u>thing</u>.
   Feed it good food.
9. Put food in a <u>thing</u>.
   Put food in a dish.
10. Play in the <u>place</u> with your dog.
    Play in the yard with your dog.
11. Wash your pet in a <u>thing</u>.
    Wash your pet in a tub.
12. Take your dog to a <u>person</u>.
    Take your dog to a vet.

Summarize

Ask children to tell what they know
about nouns.

• A noun names a person, place,
animal, or thing.

Grammar-Writing Connection

Write the following cloze story on
the board.

A ___ was walking to the ___. It was
a lovely ___. The ___ wanted to get a
___. A tall ___ with a ___ on her ___
tapped the ___ on the ___ and asked
to borrow a ___. How odd, thought
the ___. A ___ asked me the same
thing yesterday!

*(Possible answer: A **boy** was walking
to the **store**. It was a lovely **day**. The
boy wanted to get a **newspaper**. A
tall **woman** with a **snake** on her **head**
tapped the **boy** on the **arm** and asked
to borrow a **shoelace**. How odd,
thought the **boy**. A **man** asked me
the same thing yesterday!)*

Ask children to help you fill in the
blanks in the story with nouns. Point
out that the story doesn't have to
make sense. Write children's suggested
nouns in the blanks, and then read
aloud the finished story together.

Time-order Words

- Identify characteristics of directions.
- Write directions using time-order words.
- Develop criteria for judging a piece of writing.

TEACH

Read aloud the information in the box at the top of the page. Then say: *Listen carefully for time-order words as I read these sentences.*

Think Aloud *First I got up. Next I brushed my teeth. Then I got dressed. Last I ate breakfast.* I know that *first, next, then,* and *last* are time-order words. The writer used these words to show me the order in which he does things every morning.

Guided Writing

Read items 1–4 in Exercise 1 with children. Ask them which word in the Word Bank they would use to begin each sentence. Point out that first they have to decide what order the sentences belong in.

Independent Writing

Read the directions for Exercise 2. Discuss with children things they can make or do. After they complete the exercise, ask volunteers to share what they have written.

WRITER'S CRAFT

Time-order Words

Good writers use **time-order words** to show readers the order of steps or events. Some time-order words are *first, next, then, later, now, tomorrow,* and *last.*

First I got up. **Next** I brushed my teeth.

Then I got dressed. **Last** I ate breakfast.

Choose the best order for the sentences. **Find** a word in the Word Bank to begin each sentence. **Write** the sentences in a paragraph.

First	Next	Then	Last

1. ___ Bill opens the door for Turk.
2. ___ Turk brings his leash to Bill.
3. ___ Turk rushes outside.
4. ___ Bill puts the leash on Turk.

2. First Turk brings his leash to Bill. 4. Next (or Then) Bill puts the leash on Turk. 1. Then (or Next) Bill opens the door for Turk. 3. Last Turk rushes outside.

Tell how to make or do something. **Put** your sentences in order. **Use** time-order words.

Possible answer:
First I got the bag of cat food. Next I poured the cat food into Kip's bowl. Then I put out fresh water for him. Last I called Kip.

84 Writing

RESOURCES

Writing Transparency 6

Write Directions

> **Writing Prompt** Write directions to help a new student get from your classroom to the lunchroom.

Writer tells what directions are for in first sentence.

Writer uses time-order words to show order of steps.

Details make directions clear.

How to Get to the Lunchroom

Follow these directions to get from our classroom to the lunchroom. First go out the classroom door and turn right. Next walk to the end of the hall. You will pass six classrooms and the gym. Then turn left and go down the stairs. Now turn left again. Walk to the second door on the right. Go through that door, and you are in the lunchroom.

Writing **85**

Write Directions

ANALYZE THE MODEL

Read aloud the model and the callouts to the left of it. Then prepare children to write their own directions.

> ### PROMPT
> Imagine a new student wants to go from your classroom to the lunchroom. Write directions for the student. Include time-order words.

Getting Started Children can do any of the following.
- Use an organizer (pp. TR28–TR32).
- Close their eyes and picture the route to the lunchroom in their minds.
- Draw a map to use as an aid while they write.

Editing/Revising Checklist
☑ Did I use time-order words to show the steps?

☑ Are my directions clear and easy to follow?

☑ Did I use nouns correctly?

Self-Evaluation Distribute copies of p. TR26 for children to fill out.

Scoring Rubric — Write Directions

Rubric 4 3 2 1	4	3	2	1
Focus/Ideas	Directions focused on topic; give all important steps	Directions generally focused on topic; give most steps	Directions not clearly focused; give few steps	Directions with no focus or steps
Organization/ Paragraphs	Steps organized in correct order; easy to follow	Steps mostly organized in correct order	Some steps not in order or missing; hard to follow	No order
Voice	Clear, knowledgeable voice	Fairly clear, knowledgeable voice	No clear voice	Uninvolved or indifferent
Word Choice	Uses time-order words and strong verbs	Uses some time-order words and strong verbs	Few time-order words or strong verbs	Incorrect or limited word choice
Sentences	Clear sentences; use of commands	Mostly clear sentences; some commands	Sentences unclear; few commands	Incoherent sentences; no commands
Conventions	Few or no errors	No serious errors	Many errors	Too many errors

Proper Nouns

- Recognize proper nouns.
- Use proper nouns correctly in writing.
- Become familiar with proper nouns on standardized tests.

TEACH

Read aloud the definition, instruction, and examples in the box on p. 86. Then say:

We know that nouns are words that name people, places, animals, or things. Proper nouns are special names for people, places, animals, and things. They begin with capital letters.

Write the example paragraph on the board. Circle the proper nouns as you talk about them.

Think Aloud

Model I see the name *Mr. Morgan*. This is a proper noun because *Mr.* is the title for a person and *Morgan* is a special name for a person. I also see the name *Ronald Morgan*. It is the special name for a person too, so it is a proper noun. Here are some more proper nouns. *Tuesday* is a day of the week, *May* is a month of the year, and *Walker Park* is the special name of a place. How else can I tell that these are proper nouns? I see that they begin with capital letters.

Proper Nouns

Proper nouns are special names for people, places, animals, and things. They begin with capital letters. **Days of the week, months of the year,** and **holidays** also begin with capital letters. **Titles** for people begin with capital letters. Many titles end with a **period (.).** Some proper nouns have more than one word.

Mr. Morgan threw the ball. **Ronald Morgan** swung at it. He got his first hit on **Tuesday, May** 10, in **Walker Park.**

A **Write** the two proper nouns in each sentence.

1. Alicia Ortiz broke her arm on July 1.
   Alicia Ortiz, July
2. Dr. Lee said not to play baseball until Labor Day. Dr. Lee, Labor Day
3. On Friday the girl was back at Pioneer Park.
   Friday, Pioneer Park
4. Her team, the Patton Panthers, was playing the Terry Tigers. Patton Panthers, Terry Tigers
5. "Go, Roberto! Come on, Cindy!" she shouted.
   Roberto, Cindy
6. The next game is at Anders Field on the Fourth of July. Anders Field, Fourth of July

86 Grammar

RESOURCES

Daily Fix-It Lesson 7
    See p. TR3.
    See also Daily Fix-It Transparency 7.
Grammar Transparency 7

B **Write** the two proper nouns in each sentence correctly. Some proper nouns have more than one word.

1. Our new coach, mrs. alice ray, moved here in june. Mrs. Alice Ray, June

2. On monday morning she met us at morgan field. Monday, Morgan Field

3. This park is on doyle road, near the town of amber. Doyle Road, Amber

4. Our game with the raytown ravens will be on flag day. Raytown Ravens, Flag Day

5. My friends marcus and leo are great players. Marcus, Leo

6. Our old coach, mr. franklin, moved to cleveland. Mr. Franklin, Cleveland

C **Complete** each sentence with a proper noun of your own. The word in ( ) tells you what kind of proper noun to use. **Write** the sentences.

Possible answers:

7. I have a friend named ___. (person's name)
I have a friend named Shawn.

8. Our birthdays are in ___. (month)
Our birthdays are in October.

9. We both like ___. (holiday)
We both like Memorial Day.

10. We both have pets named ___. (animal's name)
We both have pets named Flash.

Grammar **87**

Guided Practice Ⓐ

Go through the exercise with children. Ask volunteers to tell how they decided which words in the sentences were proper nouns. Remind children that there are two proper nouns in each sentence, but that each noun may have one or more words.

TEACHING TIP

Help children distinguish proper nouns from other nouns.

- On the board, write common and proper nouns: *pig, Mr., Jack, raincoat, Tuesday, house, March, lake,* and *New York.*

- Point to each noun and ask if it is a proper noun. When children say yes, ask them how they know that.

Independent Practice
Ⓑ and Ⓒ

Have children complete the exercises. For Differentiated Instruction and Extra Practice, see p. TR12.

Differentiated Instruction

Strategic Intervention

Give each child part of a newspaper page. Have children circle proper nouns in the text. When they are finished, ask them to share some of the proper nouns with the group and explain how they knew these words were proper nouns.

Advanced

Have children write several sentences about a recent family outing they enjoyed. Tell them to use at least three proper nouns in their sentences. Ask children to exchange papers with another child and circle the proper nouns in each other's work.

ELL

On the board, write titles for people: *Mr., Ms., Mrs., Dr., Rev.* Read the titles together. Ask children to offer names to go with the titles. Write their suggestions on the board: *Mr. Gomez, Ms. Wong.* Then ask children to share titles for people in their home languages. Add the names and say those together as well.

Point out to children that they are looking for proper nouns to complete the sentences. Remind them that proper nouns begin with capital letters.

Monitor Progress

Check Grammar

If... children have difficulty identifying proper nouns,	**then...** have them look for examples in their science, reading, or social studies textbook.

Test Preparation

✓ Write the letter of the correct answer.

1. One baseball team is the ___.
   - ○ **A** Chicago cubs
   - ○ **B** chicago cubs
   - ⊗ **C** Chicago Cubs

2. There are baseball teams in ___.
   - ○ **A** boston and dallas
   - ⊗ **B** Boston and Dallas
   - ○ **C** Boston and dallas

3. One famous baseball player was ___.
   - ○ **A** Mr. babe ruth
   - ⊗ **B** Mr. Babe Ruth
   - ○ **C** mr. Babe Ruth

4. The season ends after ___.
   - ⊗ **A** Labor Day
   - ○ **B** Labor day
   - ○ **C** labor day

5. The World Series begins in ___.
   - ○ **A** october
   - ○ **B** OCTOBER
   - ⊗ **C** October

6. ___ want to go to a game.
   - ⊗ **A** Liz and Tom
   - ○ **B** Liz and tom
   - ○ **C** liz and tom

Review

✓ **Write** the proper nouns in the sentences correctly. The number in ( ) tells how many proper nouns are in the sentence.

1. mrs. smith helps me with math. (1)
   Mrs. Smith
2. She also coaches the bayfield bears. (1)
   Bayfield Bears
3. I go to her house every monday. (1)
   Monday
4. It is on maple street next to lincoln school. (2)
   Maple Street, Lincoln School
5. The smiths have a cat called mr. fluffy. (2)
   Smiths, Mr. Fluffy
6. alex smith got the cat in april. (2)
   Alex Smith, April

✓ **Complete** each sentence with a proper noun from the box. **Write** the sentences. **Write** the proper nouns correctly.

| ms. brown | labor day |
| atlantic ocean | florida |

7. Ben lives in the state of ___.
   Ben lives in the state of Florida.
8. He swims in the ___. He swims in the Atlantic Ocean.
9. ___ is teaching him. Ms. Brown is teaching him.
10. By ___, he will swim well. By Labor Day, he will swim well.

Summarize

Ask children what they know about proper nouns.

- Proper nouns are special names for people, places, animals, or things.
- Days of the week, months of the year, holidays, and titles for people are also proper nouns.
- All proper nouns begin with capital letters.

Grammar-Writing Connection

Explain to children that using proper nouns will help make their writing more vivid and interesting because proper nouns add details.

Less vivid: The family spent the holiday at a beach.

More vivid: The Camerons spent Labor Day at White Sands Beach.

Use Precise Nouns

- Identify characteristics of a paragraph.
- Write a paragraph using precise nouns.
- Develop criteria for judging a piece of writing.

TEACH

Read aloud the information in the box at the top of the page. Then say: *Listen as I read these sentences.*

 Think Aloud When I read the sentence *Those people are the team,* I do not get a clear picture. Why not? *People* and *team* are not precise nouns. They do not tell me very much. When I read the sentence *Those players are the Midville Mavericks,* I get a much clearer picture. *Players* and *Midville Mavericks* are more precise nouns than *people* and *team.* They tell me more.

 Guided Writing

Read items 1–5 in Exercise 1 with children. Have them tell which noun from the Word Bank they would use in each sentence. Ask volunteers to read their sentences aloud.

 Independent Writing

Read the directions for Exercise 2. Discuss games and activities children might write about and help them think of precise nouns to use. Ask volunteers to read aloud their paragraphs.

  WRITER'S CRAFT

Use Precise Nouns

Use **precise nouns** in your writing. Precise nouns give your readers clear pictures.

Those <u>people</u> are the <u>team</u>.

↓ ↓

Those <u>players</u> are the <u>Midville</u> <u>Mavericks</u>.

Choose a noun from the box to replace the underlined words in each sentence. **Write** the sentences.

uniforms	gloves	dugout
Dave Wilson	Riverside Field	

1. The Mavericks play at <u>the park</u>.
   The Mavericks play at Riverside Field.
2. They wear <u>clothes</u> with red stripes.
   They wear uniforms with red stripes.
3. <u>That man</u> is their best pitcher.
   Dave Wilson is their best pitcher.
4. The players sit in the <u>place</u>.
   The players sit in the dugout.
5. They carry their <u>things</u> onto the field.
   They carry their gloves onto the field.

 Write a paragraph about a game or activity. **Use** precise nouns to make a clear picture.
Possible answer is on page TR34.

90 Writing

RESOURCES

Writing Transparency 7

Tell How to Pick a Fantasy Team

Writing Prompt Imagine you are picking players for a baseball team. The players on this fantasy team must be animals. Choose several animals, and tell why they can or cannot be on your team.

First sentence tells what the paragraph is about.

Writer uses exact nouns to make a clear picture.

Ending is funny.

A Fantasy Team

What animals would I choose to play on my fantasy baseball team? An octopus can throw, catch, and hit, but it cannot run. A horse cannot throw, catch, or hit, but it can run. The octopus could be the pitcher. The horse could run in place of the octopus. Monkeys would make good players. They can run, hit, catch, and throw. They could play on the bases and in the field. Fish would be terrible players. They cannot run, hit, catch, or throw!

Writing 91

Tell How to Pick a Fantasy Team

ANALYZE THE MODEL

Read aloud the model and the callouts to the left of it. Then prepare children to write their own paragraphs.

PROMPT

Now think of animals that can or cannot be on your fantasy baseball team. Use precise nouns to make a clear picture of your team.

Getting Started Children can do any of the following.

- Use an organizer (pp. TR28–TR32).
- List animals and how they move.
- Review what baseball players do in the game.

Editing/Revising Checklist

☑ Did I use precise nouns to give a clear picture?

☑ Did I include a beginning and an ending?

☑ Did I begin proper nouns with capital letters?

Self-Evaluation Distribute copies of p. TR26 for children to fill out.

Scoring Rubric
Fantasy Team Paragraph

Rubric 4 3 2 1	4	3	2	1
Focus/Ideas	Strongly focused on topic; excellent supporting details	Generally focused on topic; good supporting details	Somewhat unfocused; few supporting details	No focus on topic; no supporting details
Organization/ Paragraphs	Well-organized paragraph; ideas in order	Good paragraph; ideas in some order	Weak paragraph; little order to ideas	Not a paragraph; no order to ideas
Voice	Imaginative, lively; shows how writer feels	Mostly imaginative, lively; shows some feelings	Not very imaginative or lively; shows few feelings	Not imaginative or lively; shows no feelings
Word Choice	Vivid, clear word picture; uses precise nouns	Clear word picture; some precise nouns	Dull or unclear word picture; few precise nouns	No word picture; no precise nouns
Sentences	Complete sentences; different kinds	Most sentences complete; some different kinds	Many stringy or choppy sentences	Incomplete or choppy sentences
Conventions	Few or no errors	No serious errors	Many errors	Too many errors

Singular and Plural Nouns

- Recognize singular and plural nouns.
- Use singular and plural nouns correctly in writing.
- Become familiar with singular and plural nouns on standardized tests.

TEACH

Read aloud the definitions, instruction, and examples in the box on p. 92. Then say:

Nouns that name one person, place, animal, or thing are called singular nouns. Nouns that name more than one person, place, animal, or thing are called plural nouns. To make a singular noun plural, you usually add -s at the end. However, if the noun ends in s, ch, sh, or x, you add -es.

Write the example nouns from the box (*turtle, bears, rabbits, foxes*) on the board.

Think Aloud **Model** I know that the word *turtle* is a singular noun. It names one animal, so it does not have -s or -es at the end. The words *bears, rabbits,* and *foxes* are plural nouns. They name more than one animal. *Bears* and *rabbits* have -s at the end. *Foxes* has -es at the end. Why? Because the singular noun, *fox,* ends with x.

LESSON 8

Singular and Plural Nouns

A **singular noun** names one person, place, animal, or thing. A noun that names more than one is called a **plural noun**.

turtle (one)   bears (more than one)

You add **-s** to most nouns to show more than one. If a noun ends in **s, ch, sh,** or **x**, add **-es** to the noun to show more than one.

rabbits (add **-s**)   foxes (add **-es**)

A **Add** *-s* or *-es* to each singular noun. **Write** the plural noun.

1. tree trees
2. bus buses
3. shoe shoes
4. box boxes
5. lamp lamps
6. dish dishes

92 Grammar

RESOURCES

Daily Fix-It Lesson 8
   See p. TR3.
   See also Daily Fix-It Transparency 8.
Grammar Transparency 8

B **Write** each sentence. **Underline** the singular noun. **Circle** the plural noun.

1. A <u>rabbit</u> raced with (turtles).

2. Only one <u>raccoon</u> watched from the (benches).

3. The (squirrels) rested under a <u>tree</u>.

4. The <u>cow</u> was eating some tall (grasses).

5. The <u>race</u> had no (winners).

6. The (animals) gave up and had a <u>party</u>.

C **Add** -s or -es to each word in ( ). **Write** the sentences.

7. The (bear) were not happy. bears

8. Some (branch) fell into the stream. branches

9. Two (beaver) helped. beavers

10. They chewed the wood into (piece). pieces

11. (Fox) pulled the wood from the stream. Foxes

12. The rabbits under the (bush) were glad. bushes

Grammar **93**

PRACTICE

Guided Practice A

Go through the exercise with children. Ask them to explain why they added -s to some of the words and -es to others.

TEACHING TIP

Help children identify singular nouns to which we add -es to make their plural forms.

• Write s, ch, sh, and x in four columns on the board.

• With children, brainstorm singular nouns that end with these letters.

• Begin with the words bus, dish, and box from Exercise A. Offer other words, such as glass, ash, peach, bench, and tax. Encourage children to suggest other words.

• Leave the lists on the board for this lesson.

Independent Practice
B **and** C

Have children complete the exercises. For Differentiated Instruction and Extra Practice, see p. TR12.

Differentiated Instruction

Strategic Intervention

Write singular and plural nouns on index cards, one noun per card. Have children take turns drawing a card, reading the word aloud, and identifying it as singular or plural. If the word is singular, they write its plural form on the board. If it is plural, they write the singular form.

Advanced

Give pairs of children pages from old newspapers or magazines and a sheet of construction paper. Have them divide the construction paper into two sections and label the sections *Plural Nouns with -s* and *Plural Nouns with -es*. Then have them find, cut out, and paste plural nouns in the correct section. Ask children what they notice about their charts. *(There are more words in the Plural Nouns with -s section.)*

ELL

Pair English language learners with children who understand the concept. Give each pair a sheet of paper. Have one child in each pair write two singular nouns on the paper and then give it to his or her partner, who writes the plural forms of the nouns. That child then writes two more singular nouns and gives the paper back to his or her partner. Continue until children have written many singular and plural nouns.

TEST-TAKING TIP

Remind children that singular nouns that end in s, ch, sh, or x add -es at the end to make their plural forms. Singular nouns that end in all other letters add -s. Point out that children need to identify the singular form of the answer word before they can identify its correct plural form.

Monitor Progress
Check Grammar

If... children have difficulty recognizing correct plural nouns,	**then...** go through the test items with them and show them how to eliminate the incorrect answers.

Test Preparation

✓ **Write** the letter of the correct answer.

1. In a story, ___ may do silly things.
- ○ **A** animalz
- ⊗ **B** animals
- ○ **C** animales

2. A turtle may make some ___.
- ○ **A** sandwich
- ○ **B** sandwichs
- ⊗ **C** sandwiches

3. Squirrels may wrap ___ of nuts.
- ○ **A** boxses
- ○ **B** boxss
- ⊗ **C** boxes

4. One ___ sings silly songs.
- ⊗ **A** chipmunk
- ○ **B** chipmunks
- ○ **C** chipmunkes

5. Beavers might ride in ___.
- ○ **A** busez
- ⊗ **B** buses
- ○ **C** buss

6. Bears might paint with ___.
- ⊗ **A** brushes
- ○ **B** brush
- ○ **C** brushs

94 Grammar

Review

✓ **Add** -s or -es to each singular noun. **Write** the plural noun.

1. stick sticks   **5.** bush bushes
2. lunch lunches   **6.** rock rocks
3. bus buses   **7.** mailbox mailboxes
4. bird birds   **8.** dish dishes

✓ **Choose** the correct noun in ( ). **Write** the sentences.

9. Turtle stood on a (<u>rock</u>, rocks).
10. He made (speechs, <u>speeches</u>) there.
11. Squirrels peeked out of (bushs, <u>bushes</u>).
12. (<u>Foxes</u>, Foxs) sat on logs.
13. The (<u>rabbits</u>, rabbites) listened too.
14. They were hiding in the (ditchs, <u>ditches</u>).

Grammar **95**

Summarize

Ask children what the difference is between singular and plural nouns.

- A singular noun names one person, place, animal, or thing. A plural noun names more than one.
- Add -s to most singular nouns to make them plural. Add -es to singular nouns that end in s, ch, sh, and x.

Grammar-Writing Connection

Point out to children that not all nouns that end in s are plural. Some singular nouns also end in s.

Singular nouns: Our <u>class</u> is on that <u>bus</u>.

Plural nouns: Four <u>classes</u> waited for two <u>buses</u>.

Organization

TEACH

Read aloud the information in the box at the top of the page. Then say: *Listen as I read the following. Tell me how the writer organized her ideas.*

 Think Aloud I have a lot to do this morning. First I'll get dressed. Then I'll eat breakfast. Next I'll brush my teeth. After that, I'll pack my backpack. Finally, I'll catch the bus.

Review with children how the writer organized her ideas. *(She used time-order words to tell the order of the events.)* Write the time-order words on the board. *(First, Then, Next, After that, Finally)*

 ### Guided Writing

Read items 1–3 in Exercise 1 with children. Have them tell how they used the time-order words to help them. Then read items 4–5 In Exercise 2. Ask volunteers to read their sentences.

 ### Independent Writing

Read the directions for Exercise 3. Talk with children about things they might do. After they have completed their writing, ask volunteers to share their plans.

Organization

> Before you write, think about how you will **organize** your ideas. Here are some ways you can organize.
>
> - Use time-order words such as *first*, *next*, *then*, *later*, *now*, and *last*.
> - Put your ideas in a list, diagram, or chart.

 Write the sentences in the correct order to tell what happened.

1. Next, we looked for facts in the library.
2. First, Beth and I chose butterflies for our topic.
3. Then we wrote a draft of our report.
Sentence order: 2, 1, 3

 Add a time-order word to each sentence. **Write** the sentences in the correct order.
Possible answers:

4. ___ I painted the picture.
   Then
5. ___, I got my paints and white paper.
   First   Sentence order: 5, 4

 Make a plan for what you will do next weekend. **Use** a chart to help you organize your writing.
Possible answer is on page TR34.

96 Writing

RESOURCES

Writing Transparency 3

Write a Plan

Writing Prompt Imagine you have to share a room with Alex. Alex is very different from you. Write a plan. Tell what you can do to help you get along with Alex.

Writer uses a list to organize his ideas. A bullet marks each point.

Writer begins each point with statement of an idea.

Writer gives details that explain his ideas.

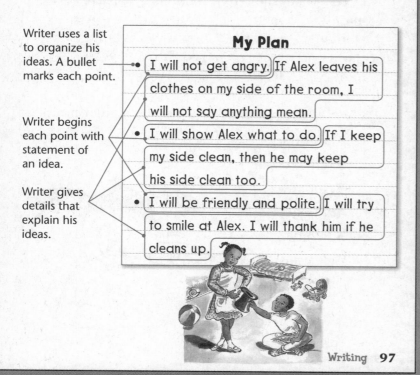

My Plan

- I will not get angry. If Alex leaves his clothes on my side of the room, I will not say anything mean.

- I will show Alex what to do. If I keep my side clean, then he may keep his side clean too.

- I will be friendly and polite. I will try to smile at Alex. I will thank him if he cleans up.

Writing **97**

Write a Plan
ANALYZE THE MODEL

Read aloud the model and the callouts to the left of it. Then prepare children to write their own plans.

PROMPT

Write your own plan about how you can share a room with Alex. You can make a list, diagram, or chart to help you organize your ideas.

Getting Started Children can do any of the following.

- Use an organizer (pp. TR28–TR32).
- List their ideas and think of an example for each one.
- Try out their ideas on a partner, who then gives them feedback.

Editing/Revising Checklist

☑ Did I organize my ideas before I began writing?

☑ Did I include enough details to explain my plan?

☑ Did I use singular and plural nouns correctly?

Self-Evaluation Distribute copies of p. TR26 for children to fill out.

Scoring Rubric Plan

Rubric 4 3 2 1	4	3	2	1
Focus/Ideas	Focused plan with clear ideas and strong supporting details	Focused plan with good ideas and supporting details	Plan sometimes unfocused; some supporting details	Plan with no focus or details
Organization/ Paragraphs	Ideas clearly organized; easy to follow	Ideas organized	Ideas somewhat disorganized	No organization
Voice	Serious; shows writer's feelings	Mostly serious; shows some feelings	Not serious; shows few feelings	Careless with no feelings
Word Choice	Clear, well-chosen words	Mostly good word choices	Some words not suitable to topic	Words often not suitable to topic
Sentences	Smooth sentences; different lengths and kinds	Most sentences smooth; some different lengths and kinds	Many stringy or choppy sentences; some incomplete	Many incomplete sentences or choppy sentences
Conventions	Few or no errors	No serious errors	Many errors	Too many errors

Plural Nouns That Change Spelling

TEACH

Read aloud the definition, instruction, and examples in the box on p. 98. Then say:

We know that plural nouns name more than one person, place, animal, or thing. We also know that most singular nouns add -s or -es to name more than one. Sometimes, though, nouns change their spelling to name more than one.

Write the singular nouns *child, foot,* and *mouse* and the plural nouns *children, feet,* and *mice* on the board. Point to them as you talk.

Model This is the singular noun *child.* If I want to make it plural, do I add -s or -es? No, the plural of *child* is *children.* What about *foot* and *mouse?* Do I add -s or -es to make them plural? No, the plural of *foot* is *feet,* and the plural of *mouse* is *mice.* The singular nouns change their spellings in different ways to make the plurals. I will have to learn these spellings.

LESSON 9

Plural Nouns That Change Spelling

A **plural noun** names more than one person, place, animal, or thing. Some nouns change spelling to name more than one.

Singular	Plural	Singular	Plural
child	children	leaf	leaves
man	men	wolf	wolves
woman	women	mouse	mice
tooth	teeth	goose	geese
foot	feet		

A **Write** the plural noun for each singular noun.

1. tooth teeth
2. child children
3. foot feet
4. mouse mice
5. woman women
6. leaf leaves

98 Grammar

RESOURCES

Daily Fix-It Lesson 9
See p. TR3.
See also Daily Fix-It Transparency 9.
Grammar Transparency 9

B **Choose** the correct noun in ( ) to complete each sentence. **Write** the sentences.

1. What sound do (gooses, <u>geese</u>) make?

2. A goose has flat (<u>feet</u>, foots).

3. What sound do (<u>mice</u>, mouses) make?

4. A mouse has sharp (tooths, <u>teeth</u>).

5. What sounds do (childs, <u>children</u>) make?

6. How many shoes do two (mans, <u>men</u>) need?

C **Change** the noun in ( ) to a plural noun. **Write** the question. **Write** an answer to the question.

Example　　How are (wolf) like the wind?
　　　　　　　How are wolves like the wind?
　　　　　　　Wolves and the wind howl.

7. How are (goose) like car horns?
Possible answer: How are geese like car horns? Geese and car horns honk.

8. How are (foot) like socks?
Possible answer: How are feet like socks? Feet and socks have toes.

9. How are (tooth) like pins?
Possible answer: How are teeth like pins? Teeth and pins are sharp.

10. How are (leaf) like snowflakes?
Possible answer: How are leaves like snowflakes? Leaves and snowflakes fall.

Grammar　**99**

PRACTICE

Guided Practice Ⓐ

Go through the exercise with children. Remind them that they can use the chart at the top of p. 98 to help them write the plural nouns. Have volunteers explain the differences in spelling between the singular nouns and their plural forms.

TEACHING TIP

Give children additional practice in learning the plural nouns that change spelling.

- Say phrases such as the following and let children complete them.

  One foot, two ____
  One man, many ____
  One goose, twenty ____

- You might also write the phrases on the board and have children write the plural nouns.

Independent Practice
Ⓑ and Ⓒ

Have children complete the exercises. For Differentiated Instruction and Extra Practice, see p. TR12.

Differentiated Instruction

Strategic Intervention

Write each singular and plural noun in the chart on p. 98 on an index card. Give each child a card with a singular noun. Mix the plural noun cards and place them face down on a table. Have a child turn over a card. If it shows the plural form of his or her noun, the child takes both cards. If not, the child turns the card down, and another child takes a turn.

Advanced

Write the words *child, tooth,* and *leaf* on the board. Challenge children to write a paragraph in which they use the plural forms of these three words. When they finish writing, have them read aloud their paragraphs to the group. Check their spelling of plural nouns.

ELL

Play an auditory game. Say a sentence such as *I see the child.* Let children respond with the same sentence, only using the plural form, *I see the children.* Continue using other nouns that change spelling in their plural form.

Test Preparation

✓ **Write** the letter of the correct answer.

1. Three ___ listened for sounds.
   - ⊗ **A** children
   - ○ **B** child
   - ○ **C** childs

2. They heard many ___ honking.
   - ○ **A** gooses
   - ⊗ **B** geese
   - ○ **C** goose

3. Horses were stamping their ___.
   - ○ **A** feets
   - ○ **B** foots
   - ⊗ **C** feet

4. Some ___ fed clucking hens.
   - ○ **A** womans
   - ⊗ **B** women
   - ○ **C** womens

5. A family of ___ squeaked in the barn.
   - ○ **A** mices
   - ○ **B** mouses
   - ⊗ **C** mice

6. Four ___ milked mooing cows.
   - ⊗ **A** men
   - ○ **B** mans
   - ○ **C** mens

Review

✓ **Choose** the correct noun in ( ) to complete each sentence. **Write** the noun.

1. The (mouses, <u>mice</u>) were fine musicians.
2. The (childs, <u>children</u>) clapped to the beat.
3. They tapped their (<u>feet</u>, foots).
4. The (<u>geese</u>, gooses) honked the tune.
5. The donkey smiled and showed his (tooths, <u>teeth</u>).
6. Many (womans, <u>women</u>) came for the concert.

✓ **Change** each noun in ( ) to a plural noun. **Write** the sentences.

7. Two ___ have a big barn. (man)
   men
8. They care for sick ___. (goose)
   geese
9. That runner has sore ___. (foot)
   feet
10. The old dog has few ___. (tooth)
    teeth
11. Many tiny ___ find a home. (mouse)
    mice
12. ___ help with the animals. (child)
    Children

Grammar **101**

Summarize

Ask children to name two important things about plural nouns.

- Plural nouns name more than one person, place, animal, or thing.
- Some nouns change spelling to name more than one.

Grammar-Writing Connection

Explain to children that it is important to use the correct plural nouns in their writing so that their readers will not get confused or distracted by incorrect words.

Incorrect: I found a nest of baby <u>mouses</u> in a pile of <u>leafs</u>.

Correct: I found a nest of baby <u>mice</u> in a pile of <u>leaves</u>.

Put Ideas in Order

TEACH

Read aloud the information in the box at the top of the page. Then say: *As I read the following, think about how I put my ideas in order.*

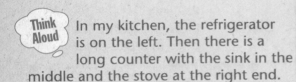 **Think Aloud** In my kitchen, the refrigerator is on the left. Then there is a long counter with the sink in the middle and the stove at the right end.

Ask children whether you used space order or compare and contrast order. *(space order)* Review the clues in the sentences. *(on the left, in the middle, at the right end)*

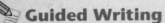 Guided Writing

Read each paragraph in Exercise 1. Ask children if the paragraph is in space order or compare and contrast order and how they know that.

Independent Writing

Read the directions for Exercise 2. Talk with children about two people, books, or animals they can write about. Invite volunteers to share their writing with the class.

 WRITER'S CRAFT

Put Ideas in Order

One way to **put ideas in order** is to use time order. Here are two more ways.

- Use **space order**. Tell about something from top to bottom or from left to right.
- Use **compare and contrast order**. Tell how things are alike. Tell how they are different.

 Read each paragraph. **Write** the letter of the order of the ideas in the paragraph.

   A   space order
   B   compare and contrast order

1. Vince and Joe have dark hair and brown eyes. They are both good at math. Vince likes movies. He wants to be an actor. Joe likes books. He wants to be a teacher. B

2. Angela arranged her books in her new bookcase. She put sports books on the top shelf. Nature books are on the middle shelf. Mysteries are on the bottom shelf. A

 Describe two family members, two books, or two animals. **Use** compare and contrast order.

102 Writing   Posssible answer is on page TR35.

RESOURCES

Writing Transparency 9

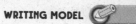

Make a Poster

Writing Prompt Think about how you would form a book club. Make a poster to tell people how they can form a book club.

Title tells the topic of the poster.

The writer spells plural nouns correctly.

Steps are arranged in order.

How to Form a Book Club

1. **Find** other **children** who like to read. Ask your friends, and have them ask their friends.
2. **Choose** a place to meet. Your home could be the first meeting place.
3. **Pick** a date and time for the meeting.
4. **Vote** on a book for everyone to read.
5. **Meet** and talk about the book.

Writing **103**

Make a Poster

ANALYZE THE MODEL

Read aloud the model and the callouts to the left of it. Then prepare children to write their own posters.

PROMPT

Now create your own poster about forming a book club. Put your ideas in order.

Getting Started Children can do any of the following.

- Use an organizer (pp. TR28–TR32).
- Make notes of their ideas.
- Decide in what order they want to put their ideas.

Editing/Revising Checklist

☑ Did I put my ideas in an order that makes sense?

☑ Are my ideas explained clearly?

☑ Did I spell plural nouns correctly?

Self-Evaluation Distribute copies of p. TR26 for children to fill out.

Scoring Rubric Poster

Rubric 4 3 2 1	4	3	2	1
Focus/Ideas	Poster focused on topic; clear ideas and details	Poster generally focused on topic; some good ideas and details	Poster not clearly focused on topic; needs more ideas and details	Poster with no focus; no ideas or details
Organization/ Paragraphs	Ideas in clear order	Ideas in mostly clear order	Ideas not always clearly ordered	No recognizable order
Voice	Clear, knowledgeable voice	Fairly clear, knowledgeable voice	No clear voice	Uninvolved or indifferent voice
Word Choice	Clear, well-chosen words; strong verbs	Generally well-chosen words; some strong verbs	Few clear words or strong verbs	Incorrect or limited word choice
Sentences	Complete sentences; includes statements and questions	Mostly clear sentences; some commands	Sentences unclear; few commands	Incoherent sentences; no commands
Conventions	Few or no errors	No serious errors	Many errors	Too many errors

Possessive Nouns

- Recognize possessive nouns.
- Use possessive nouns correctly in writing.
- Become familiar with possessive nouns on standardized tests.

TEACH

Read aloud the definition, instruction, and examples in the box on p. 104. Then say:

We know that a singular noun names one person, place, animal, or thing, and a plural noun names more than one person, place, animal, or thing. A possessive noun shows who or what owns something. To show ownership, a singular noun adds an apostrophe and -s, and a plural noun adds only an apostrophe.

Write the example possessive phrases from the box *(the turkey's wings, rabbits' tails)* on the board.

Think Aloud **Model** In the phrase *the turkey's wings,* I see an apostrophe and -s at the end of *turkey.* Because *turkey* is singular, an apostrophe and -s is added to make the possessive noun. The wings belong to one turkey. In the phrase *rabbits' tails,* I see only an apostrophe at the end of *rabbits.* Because *rabbits* is plural, an apostrophe is added to make the possessive noun. The tails belong to more than one rabbit.

LESSON 10

Possessive Nouns

A noun that shows who or what owns something is a **possessive noun**. To show ownership, add an **apostrophe (')** and **-s** when the noun is singular. Add just an **apostrophe (')** when the noun is plural.

the turkey's wings

rabbits' tails

A **Add** *'s* to each singular noun in ( ). **Write** the words.

   1. the (horse) head the horse's head

   2. the (goat) legs the goat's legs

   3. the (bear) fur the bear's fur

Add *'* to each plural noun in ( ). **Write** the words.

   4. the (monkeys) tails the monkeys' tails

   5. the (giraffes) necks the giraffes' necks

   6. the (birds) wings the birds' wings

104 Grammar

RESOURCES

Daily Fix-It Lesson 10
  See p. TR4.
  See also Daily Fix-It Transparency 10.
Grammar Transparency 10

B **Write** the possessive noun in ( ) to complete each sentence.

1. Watch out for a (porcupines, <u>porcupine's</u>) quills.

2. All the (quill's, <u>quills'</u>) tips are sharp.

3. The quills stick to an (attacker, <u>attacker's</u>) body.

4. We pulled quills out of our (dogs, <u>dogs'</u>) noses.

5. They stay away from that (<u>animal's</u>, animals') home!

6. Do (skunk, <u>skunks'</u>) odors protect them too?

C **Rewrite** each sentence. **Use** *'s* or *'* to write the underlined words as a possessive noun.

7. We had Thanksgiving dinner at <u>the house of our neighbors</u>.
   We had Thanksgiving dinner at our neighbors' house.

8. Mr. Brown wore his <u>outfit of a Pilgrim</u>.
   Mr. Brown wore his Pilgrim's outfit.

9. Mrs. Brown made <u>the cake of her grandmother</u>.
   Mrs. Brown made her grandmother's cake.

10. The turkey came from <u>the yard of a farmer</u>.
    The turkey came from a farmer's yard.

11. Dad liked the <u>taste of yams</u>.
    Dad liked the yams' taste.

12. The pumpkin pie was <u>the favorite of Mom</u>.
    The pumpkin pie was Mom's favorite.

Guided Practice **A**

Go through the exercise with children. Ask volunteers to read aloud the phrases and tell how they made the noun possessive in each.

TEACHING TiP

Children may ask about making the possessive forms of irregular plural nouns or singular nouns that end in -s.

- Irregular plural nouns form their possessives as singular nouns do, by adding an apostrophe and -s: *children, children's; mice, mice's.*

- Singular nouns that end in -s form their possessives as other singular nouns do, by adding an apostrophe and -s: *dress, dress's; Gus, Gus's.*

Independent Practice **B** and **C**

Have children complete the exercises. For Differentiated Instruction and Extra Practice, see p. TR12.

Differentiated Instruction

Strategic Intervention

Have a volunteer hold up something that belongs to him or her, such as a pencil. Ask: *Who owns the pencil? ([Child's name] owns it.)* Say: *(Child's name) owns the pencil. It is (Child's name)'s pencil.* Write the sentence with the possessive noun on the board. Ask the child to underline the apostrophe and -s that shows ownership. Continue with other volunteers and their possessions.

Advanced

Ask children to write several sentences about things that they and their friends own. Tell them to use at least two possessive nouns in their sentences. Have volunteers read aloud their sentences and listeners point out the possessives.

ELL

Many languages do not form possessives as English does. Write the following on the board:

fur of the dog   *dog's fur*

nests of the birds   *birds' nests*

Explain that each pair of phrases means the same thing. Then ask children to show how possessives are formed in their home languages.

Test Preparation

☑ **Write** the letter of the correct answer.

1. The two ___ plan was great!
- ○ **A** rabbit
- ⊗ **B** rabbits'
- ○ **C** rabbit's

2. They had a party for ___ birthday.
- ○ **A** Moose
- ○ **B** Moose'
- ⊗ **C** Moose's

3. The ___ surprise was a big cake.
- ⊗ **A** friends'
- ○ **B** friends
- ○ **C** friend

4. The ___ top had 18 candles.
- ○ **A** cake
- ○ **B** cakes'
- ⊗ **C** cake's

5. All the ___ flames glowed brightly.
- ⊗ **A** candles'
- ○ **B** candle'
- ○ **C** candle's

6. The ___ party surprised Moose.
- ○ **A** animals
- ⊗ **B** animals'
- ○ **C** animals's

Review

✓ **Add** '*s* or ' to each word in ( ). **Write** the sentences.

1. Cheese can be made from a (goat) milk.
  Cheese can be made from a goat's milk.

2. A (sheep) wool is made into yarn.
  A sheep's wool is made into yarn.

3. You can boil, fry, or scramble (hens) eggs.
  You can boil, fry, or scramble hens' eggs.

4. (Bees) honey tastes great on toast.
  Bees' honey tastes great on toast.

5. A (cow) milk can make you healthy.
  A cow's milk can make you healthy.

6. (Ostriches) eggs can feed many people.
  Ostriches' eggs can feed many people.

✓ **Choose** the word in ( ) that completes each sentence. **Write** the sentences.

7. One (<u>turkey's</u>, turkeys') feathers are black.

8. Most (turkey's, <u>turkeys'</u>) feathers are white.

9. Three (<u>kittens'</u>, kitten's) fur is white.

10. One (kittens', <u>kitten's</u>) fur is brown.

11. Many (goat's, <u>goats'</u>) hair is long.

12. That (<u>goat's</u>, goats') hair is short.

13. Your (<u>cat's</u>, cats') tail is bushy.

14. Those two (dog's, <u>dogs'</u>) tails are wagging.

Summarize

Have children tell what they know about possessive nouns.

- A possessive noun shows who or what owns something.
- Add an apostrophe and -*s* to a singular noun to show ownership.
- Add only an apostrophe to a plural noun to show ownership.

Grammar-Writing Connection

Explain to children that using possessive nouns is one way to make their writing less wordy.

Wordy: <u>The friends of Ms. Herne</u> came to <u>the house of my uncle</u>.

Less wordy: <u>Ms. Herne's friends</u> came to <u>my uncle's house</u>.

Include All the Information

TEACH

Read aloud the information in the box at the top of the page. Then say: *Listen as I read this note.*

Think Aloud

Jake

Don't forget. Your baseball game is at Johnson Park at 6:30 P.M.

Ellen

Ask children whom the note is for *(Jake)*, whom it is from *(Ellen)*, and what it is about. *(reminding Jake about the time and place of his baseball game)* Discuss whether Ellen included all the information Jake needs to know.

Guided Writing

Read the invitation and note in Exercise 1. Have children identify what information is missing. Ask volunteers to tell what they added.

Independent Writing

Read the directions for Exercise 2. Discuss with children what their friend would need to know. Invite volunteers to read aloud their notes to the group.

Include All the Information

Writers should **include all the information** that readers need to know. In an invitation, include the date, time, and place. In a note, include whom the note is for, whom it is from, and what it is about.

 Read the invitation and the note below. **Write** the missing information.

> **Lucy Hall** Is Having a Party!
>
> For Valentine's Day
>
> Date
>
> Time
>
> Place 3431 Third Street

Possible answer: **Date** Saturday, February 13; **Time** 1:00 P.M.

> **To** Mom
> **From**
> Wants to change Tuesday
> appointment to Thursday.
> Call him at 616-555-3678.
> **Message taken by**

Possible answer: **From** Mr. Kurt Jaworski; **Message taken by** Scott

 Write a note inviting a friend to do something. **Include** all the information.

Possible answer is on page TR35.

108 Writing

RESOURCES

Writing Transparency 10

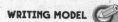

Write an Invitation

Writing Prompt Your class is giving a party. Write an invitation asking other people at your school to come. Be sure to include all the information that the people need to know.

Come to Our Party!

Purpose of party is given in first sentence.

The students in Mrs. McAvie's second grade class are having a Thanksgiving party. You are invited! The party is on Wednesday, November 20, at 2:30 P.M. in Room 105. Dress up like a Pilgrim if you like. There will be pumpkin cookies, orange punch, and games. Please let us know if you can come.

Writer gives information that readers need to know in second sentence.

Additional details are given in later sentences.

Writing **109**

Write an Invitation

ANALYZE THE MODEL

Read aloud the model and the callouts to the left of it. Then prepare children to write their own invitations.

PROMPT

Write an invitation for your class party. Include all the information your guests need to know.

Getting Started Children can do any of the following.

- Use an organizer (pp. TR28–TR32).
- Make notes about things they need to include.
- Use the models on pp. 108 and 109 to help them.

Editing/Revising Checklist

☑ Did I include all the information readers need to know?

☑ Is the information organized clearly?

☑ Are possessive nouns written correctly?

Self-Evaluation Distribute copies of p. TR26 for children to fill out.

Scoring Rubric — Write an Invitation

Rubric 4 3 2 1	4	3	2	1
Focus/Ideas	Invitation with strong focus on topic; includes all information	Invitation with good focus on topic; includes most information	Invitation unfocused; missing important information	Invitation with no focus or important information
Organization/ Paragraphs	Information well organized; easy to follow	Information mostly organized	Information not organized in logical order	No organization
Voice	Clear, knowledgeable voice	Fairly clear, knowledgeable voice	No clear voice; lacks knowledge	Careless; no knowledge
Word Choice	Clear, well-chosen words	Generally clear words	Some vague words	Incorrect or limited word choice
Sentences	Clear, complete sentences; variety of kinds	Most sentences complete; some variety	Some incomplete sentences; little variety	Many incomplete sentences; no variety
Conventions	Few or no errors	No serious errors	Many errors	Too many errors

Verbs

OBJECTIVES

- Recognize verbs.
- Use verbs correctly in writing.
- Become familiar with verbs on standardized tests.

TEACH

Read aloud the definition, instruction, and examples in the box on p. 110. Then say:

What is a verb? A verb is a word that shows action.

Write on the board the sentence from the box. *(Ahmed makes a present for his dad.)* Point to it.

Think Aloud **Model** As I look at this sentence, I see that the word makes is a verb. How do I know that *makes* is a verb? I know it is a verb because it tells what Ahmed does. If I ask, *What does this sentence say Ahmed does?* the answer is *Ahmed makes.*

LESSON 11

Verbs

A word that shows action is a **verb**.

Ahmed **makes** a present for his dad.

The word **makes** is a verb. It tells what Ahmed does.

A **Write** the verb in each sentence.

1. Ahmed <u>finds</u> a small flat piece of wood.
2. He <u>sands</u> the wood.
3. Next Ahmed <u>cuts</u> the edges.
4. He <u>picks</u> his dad's favorite color.
5. Ahmed <u>paints</u> the wood yellow.
6. He <u>prints</u> "The Best Dad" in black.
7. Then he <u>wraps</u> the gift.
8. Ahmed's dad <u>opens</u> the present.
9. Dad <u>thanks</u> Ahmed.
10. Dad and Ahmed <u>hug</u> each other.

110 Grammar

RESOURCES

Daily Fix-It Lesson 11
    See p. TR4.
    See also Daily Fix-It Transparency 11.
Grammar Transparency 11

B **Add** a word in ( ) to each sentence.
Write the sentences.

1. Henry (<u>buys</u>, plays) two plants.

2. He (wears, <u>puts</u>) one plant in the sun.

3. He (<u>sets</u>, tells) one plant in the dark.

4. One plant (sleeps, <u>grows</u>) tall.

5. One plant (<u>dies</u>, makes).

6. Plants (<u>need</u>, cut) light.

C **Write** a verb from the box to complete each sentence.

kicks	paints	hums
writes	builds	bakes

7. Lucy ___ a story at school.
writes

8. Walter ___ pictures.
paints

9. Henry ___ happy tunes.
hums

10. Maria ___ a pie.
bakes

11. Ling ___ a football.
kicks

12. Ann ___ a robot.
builds

Grammar **111**

Guided Practice **A**

Go through the exercise with children. Ask volunteers to tell how they identified the verb in each sentence. Let them demonstrate the action that each verb shows.

TEACHING TiP

Reinforce the idea that verbs show actions.

- Pantomime actions for verbs such as *jump, sing, clap, wave,* and *sit.* Ask children to do the actions with you.

- Ask them to identify each action and complete this sentence: *We ___.*

- Write the verbs children give in a list on the board. Read them together. Explain that these words are verbs because they show actions.

Independent Practice **B** and **C**

Have children complete the exercises. For Differentiated Instruction and Extra Practice, see p. TR13.

Differentiated Instruction

Strategic Intervention

Write verbs such as *cut, paste, fold, drop,* and *walk* on cards. Ask each child to take a card and make up a sentence with the verb, but instead of using the verb, pantomime the action. For example, *You ___ (model cutting, using your fingers as scissors) paper.* Have the other students guess the action and repeat the sentence filling in the blank: *You cut paper.*

Advanced

Find pictures in magazines that show people or animals in action. Give each child a picture. Ask children to write sentences about their picture using verbs to describe what the people or animals are doing. Ask volunteers to read aloud their sentences. Write the verbs they use on the board.

ELL

Help children make a verb book. On the board, write verbs that they can illustrate, such as *paint, write, open, run, sleep,* and *hop.* Read the verbs together and discuss how each verb shows action. Then have children draw and label pictures for the verbs, each on a separate sheet of paper. Put their papers between two sheets of construction paper and staple them together to make a verb book.

Monitor Progress	
Check Grammar	
If... children have difficulty identifying verbs,	**then...** go through the test items with them and show how you would eliminate the incorrect answers.

Test Preparation

✓ **Write** the letter of the correct answer.

1. An ant ___ on six legs.
   - ○ **A** bug
   - ⊗ **B** walks
   - ○ **C** feet

2. Some ants ___ in tunnels.
   - ○ **A** tiny
   - ○ **B** dirt
   - ⊗ **C** live

3. Ants ___ in long lines.
   - ○ **A** red
   - ○ **B** surprise
   - ⊗ **C** march

4. A queen ant ___ many eggs.
   - ⊗ **A** lays
   - ○ **B** round
   - ○ **C** small

5. A worker ant ___ for food.
   - ○ **A** busy
   - ⊗ **B** looks
   - ○ **C** good

6. An ant ___ heavy things.
   - ⊗ **A** lifts
   - ○ **B** hill
   - ○ **C** big

Review

☑ **Write** each sentence. **Underline** the verb.

1. Bess and Ella <u>pick</u> a science project.

2. They <u>build</u> a robot dog.

3. The robot dog <u>barks</u>.

4. It <u>hops</u> into the air.

5. The dog <u>wags</u> its metal tail.

6. The girls <u>win</u> a prize at the science fair.

☑ **Complete** each sentence with a word in ( ). **Write** the sentences.

7. Andy (<u>makes</u>, helps) a baked potato.

8. He (glues, <u>washes</u>) the potato.

9. He (sends, <u>pokes</u>) holes in it with a fork.

10. He and Mom (<u>wrap</u>, stop) the potato in foil.

11. They (think, <u>bake</u>) the potato in the oven.

12. Then Andy (draws, <u>eats</u>) the potato.

Grammar **113**

Summarize

Ask children to tell you what they know about verbs.

• A verb is a word that shows action.

Grammar-Writing Connection

Explain that although words such as *has* and *get* show action and therefore are verbs, they are not strong verbs. Strong verbs tell more about actions than weak verbs. They give a clearer, more vivid picture.

Weak verb: Zach <u>has</u> a new cap.
Strong verb: Zach <u>wears</u> a new cap.

Strong Verbs

OBJECTIVES

- Identify characteristics of a plan to make a robot.
- Write a plan for a robot using strong verbs.
- Develop criteria for judging a piece of writing.

TEACH

Read aloud the information in the box at the top of the page. Then say: *As I read two sentences, listen to the verbs.*

 Think Aloud *Sara gets red beads.* The verb in this sentence is *gets.* It doesn't tell me how Sara got the beads. *Sara buys the red beads.* Now I know exactly how Sara got the beads. She bought them. *Buys* is a stronger verb than *gets.*

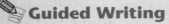 **Guided Writing**

Read items 1–5 in Exercise 1 with children. Have them tell which verb in the box they would use to replace each underlined verb. Ask volunteers to read aloud each revised sentence.

 **Independent Writing**

Read the directions for Exercise 2. Ask children to name things they have made. After they have finished writing, ask volunteers to share their work.

Strong Verbs

Use **strong verbs**. They give readers a clear picture of exactly what is happening.

Weak Verb	Sara <u>gets</u> red beads.
Strong Verb	Sara <u>buys</u> red beads.

Replace the underlined verb with a strong verb from the box. **Write** the new sentences.

declares	race	squeeze	builds	carry

1. On Saturday the girls <u>walk</u> over to Sara's house.
   race
2. Each girl <u>makes</u> part of a model castle.
   builds
3. The girls <u>take</u> the model to the backyard.
   carry
4. They <u>go</u> through a tight doorway.
   squeeze
5. Sara <u>says</u> our model is the best ever.
   declares

 Write about something you have made. **Use** strong verbs.

Possible answer: I collected 36 craft sticks and painted them blue. I glued them together to make a box. Then I glued the sides and bottom together. I donated the box to the school sale.

114 Writing

RESOURCES

Writing Transparency 11

Make a Robot

Writing Prompt Imagine that you are creating a robot for a science project. Write a plan for your robot. Tell what it looks like, how it moves, and what it can do.

First sentence shows that plan will focus on the robot.

Writer uses strong verbs to describe robot's actions.

Best of all signals most important thing robot will do.

My Robot

My robot will look like me, with brown eyes and black hair. It will walk and run like me, so it can go to school and play games with me. It will carry my backpack. My robot will obey only me. Best of all, it will help me do my homework. But my robot won't talk, laugh, or smile like I do. I don't want it to be too much like me!

Writing **115**

Make a Robot

ANALYZE THE MODEL

Read aloud the model and the callouts to the left of it. Then prepare children to write their own plan for a robot.

PROMPT

Now write a plan for your own robot. Use strong verbs as you tell about your robot.

Getting Started Children can do any of the following.

- Use an organizer (pp. TR28–TR32).
- Draw a picture of their robot and write about the picture.
- List things they would like their robot to be able to do.

Editing/Revising Checklist

- ☑ Did I focus on the topic of making a robot?
- ☑ Did I use strong verbs in my plan?
- ☑ Did I use verbs in my sentences?

Self-Evaluation Distribute copies of p. TR26 for children to fill out.

Scoring Rubric — Make a Robot

Rubric 4 3 2 1	4	3	2	1
Focus/Ideas	Plan with strong focus on topic; excellent details about robot	Plan with good focus on topic; good details about robot	Plan sometimes not focused on topic; some details about robot	Plan with no focus and no details about robot
Organization/ Paragraphs	Topic in first sentence; details in logical order	Topic in first sentence; details in mostly logical order	Topic somewhat vague; details not in discernible order	Topic not mentioned; no order
Voice	Lively, imaginative; shows writer's feelings on topic	Generally lively, imaginative; shows some feelings	Not very lively or imaginative; shows few feelings	Not very lively or imaginative; shows few feelings
Word Choice	Vivid, clear word pictures; uses strong verbs	Clear word pictures; uses some strong verbs	Word pictures unclear; few strong verbs	No word pictures; no strong verbs
Sentences	Smooth sentences; good variety	Most sentences smooth; some variety	Many choppy sentences; little variety	Many choppy sentences; little variety
Conventions	Few or no errors	No serious errors	Many errors	Too many errors

Verbs with Singular and Plural Nouns

TEACH

Read aloud the instruction and examples in the box on p. 116. Then say:

We know that a verb is a word that shows action. When we want to tell what one person, animal or thing does, we add -s to the verb. When we want to tell what two or more people, animals, or things do, we do not add -s to the verb.

Write on the board the three example sentences from the box. (*One child draws a car. Two children draw flowers. Lulu and Pedro draw a house.*)

Think Aloud **Model** As I read the first sentence, I ask myself, "How many children are drawing?" and I answer, "One child." The verb *draw* ends with -s because it tells what one child does. Then I ask myself how many children are drawing in the second and third sentences. Two children are drawing. The verb *draw* does not end with -s because it tells what two children do.

Verbs with Singular and Plural Nouns

Add **-s** to a verb to tell what one person, animal, or thing does. Do **not** add **-s** to a verb that tells what two or more people, animals, or things do.

One child **draws** a car.

Two children **draw** flowers.

Lulu and Pedro **draw** a house.

A **Write** the verb in ( ) that completes each sentence.

1. The children (paints, <u>paint</u>) a big picture.
2. One girl (<u>makes</u>, make) a road.
3. Two boys (adds, <u>add</u>) cars and trucks.
4. Three girls (colors, <u>color</u>) the sky blue.
5. Al (<u>uses</u>, use) yellow for a sun.
6. The teacher (<u>hangs</u>, hang) the picture on the wall.
7. The picture (<u>covers</u>, cover) the whole wall.
8. The students (loves, <u>love</u>) their beautiful picture.

116 Grammar

RESOURCES

Daily Fix-It Lesson 12
  See p. TR4.
  See also Daily Fix-It Transparency 12.
Grammar Transparency 12

B Write the verb in ( ) if it is correct. **Change** the verb if it is not correct. **Add** -s.

1. Juno and his mom (walk) to the mailbox.
   walk
2. Many letters (sit) inside the box.
   sit
3. Juno (take) out the mail.
   takes
4. Mom (hope) one letter is for her.
   hopes
5. A letter (come) for Juno.
   comes
6. Mom and Dad (get) five bills.
   get

C Choose a verb from the box to complete each sentence. **Add** -s to the verb if the subject is one person or thing. **Write** the sentence.

peek	soar	hug	land	drift	stare

Possible answers:

7. A plane ___ through the sky.
   soars
8. Jenny ___ out a window.
   peeks
9. Clouds ___ past.
   drift
10. She ___ at tiny houses below.
    stares
11. The plane ___ at the airport.
    lands
12. Grandma and Grandpa ___ Jenny.
    hug

Guided Practice Ⓐ

Go through the exercise with children. Ask volunteers to tell how they decided which verb to choose. Read aloud the completed sentences together.

TEACHING TIP

Give children additional practice in deciding when to add -s to verbs.

- In a column on the board, write singular and plural subjects.
- In two more columns, write verbs with and without -s.

Jane	sit	sits
Dogs	run	runs
The car	stop	stops
Boys	laugh	laughs

- Ask volunteers to circle the correct verb form for each subject.

Independent Practice
Ⓑ and Ⓒ

Have children complete the exercises. For Differentiated Instruction and Extra Practice, see p. TR13.

Differentiated Instruction

Strategic Intervention

Write this sentence on the board.

Sarah skate__ on the icy pond.

Ask children if Sarah is one person or more than one person. *(one person)* Ask them if you should add -s to *skate*. (yes) Add -s and read the sentence together. Write this sentence on the board.

The girls skate__ for hours.

Ask children similar questions. *(more than one; no)* Continue with verbs in other sentences.

Advanced

Give each child part of a student newspaper page. Ask children to find verbs with singular and plural nouns. Have them circle verbs with singular nouns and underline verbs with plural nouns. Ask volunteers to read some of their sentences and explain why the verbs end or do not end with -s.

ELL

Write singular and plural subjects on one set of cards and verbs for the singular and plural subjects on another set. Have pairs of children work together to match the subjects with the appropriate verb forms.

Boys	swim
Jill	swims
The children	sing
A child	sings

TEST-TAKING TiP

Point out that children need to decide first whether the subject of the sentence is singular or plural. This will help them eliminate some answers. Then they can try the remaining answers in the sentence to see which makes sense.

Monitor Progress

Check Grammar

If... children have difficulty deciding when to add -s to verbs,	then... have them look in favorite stories for examples of verbs for singular and plural subjects.

Test Preparation

✓ **Write** the letter of the correct answer.

1. Pedro ___ pictures with a camera.
   - ○ **A** fold
   - ⊗ **B** takes
   - ○ **C** take

2. Some pictures ___ his dog.
   - ○ **A** shows
   - ⊗ **B** show
   - ○ **C** colors

3. Three pictures ___ too dark.
   - ⊗ **A** look
   - ○ **B** looks
   - ○ **C** opens

4. The boy ___ some pictures in a book.
   - ○ **A** read
   - ○ **B** glue
   - ⊗ **C** glues

5. Rosa and Ida ___ two pictures
   - ○ **A** meets
   - ○ **B** gets
   - ⊗ **C** get

6. The girls ___ the pictures.
   - ⊗ **A** like
   - ○ **B** likes
   - ○ **C** pins

118 Grammar

Review

✓ **Choose** the verb in ( ) that completes each sentence. **Write** the sentences.

1. My grandma (live, <u>lives</u>) in Korea.

2. Aunt Keiko (write, <u>writes</u>) to her.

3. Two cousins (<u>visit</u>, visits) us.

4. Mom (call, <u>calls</u>) her sister in China.

5. My uncles (<u>teach</u>, teaches) in California.

6. Grandpa (lose, <u>loses</u>) his pictures of Japan.

✓ **Write** the verb in ( ) if it is correct. **Change** the verb if it is not correct. **Add** -s.

7. Ling (draw) many pictures.
   draws

8. Some pictures (show) Ling with her flute.
   show

9. Dad and Ling (find) magnets.
   find

10. A magnet (stick) to metal.
    sticks

11. One picture (hang) on the door.
    hangs

12. Mom (give) Ling a hug.
    gives

13. Mom (read) her book.
    reads

14. They (like) the pictures.
    like

Grammar **119**

Summarize

have them look in favorite stories for examples of verbs for singular and plural subjects.

- Add -s to a verb that tells what one person, animal, or thing does.
- Do not add -s to a verb that tells what two or more people, animals, or things do.

Grammar-Writing Connection

Display a picture that shows both singular and plural subjects doing things. Ask children to write sentences about what is happening in the picture. *(The girl runs on the path. The two men fish in the pond.)* You may wish to have children answer specific questions about the picture. *(What does the girl do? What do the two men do?)* Remind children to add -s to verbs with singular subjects and to not add -s to verbs with plural subjects. Invite volunteers to read aloud their sentences. Check their work.

Words That Compare and Contrast

OBJECTIVES

- Identify characteristics of a comparison.
- Write a comparison using words that compare and contrast.
- Develop criteria for judging a piece of writing.

TEACH

Read aloud the information in the box at the top of the page. Then say: *As I read, listen for words that compare or contrast.*

Think Aloud *Both Joy and I take dance lessons. Joy likes ballet, but I like tap.* How are Joy and I alike? We both take dance lessons. The word *both* compares Joy and me. How are Joy and I different? Joy likes ballet. I like tap. The word *but* contrasts Joy and me.

 ### Guided Writing

Read items 1–4 in Exercise 1 with children. Ask volunteers to explain how they chose the word for each sentence. Discuss the clues in the sentences.

 ### Independent Writing

Read the directions for Exercise 2. Suggest children make a chart of ways they and the friend are alike and different. After they have finished writing, call on volunteers to read their work.

 WRITER'S CRAFT

Words That Compare and Contrast

> When you **compare,** you tell how things are alike. Use the words *and, like, too,* and *both* to compare things. When you **contrast,** you tell how things are different. Use *but* and *unlike* to contrast things.
>
> **Alike** Both Joy and I take dance lessons.
>
> **Different** Joy likes ballet, but I like tap.

 Write the word in ( ) that works in each sentence.

1. I like my piano lessons, (but, both) Joy does not like hers.
   but
2. (Both, Unlike) Joy and I practice every day for an hour.
   Both
3. Joy begins practicing at 3 o'clock. (Like, Unlike) her, I begin at 2 o'clock.
   Unlike
4. My teacher is Mr. Nathan. He teaches Joy (and, too).
   too

 Write about you and a friend. **Tell** how you are alike and different.

Possible answer: Both Lucy and I like movies. She likes action movies, but I like comedies. We like books too. She likes science fiction. Unlike Lucy, I like mysteries best.

120 Writing

RESOURCES

Writing Transparency 12

Compare Two Animals

Writing Prompt Choose two animals. Compare the ways these animals communicate. How are they alike? How are they different?

Writer uses *Both* to signal ways the animals are alike.

Writer first tells how cats and dogs are alike and then tells how they are different.

Writer uses *but* to show a difference.

Animal Talk

Both cats and dogs use sounds to tell you things. Cats hiss and dogs growl when they are angry. Cats meow and dogs bark when they want something.

Cats and dogs do different things to let you know how they feel. Cats fluff their tails when they are scared. Dogs wag their tails when they are happy.

Most animals like to be petted. Dogs nudge you with a paw to ask for love. Cats like to be petted too, but they may not beg you.

Writing **121**

Compare Two Animals

ANALYZE THE MODEL

Read aloud the model and the callouts to the left of it. Then prepare children to write their own compare/contrast paragraphs.

PROMPT

Choose two animals. Tell how they are alike and different. Use words such as *and, like, too, both, but,* and *unlike*.

Getting Started Children can do any of the following.

- Use an organizer (pp. TR28–TR32).
- Draw pictures of the two animals.
- Look for information about them in the library or on the Internet.

Editing/Revising Checklist

☑ Did I organize my details in a way that makes sense?

☑ Did I use compare and contrast words?

☑ Did I use verbs with singular and plural nouns correctly?

Self-Evaluation Distribute copies of p. TR26 for children to fill out.

Scoring Rubric — Compare Two Animals

Rubric 4 3 2 1	4	3	2	1
Focus/Ideas	Strong focus on topic; many details that compare/contrast	Good focus on topic; some details that compare/contrast	Weak focus on topic; few details that compare/contrast	Weak focus on topic; few details that compare/contrast
Organization/ Paragraphs	Similarities/differences organized clearly, logically	Similarities/differences organized logically	Similarities/differences somewhat disorganized	No order
Voice	Lively, thoughtful; shows writer's feelings	Somewhat lively, thoughtful; shows some feelings	Not very lively or thoughtful; shows few feelings	Careless; does not show feelings
Word Choice	Vivid word pictures; uses compare/contrast words	Good word pictures; uses some compare/contrast words	Few word pictures; few compare/contrast words	Good word pictures; uses some compare/contrast words
Sentences	Smooth sentences; good variety	Most sentences smooth; some variety	Many choppy or stringy sentences; little variety	Choppy or incomplete sentences; no variety
Conventions	Few or no errors	No serious errors	Many errors	Too many errors

Verbs for Present, Past, and Future

- Recognize verbs for present, past, and future.
- Use verbs for present, past, and future correctly in writing.
- Become familiar with verbs on standardized tests.

TEACH

Read aloud the instruction and examples in the box on p. 122. Then say:

We can use verbs to tell about actions that happen now, actions that happened in the past, or actions that will happen in the future. To do this, we add an ending or a word to the verb.

Write on the board the example sentences from the box. *(Today Jeb bakes muffins. Yesterday Jeb baked muffins. Tomorrow Jeb will bake muffins.)*

Think Aloud **Model** As I look at the first sentence, I see the verb *bakes*. I know that -s at the end means that the verb tells about now. In the second sentence, I see the verb *baked*. I know that *-ed* at the end means that the verb tells about the past. In the third sentence, the verb is *will bake*. I know that the word *will* added to a verb means that the verb tells about the future.

Verbs for Present, Past, and Future

Today Jeb **bakes** muffins.

The verb **bakes** tells about now. It ends with **-s**.

Yesterday Jeb **baked** muffins.

The verb **baked** tells about the past. It ends with **-ed**.

Tomorrow Jeb **will bake** muffins.

The verb **will bake** tells about the future. It begins with **will**.

A **Write** the verb in each sentence. **Write** *N* if the verb tells about now. **Write** *P* if the verb tells about the past. **Write** *F* if the verb tells about the future.

1. Jeb makes new kinds of muffins.
   makes; N
2. Today he puts in nuts.
   puts; N
3. Last week he mixed in oranges.
   mixed; P
4. Yesterday he added pineapple.
   added; P
5. Next week he will use squash.
   will use; F
6. In the future, I will cook my own muffins.
   will cook; F

122 Grammar

RESOURCES

Daily Fix-It Lesson 13
   See p. TR5.
   See also Daily Fix-It Transparency 13.
Grammar Transparency 13

B **Add** *-s, -ed,* or *will* to the underlined verb. **Follow** the directions in ( ). **Write** the sentences.

1. Last night Travis <u>yawn</u>. (past)
Last night Travis yawned.

2. Then he <u>climb</u> into bed. (past)
Then he climbed into bed.

3. Soon Travis <u>take</u> a walk. (future)
Soon Travis will take a walk.

4. Now he <u>spot</u> his friend Nixon. (present)
Now he spots his friend Nixon.

5. Later he <u>meet</u> another friend. (future)
Later he will meet another friend.

6. Last week all the friends <u>race</u> their bikes. (past)
Last week all the friends raced their bikes.

C **Choose** the verb from the box that completes each sentence. **Add** *-s, -ed,* or *will* to each verb. **Write** the sentences.

pick	help	look
want	bake	invite

7. Tomorrow Carmen ___ cherry pies.
Tomorrow Carmen will bake cherry pies.

8. Yesterday she ___ the cherries.
Yesterday she picked the cherries.

9. Chiyo ___ Carmen with that job.
Chiyo helped Carmen with that job.

10. Today Carmen ___ her friends for dinner.
Today Carmen invites her friends for dinner.

11. Artie ___ pie right now!
Artie wants pie right now!

12. Next week Carmen ___ for more cherries.
Next week Carmen will look for more cherries.

Grammar **123**

Go through the exercise with children. Ask children what clues they used to identify whether the verb in each sentence tells about the present, past, or future.

TEACHING TIP

Point out that sometimes sentences have other clues about when the actions happen. Review with children these words and phrases and the verb tenses they indicate.

- Present—*now, today, right now*
- Past—*yesterday, last week*
- Future—*tomorrow, next week, soon, later*

Independent Practice
Ⓑ and Ⓒ

Have children complete the exercises. For Differentiated Instruction and Extra Practice, see p. TR13.

Differentiated Instruction

Strategic Intervention

Write these sentences on the board:

Celia opened the window.
Celia shuts the door.
Celia will clean her room.

Ask children which sentence tells what Celia does now *(2)*, what she did in the past *(1)*, and what she will do. *(3)* Circle *-s, -ed,* and *will* in the sentences and discuss how these tell when the actions happen.

Advanced

Ask children to think of something they did yesterday, something they do now, and something they will do tomorrow. Have them write sentences about these activities. Remind them to use verbs that tell about now, the past, or the future. Ask children to read aloud their sentences. Check their verb forms.

ELL

To provide scaffolding, make a chart like the one below. Write the present tense form of a verb in the first column and use the verb in a sentence. *(Dad cooks rice.)* Have children help you fill in the other two columns. Change the sentence using the new verb forms: *Dad cooked rice. Dad will cook rice.* Have children repeat the sentences. Continue with other verbs.

Present (now)	Past (yesterday)	Future (tomorrow)
cooks	cooked	will cook
plays	played	will play
climb	climbed	will climb

Monitor Progress

Check Grammar

If... children have difficulty recognizing verbs for present, past, and future,	then... write additional verbs on the board and together write their present, past, and future forms.

Test Preparation

✔ **Write** the letter that tells the time of the verb.

1. Yesterday Leroy watched a spider.

- ○ **A** now
- ⊗ **B** past
- ○ **C** future

2. The spider's web looks beautiful.

- ⊗ **A** now
- ○ **B** past
- ○ **C** future

3. Then Leroy checked the spider web.

- ○ **A** now
- ⊗ **B** past
- ○ **C** future

4. The spider will run away from him.

- ○ **A** now
- ○ **B** past
- ⊗ **C** future

5. Maybe later the spider will stay.

- ○ **A** now
- ○ **B** past
- ⊗ **C** future

6. Now Leroy visits the web again.

- ⊗ **A** now
- ○ **B** past
- ○ **C** future

124 Grammar

Review

✓ **Write** the sentences. **Underline** the verb in each sentence. **Write** *N* if the verb tells about now. **Write** *P* if the verb tells about the past. **Write** *F* if the verb tells about the future.

1. Last week Ted <u>fished</u>. P
2. Next week he <u>will play</u> soccer. F
3. Right now he <u>helps</u> his sister. N
4. He <u>reads</u> to her. N
5. Later he <u>will wash</u> dishes. F
6. Yesterday he <u>cleaned</u> his room. P

✓ **Choose** the correct verb in ( ) for each sentence. **Write** the sentences.

7. Yesterday we (<u>laughed</u>, will laugh) at a funny story.
8. Now we (<u>listen</u>, listened) to a new story.
9. Tomorrow we (visited, <u>will visit</u>) the library.
10. I (picked, <u>will pick</u>) an animal book there.

Grammar **125**

Summarize

Ask children to tell what they know about verbs for present, past, and future.

- A verb that has *-s* at the end tells about now.
- A verb that has *-ed* at the end tells about the past.
- A verb that begins with *will* tells about the future.

Grammar-Writing Connection

Explain to children that using verbs for present, past, and future tells readers exactly when actions happen.

Example: Derek <u>will visit</u> his cousins.

By using *will visit* in this sentence, the writer tells readers that the action will happen in the future.

Use Different Sentences

- Identify characteristics of writing advice.
- Write advice using different kinds of sentences and sentence beginnings.
- Develop criteria for judging a piece of writing.

TEACH

Read aloud the information in the box at the top of the page. Then say: *As I read, listen for different kinds of sentences and sentence beginnings.*

Think Aloud Our family is going to California. Ethan and I are so excited! Do you know why? We will see the ocean for the first time.

Review with children the different kinds of sentences and sentence beginnings the writer used.

 Guided Writing

Read items 1–4 in Exercise 1 with children. Ask them how they identified what kind of sentence each is. After children rearrange the sentences in Exercise 2, ask a volunteer to read aloud the new sentences.

 Independent Writing

Read the directions for Exercise 2. Discuss with children activities they might write about. Ask volunteers to read aloud their sentences. Listeners can identify the commands, exclamations, and different sentence beginnings.

 WRITER'S CRAFT

Use Different Sentences

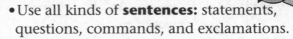

- Use all kinds of **sentences**: statements, questions, commands, and exclamations.
- Use different beginnings. Don't start too many sentences with *the, he, she, it,* or *I*.

 Write what kind of sentence each one is: *statement, question, command,* or *exclamation.*

1. That is an amazing car! **2.** Tell me about it. **3.** How fast can it go? **4.** Someday I want a car like that. 1. exclamation 2. command 3. question 4. statement.

 Rearrange the words in each sentence so that it begins with the underlined words. **Write** the new sentences.

I look at paintings by a different artist <u>each time</u>. I looked at paintings by Monet <u>last week</u>. I will see paintings by Picasso <u>next time</u>.

Each time I look at paintings by a different artist. Last week I looked at paintings by Monet. Next time I will see paintings by Picasso.

 Write about two things you have done in the last week. **Use** a command and an exclamation. **Begin** each sentence with a different word.

Possible answer is on page TR35.

126 Writing

RESOURCES

Writing Transparency 13

Write Advice

Writing Prompt What does it mean to be a good friend? Write advice about what a good friend does and does not do.

Writer begins each paragraph with a question and then answers it.

First paragraph tells things that good friends do.

Second paragraph tells things that good friends do not do.

Writer uses different kinds of sentences.

Good Friends

What do good friends do? Good friends listen to what you say. They laugh at your jokes. They share their food and toys with you. You can borrow their things because they trust you.

What do good friends not do? Good friends don't tell your secrets. They don't make fun of you, and they don't lie to you. They never pick you last for a team because you are always first with them.

Keep your good friends. They are a great treasure!

Writing 127

Write Advice

ANALYZE THE MODEL

Read aloud the model and the callouts to the left of it. Then prepare children to write their own advice.

PROMPT

Now write your own advice about being a good friend. Use all kinds of sentences and different sentence beginnings.

Getting Started Children can do any of the following.

- Use an organizer (pp. TR28–TR32).
- Think about how they have been a good or not-so-good friend.
- List things they like and don't like about their friends.

Editing/Revising Checklist

☑ Did I use different kinds of sentences?

☑ Did I begin my sentences with different words?

☑ Did I use verbs for present, past, and future correctly?

Self-Evaluation Distribute copies of p. TR26 for children to fill out.

Scoring Rubric Write Advice

Rubric 4 3 2 1	4	3	2	1
Focus/Ideas	Advice with strong focus on topic; excellent supporting details	Advice with reasonable focus on topic; good supporting details	Advice not always focused on topic; some supporting details	Advice with no focus on topic and few details
Organization/ Paragraphs	Details in clear, logical order; easy to follow	Details in logical order	Details somewhat disorganized; hard to follow	No order
Voice	Lively, thoughtful; shows writer's feelings	Fairly lively, thoughtful; shows some feelings	Not very lively or thoughtful; shows few feelings	Careless; does not show feelings
Word Choice	Clear, well-chosen words	Words mostly well chosen	Some words that do not fit topic	Many words that do not fit topic
Sentences	Smooth sentences; different kinds of sentences and beginnings	Most sentences smooth; some different kinds and beginnings	Many choppy sentences; little variety; repetitive beginnings	Many incomplete sentences; no variety; same beginnings
Conventions	Few or no errors	No serious errors	Many errors	Too many errors

More About Verbs

TEACH

Read aloud the instruction and examples in the box on p. 128. Then say:

We know that verbs that end with -s tell about now, verbs that end with -ed tell about the past, and verbs that start with will tell about the future. Now we will practice using the correct verbs to show something happening now, in the past, or in the future.

Write on the board the three example sentences from the box. (Today Chris plays the piano. Yesterday Chris played the piano. Tomorrow Chris will play the piano.)

Think Aloud **Model** As I look at the first sentence, I see the word Today, so I know that the action is happening now. The verb plays ends with -s. That is correct. A verb that ends with -s tells about something happening now.

Continue in a similar way with the other sentences. Point out the words Yesterday and Tomorrow and explain how the ending -ed and the word will show something is happening in the past and in the future, respectively.

More About Verbs

Use the correct verb in each sentence to show something happening now, in the past, or in the future.

Today Chris **plays** the piano. (now)
Yesterday Chris **played** the piano. (in the past)
Tomorrow Chris **will play** the piano. (in the future)

A **Write** the sentences. **Use** the verb in ( ) that completes the sentence.

1. Chris (started, will start) piano lessons three years ago.

2. Now she (practices, practiced) an hour each day.

3. Last week her sister (dances, danced) in the school show.

4. Today their mother (cooks, cooked) soup for the girls.

5. Next year she (takes, will take) them to music camp.

128 Grammar

RESOURCES

Daily Fix-It Lesson 14
   See p. TR5.
   See also Daily Fix-It Transparency 14.
Grammar Transparency 14

B Add -s, -ed, or *will* to each verb in ( ).
Write each sentence.

1. Brad (stir) some corn soup now.
   Brad stirs some corn soup now.
2. Yesterday he (boil) corn on the cob.
   Yesterday he boiled corn on the cob.
3. Tomorrow he (bake) cornbread.
   Tomorrow he will bake cornbread.
4. Next Saturday he (pop) popcorn.
   Next Saturday he will pop popcorn.
5. Last week he (fix) corn muffins.
   Last week he fixed corn muffins.
6. Now Brad (think) of more ideas for corn.
   Now Brad thinks of more ideas for corn.

C **Complete** each sentence with a verb from the box. **Write** each sentence. **Write** *now, past,* or *future* to tell when the action happened.

invites	will make	will glue
played	calls	picked

7. Last week Blanca and Rosa ___ at the beach.
   Last week Blanca and Rosa played at the beach; past
8. They ___ up shells.
   They picked up shells; past
9. Now Blanca ___ Rosa on the phone.
   Now Blanca calls Rosa on the phone; now
10. She ___ Rosa to a birthday party.
    She invites Rosa to a birthday party; now
11. Tomorrow Rosa ___ a gift for Blanca.
    Tomorrow Rosa will make a gift for Blanca; future
12. She ___ shells on a picture frame.
    She will glue shells on a picture frame; future

Grammar **129**

Guided Practice **A**

Go through the exercise with children. Ask them how they decided which verb in parentheses completed the sentence. They should mention clues such as *three years ago, now, last week, today,* and *next year.*

TEACHING TiP

Emphasize that sometimes words or phrases in a sentence give clues about which verb form is needed.

- On the board, write the sentence *Next year she will take them to music camp.* Point out that the words *Next year* indicate that the action will happen in the future, so the verb begins with *will.*

- Change the sentence to *Today she takes them to music camp.* Point out that the word *Today* indicates that the action happens now, so the verb changes; now it ends with *-s.*

Independent Practice **B** and **C**

Have children complete the exercises. For Differentiated Instruction and Extra Practice, see p. TR13.

Differentiated Instruction

Strategic Intervention

Write verbs such as *jump, walk, look,* and *smile* and the words *now, past,* and *future* on cards, one word on a card. Have a child take a verb card *(jump)* and a time card *(now),* change the verb to show that time *(jumps),* and use the verb form in a sentence.*(Jess jumps rope.)* Put both cards back and mix the cards before the next child draws.

Advanced

Give children this story starter: *Jack plays the drums. He needs new drums. What will he do?* Have children write about what Jack does. Remind them to use correct verbs. Invite volunteers to read aloud their stories. Check their verb forms.

ELL

Make three cards, each with one of the words *Yesterday, Today,* and *Tomorrow* on it. Place the cards at intervals on the chalk ledge. Write the same sentence above each card, omitting the verb: *Rosa ___ the table.* Tell children the verb *(clean)* and ask them how you should write the verb in each sentence. Say the sentence together with each heading *(Today Rosa ___ the table.)* and let children tell you what verb form to write.

Monitor Progress

Check Grammar

If... children have difficulty identifying the correct verbs,	**then...** tell them whether the action is happening now, in the past, or in the future in each sentence and ask them to choose the correct verb.

Test Preparation

✓ **Write** the letter of the correct answer.

1. Last month Ali ___ some tomatoes.
   - ○ **A** plants
   - ⊗ **B** planted
   - ○ **C** will plan

2. Now he ___ the plants.
   - ⊗ **A** plants
   - ○ **B** planted
   - ○ **C** will plant

3. Tomorrow he ___ weeds.
   - ○ **A** pulls
   - ○ **B** pulled
   - ⊗ **C** will pull

4. Last winter Ali ___ of fresh tomatoes.
   - ○ **A** dreams
   - ⊗ **B** dreamed
   - ○ **C** will dream

5. Next week he ___ big red tomatoes.
   - ○ **A** picks
   - ○ **B** picked
   - ⊗ **C** will pick

6. Now Ali ___ in the yard.
   - ⊗ **A** waits
   - ○ **B** waited
   - ○ **C** will wait

130 Grammar

Review

☑ **Choose** the correct verb in ( ).
Write the sentences.

1. The baby (crawls, crawled) now.
   The baby crawls now.
2. Soon she (walked, will walk).
   Soon she will walk.
3. Last month she (rolls, rolled) over.
   Last month she rolled over.
4. In the future, she (talked, will talk).
   In the future, she will talk.
5. Now she (makes, will make) silly sounds.
   Now she makes silly sounds.
6. Yesterday she (laughs, laughed).
   Yesterday she laughed.

☑ **Add** -s, -ed, or will to each verb in ( ).
Write the sentences.

7. Yesterday Manuel (walk) to the park.
   Yesterday Manuel walked to the park.
8. Now he (feed) his baby sister.
   Now he feeds his baby sister.
9. Now she (bang) her spoon on the table.
   Now she bangs her spoon on the table.
10. In an hour, Manuel (clean) the kitchen.
    In an hour, Manuel will clean the kitchen.
11. Last week he (visit) his aunt.
    Last week he visited his aunt.
12. Later tonight, he (call) Jeff on the phone.
    Later tonight, he will call Jeff on the phone.

Grammar **131**

Vivid Words

OBJECTIVES

- Identify characteristics of an ad.
- Write an ad using vivid words.
- Develop criteria for judging a piece of writing.

TEACH

Read aloud the instruction in the box at the top of the page. Then say: *Listen as I read.*

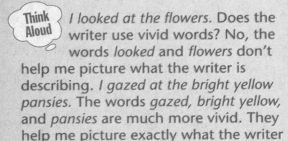

Think Aloud *I looked at the flowers.* Does the writer use vivid words? No, the words *looked* and *flowers* don't help me picture what the writer is describing. *I gazed at the bright yellow pansies.* The words *gazed, bright yellow,* and *pansies* are much more vivid. They help me picture exactly what the writer is doing and seeing.

Guided Writing

Read items 1–4 in Exercise 1 with children. Have them tell which word from the box they would use in each sentence. Ask volunteers to read aloud the revised sentences.

Independent Writing

Read the directions for Exercise 2. Brainstorm a list of classroom objects that children might write about. After they have completed their writing, ask volunteers to share what they have written.

 WRITER'S CRAFT

Vivid Words

Use **vivid words**. Help your readers see, hear, taste, smell, and touch what you are describing.

Not Vivid   I <u>looked</u> at the <u>flowers</u>.

Vivid   I <u>gazed</u> at the <u>bright yellow pansies</u>.

 Replace the underlined word in each sentence with a more vivid word from the box. **Write** the new sentences.

drifted	perfect	thrilled	tore

1. I found a <u>nice</u> gift for my mother.
   I found a perfect gift for my mother.
2. She <u>took</u> off the wrapping paper.
   She tore off the wrapping paper.
3. The paper <u>fell</u> to the ground.
   The paper drifted to the ground.
4. She was <u>happy</u> with the teacup.
   She was thrilled with the teacup.

 Describe something in your classroom. **Use** vivid words to show readers how it looks, sounds, tastes, smells, or feels.

Possible answer: Our class pet is a bright orange fish named Fred. His tail and fins are so thin you can see through them. His tiny black eyes are always open, and his mouth makes a big O.

132   Writing

RESOURCES

Writing Transparency 14

Write an Ad

> **Writing Prompt** Imagine that you have created a new food. Decide what the food looks and tastes like. Give it a name. Then write an ad for the food. Use your ideas to make people want to buy your food.

Writer mentions new food in title.

Questions get reader interested right away.

Vivid words help reader "see" the food.

Try New Broc Puffs!

Are you tired of potato chips and pretzels? Do you think all snack foods are bad for you? Try new Broc Puffs. Broc Puffs are crispy, puffy little pillows. They taste just like fresh broccoli and creamy cheese. Eat as many as you want! This snack food is good for you. Broc Puffs are full of vitamins. Yummy and healthful—that's new Broc Puffs!

Writing **133**

Write an Ad
ANALYZE THE MODEL

Read aloud the model and the callouts to the left of it. Then prepare children to write their own ads.

PROMPT

Create a new food and write an ad for it. Use vivid words to tell about the food so that people will want to buy it!

Getting Started Children can do any of the following.

- Use an organizer (pp. TR28–TR32).
- Think of foods they like and how they could combine them in a new way.
- List vivid words they could use.

Editing/Revising Checklist

☑ Did I mention my new food at the beginning of my ad?

☑ Did I use vivid words in the description of my food?

☑ Did I use the correct forms of the verbs?

Self-Evaluation Distribute copies of p. TR26 for children to fill out.

Scoring Rubric Write an Ad

Rubric 4 3 2 1	4	3	2	1
Focus/Ideas	Ad with strong focus on food; excellent descriptive details	Ad with good focus on food; good descriptive details	Ad not always focused on food; few descriptive details	Ad with no focus and no descriptive details
Organization/ Paragraphs	Details in clear, logical order	Details in logical order	Details somewhat disorganized	No order
Voice	Lively, persuasive; shows writer's feelings	Generally lively, persuasive; shows some feelings	Not very lively or persuasive; shows few feelings	Dull, not persuasive; does not show feelings
Word Choice	Uses vivid words and persuasive words	Uses some vivid and persuasive words	Uses few vivid or persuasive words	No vivid or persuasive words
Sentences	Smooth, complete sentences; good variety	Most sentences smooth, complete; some variety	Some choppy or incomplete sentences; little variety	Many choppy or incomplete sentences; no variety
Conventions	Few or no errors	No serious errors	Many errors	Too many errors

Am, Is, Are, Was, and Were

TEACH

Read aloud the definitions and examples in the box on p. 134. Then say:

Unlike verbs such as *run* and *jump,* the verbs *am, is, are, was,* and *were* do not show action. However, like those verbs, they can be used to tell about now, the past, and the future. Also, like those verbs, some are used with singular nouns and others are used with plural nouns.

Write the five example sentences from the box on the board. Point to the verbs as you talk about them.

 Model *I am an inventor. Jen is an inventor. Des and Ali are inventors.* The words *am, is,* and *are* show what these people are— inventors. All three words tell about now. However, *am* and *is* tell about singular nouns, and *are* tells about plural nouns. *Bill was an inventor. Kate and Sean were inventors.* The words *was* and *were* show what these people are too. Both words tell about the past, but *was* tells about singular nouns and *were* tells about plural nouns.

Am, Is, Are, Was, and Were

The verbs **am, is, are, was,** and **were** do not show action. They show what someone or something is or was. These verbs are forms of the verb **to be.**

The verbs **am, is,** and **are** tell about now.

I **am** an inventor.   Jen **is** an inventor.
Des and Ali **are** inventors.

The verbs **was** and **were** tell about the past.

Bill **was** an inventor.
Kate and Sean **were** inventors.

Use **am, is,** and **was** to tell about one person, place, or thing. Use **are** and **were** to tell about more than one person, place, or thing.

A **Write** each sentence. **Underline** the verb.

1. George Washington Carver <u>is</u> one of my heroes.

2. He <u>was</u> a great man.

3. Plants <u>were</u> important to him.

4. I <u>am</u> in the library.

5. These books <u>are</u> about Carver's work.

134 Grammar

RESOURCES

Daily Fix-It Lesson 15
   See p. TR5.
   See also Daily Fix-It Transparency 15.
Grammar Transparency 15

B **Write** the verb in ( ) that completes each sentence.

1. Inventors ___ clever people. (is, are)
   are
2. Zippers ___ a great invention. (was, were)
   were
3. Today inventions ___ everywhere. (is, are)
   are
4. I ___ in the Young Inventors Club. (am, are)
   am
5. George ___ in the club too. (are, is)
   is

C **Write** the sentences. **Use** a verb from the box. **Write** *N* if the verb tells about now. **Write** *P* if the verb tells about the past.

am	is	are
was	were	

6. I ___ seven years old now.
   I am seven years old now. N
7. My brother ___ nine.
   My brother is nine. N
8. Yesterday we ___ inventors.
   Yesterday we were inventors. P
9. Our invention ___ a robot.
   Our invention was a robot. P
10. Today we ___ explorers.
    Today we are explorers. N

Grammar **135**

PRACTICE

Guided Practice Ⓐ

Go through the exercise with children. Remind them that some verbs do not show action. Ask volunteers how they identified the verbs. You may wish to have children tell whether each verb tells about now or the past and whether it tells about a singular or a plural noun.

TEACHING TiP

Make a chart on the board to help children remember the important information about *am, is, are, was,* and *were.*

	Now	Past
Singular Subjects	am, is	was
Plural Subjects	are	were

Explain that *am* is used only with the word *I. Is* is used with all other singular subjects.

Independent Practice Ⓑ and Ⓒ

Have children complete the exercises. For Differentiated Instruction and Extra Practice, see p. TR13.

Differentiated Instruction

Strategic Intervention

Write this sentence on the board.

This year Jane is three.

Ask children if the verb tells about now or the past (now) and if the subject is one or more than one. (one) Write another sentence.

Last year Jane was two.

Ask the same questions (past; more than one) and continue with these sentences: *This year Jane and Rodney are three. Last year Jane and Rodney were two.*

Advanced

Ask children to write sentences that describe themselves, family members, and pets. Challenge them to use each of the verbs *am, is, are, was,* and *were* at least once in their sentences. Ask volunteers to read aloud their sentences to the class and to point out where they used *am, is, are, was,* and *were.*

ELL

Pair children who understand the concept with English language learners. Write *am, is, are, was,* and *were* in a column on the board. Then write sentences using these verbs, but leaving blanks for the verbs, for example, *Yesterday Brian ___ sad. Today Brian ___ happy.* Have partners work together to copy the sentences and complete them with the correct verbs. Read aloud the completed sentences together.

Monitor Progress

Check Grammar

If... children have difficulty choosing the correct verbs,	**then...** go through the test items with them and choose the correct answers together.

Test Preparation

✅ **Write** the letter of the correct answer.

1. A sweet potato ___ a vegetable.
   - ⊗ **A** is
   - ○ **B** are
   - ○ **C** were

2. Vegetables ___ good for you.
   - ○ **A** am
   - ⊗ **B** are
   - ○ **C** was

3. Tomatoes and beans ___ in my garden.
   - ○ **A** was
   - ○ **B** is
   - ⊗ **C** were

4. One tomato ___ very big.
   - ○ **A** are
   - ○ **B** am
   - ⊗ **C** was

5. I ___ in the kitchen now.
   - ○ **A** is
   - ⊗ **B** am
   - ○ **C** was

6. The sweet potatoes ___ in a pie.
   - ⊗ **A** are
   - ○ **B** is
   - ○ **C** was

136 Grammar

Review

✔ **Write** each sentence. **Underline** the verb. **Write** *N* if the verb tells about now. **Write** *P* if the verb tells about the past.

1. I am hungry.
<small>I am hungry. N</small>

2. Dad is in the kitchen.
<small>Dad is in the kitchen. N</small>

3. The sandwiches were on a plate.
<small>The sandwiches were on a plate. P</small>

4. My sandwich was peanut butter.
<small>My sandwich was peanut butter. P</small>

5. Dad and I are full now.
<small>Dad and I are full now. N</small>

✔ **Choose** the verb in ( ) that completes each sentence. **Write** the sentences.

6. Uncle George (is, am) a painter.
<small>Uncle George is a painter.</small>

7. Once he (was, is) a farmer.
<small>Once he was a farmer.</small>

8. I (am, is) at his farm.
<small>I am at his farm.</small>

9. First we (was, were) in the house.
<small>First we were in the house.</small>

10. Now we (were, are) in the barn.
<small>Now we are in the barn.</small>

11. His paintings (is, are) on the walls.
<small>His paintings are on the walls.</small>

12. One picture (is, are) of a cow.
<small>One picture is of a cow.</small>

Grammar **137**

Summarize

Have children tell what they have learned about the verbs *am, is, are, was,* and *were.*

- The verbs *am, is, are, was,* and *were* do not show action. They show what someone or something is or was.
- *Am, is,* and *are* tell about now, and *was* and *were* tell about the past.
- *Am, is,* and *was* tell about one person, place, animal, or thing. *Are* and *were* tell about more than one person, place, animal, or thing.

Grammar-Writing Connection

Explain that because *am, is, are, was,* and *were* have no endings, such as *-s* and *-ed,* or added words, such as *will,* to signal that they are verbs, children will have to memorize these verbs and when they are to be used. Ask children to think about favorite story characters and write sentences about these characters' feelings using the verbs *is, am, are, was,* and *were.* (*Henry is eager. Mudge is patient.*) Have volunteers read aloud their sentences to the class.

Use Precise Words

TEACH

Read aloud the instruction in the box at the top of the page. Then say: *Listen for precise words as I read about a man named Mr. Kim.*

Think Aloud *Mr. Kim is nice. Nice is a dull, vague word. It doesn't tell me much about Mr. Kim. Mr. Kim always smiles and says hello. This sentence has more precise words—always smiles, says hello. They give me a clearer, more interesting picture of Mr. Kim.*

Guided Writing

Read items 1–4 in Exercise 1 with children. Ask volunteers to identify the dull, vague words in one sentence that are replaced with precise words in the other sentence in each pair.

Independent Writing

Read the directions for Exercise 2. Talk about objects children might write about. Call on volunteers to read aloud their writing. Ask listeners to point out precise words.

 WRITER'S CRAFT

Use Precise Words
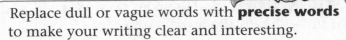

Replace dull or vague words with **precise words** to make your writing clear and interesting.

No Mr. Kim is nice.

Yes Mr. Kim always smiles and says hello.

 Which sentence in each pair uses precise words? **Write** the sentence.

1. Jose got a lot of stuff for his birthday.
   Jose got video games and a basketball for his birthday.
   Jose got video games and a basketball for his birthday.

2. We saw lions and elephants at the zoo.
   We saw animals at the zoo.
   We saw lions and elephants at the zoo.

3. I had a good time at camp.
   I paddled a canoe at camp.
   I paddled a canoe at camp.

4. Cara pushed her books into her backpack.
   Cara put her things in her bag.
   Cara pushed her books into her backpack.

 Write about something you use every day, such as a toothbrush or a pen. **Use** precise words.

Possible answer: My favorite pen is fat and blue. It has a tiny ball in its tip. When I write, it moves smoothly across the paper. I love the way I can make curves and loops with my pen.

138 Writing

RESOURCES

Writing Transparency 15

Tell About an Invention

Writing Prompt Tell about an important invention. Explain what it does and why you think it is important. Tell how the invention has changed people's lives.

The Invention of Airplanes

Writer states opinion in opening sentence. → I think airplanes are an important invention. Airplanes let people travel a long way in a short time.

Details support opinion. → Before there were airplanes, people had to travel by horse, wagon, train, or ship. These trips took a long time.

Writer compares life before and after airplanes. → Horses, wagons, trains, and ships could not go everywhere in the world. With airplanes, people can go almost anywhere they want. Also, they can get there quickly.

Writing **139**

Tell About an Invention

ANALYZE THE MODEL

Read aloud the model and the callouts to the left of it. Then prepare children to write their own explanations.

PROMPT

Think of an important invention. Write an explanation of how the invention has changed people's lives.

Getting Started Children can do any of the following.

- Use an organizer (pp. TR28–TR32).
- Make a list of inventions and choose one.
- Talk about their ideas with a partner.

Editing/Revising Checklist

✓ Did I state my opinion at the beginning of my explanation?

✓ Did I use precise words to make my writing clear?

✓ Did I use the verbs *am, is, are, was,* and *were* correctly?

Self-Evaluation Distribute copies of p. TR26 for children to fill out.

Scoring Rubric — Tell About an Invention

Rubric 4 3 2 1	4	3	2	1
Focus/Ideas	Strong focus on invention; clearly stated opinion; many details that support opinion	Good focus on invention; stated opinion; details that support opinion	Unclear focus on invention; opinion not clearly stated; few details that support opinion	No focus on invention; no opinion; no details that support opinion
Organization/ Paragraphs	Clear opening sentence; well-ordered details	Reasonable opening sentence; ordered details	Vague opening sentence; some details out of order	No opening sentence; no order
Voice	Knowledgeable, interested	Generally knowledgeable, interested	Shows lack of knowledge and/or interest	Shows no knowledge or interest
Word Choice	Good use of precise words	Uses some precise words	Few precise words	No precise words
Sentences	Smooth sentences; good variety	Most sentences smooth; some variety	Some choppy sentences; little variety	Many choppy or incomplete sentences; no variety
Conventions	Few or no errors	No serious errors	Many errors	Too many errors

Adjectives and Our Senses

OBJECTIVES

- Recognize adjectives.
- Use adjectives correctly in writing.
- Become familiar with adjectives on standardized tests.

TEACH

Read aloud the definition and example in the box on p. 140. Then say:

What is an adjective? An adjective is a word that describes a person, place, animal, or thing. An adjective can tell how something looks, sounds, tastes, feels, or smells.

Write on the board the example sentence from the box. *(My family loves hot cornbread.)*

Think Aloud **Model** As I read this sentence, I see that the writer has used the adjective *hot* to describe the noun *cornbread*. *Hot* helps me imagine what the cornbread feels like. I know I would feel its heat when I touch it with my fingers and when I put it in my mouth.

LESSON 16

Adjectives and Our Senses

An **adjective** describes a person, place, animal, or thing. An **adjective** can tell how something looks, sounds, tastes, feels, or smells.

My family loves **hot** cornbread.

Hot describes the way the cornbread tastes and feels.

A **Write** the adjective in each sentence that tells how something looks, sounds, tastes, feels, or smells.

1. Grandmother baked with yellow cornmeal.
   yellow
2. She put in flour, eggs, and cold milk.
   cold
3. Grandmother added pepper and green chilies.
   green
4. She stirred everything into a smooth batter.
   smooth
5. She poured the batter into shiny pans.
   shiny
6. Now I make delicious cornbread too.
   delicious

140 Grammar

RESOURCES

Daily Fix-It Lesson 16
    See p. TR6.
    See also Daily Fix-It Transparency 16.
Grammar Transparency 16

B **Find** the sentence with the adjective. **Write** the sentence. **Underline** the adjective.

1. We buy colorful cloth.
   Gina and I choose it. We buy <u>colorful</u> cloth.

2. Gina and I begin.
   We sew warm quilts. We sew <u>warm</u> quilts.

3. I use red squares.
   I make squares and circles. I use <u>red</u> squares.

4. Gina likes stars and triangles.
   Gina cuts big stars. Gina cuts <u>big</u> stars.

5. We sew with needles and thread.
   We hum quiet tunes. We hum <u>quiet</u> tunes.

C **Complete** each sentence with an adjective of your own. **Tell** how something looks, sounds, tastes, feels, or smells. **Write** the sentences. Possible answers:

6. Dad makes <u>crispy</u> chicken.
7. I mix <u>sour</u> lemonade.
8. Mom drives down <u>bumpy</u> roads.
9. We smell <u>fresh</u> grass.
10. Birds sing <u>noisy</u> songs.

Grammar **141**

Guided Practice Ⓐ

Go through the exercise with children. Point out that there is only one adjective in each sentence. Ask volunteers to tell how they identified each adjective.

TEACHING TIP

Help children think of adjectives.

- Draw a word web on the board and write the noun *hair* in the center circle.

- Ask children to think of adjectives that can describe hair. (*black, curly, short, red, long*) As they offer words, write them in the other circles.

- Read each adjective with the noun it modifies: *black hair, curly hair*, and so on.

Independent Practice Ⓑ **and** Ⓒ

Have children complete the exercises. For Differentiated Instruction and Extra Practice, see p. TR14.

Differentiated Instruction

Strategic Intervention

Write this sentence on the board.

I have a ___ ball.

Hold up a ball and ask children to name adjectives you could use to describe the ball. (*small, blue, round, hard*) Write the adjectives under the blank and read the sentences together. Then write another sentence about another object and repeat the activity.

Advanced

Give each child a picture of a familiar fruit such as an apple, a banana, an orange, or grapes. Challenge children to write a description of the fruit using as many of their five senses as possible. Ask volunteers to share their descriptions, and have listeners point out adjectives writers used.

ELL

In a paper bag, place common objects, such as an apple, a paper towel, a pencil, an orange, and a sponge. Ask each child to pick an object from the bag and use as many adjectives as he or she can to describe it. Model the process: *red apple, round apple, sweet apple, big apple*. Write the phrases on the board and circle the adjectives.

Monitor Progress

Check Grammar

If... children have difficulty recognizing adjectives,	**then...** have them scan paragraphs in a favorite story and find adjectives used to describe nouns.

Test Preparation

✓ **Write** the letter of the correct answer.

1. Raccoons have ___ tails.
   - ○ **A** wash
   - ○ **B** paw
   - ⊗ **C** long

2. Squirrels have ___ teeth.
   - ○ **A** nut
   - ○ **B** tree
   - ⊗ **C** sharp

3. Mice have ___ fur.
   - ○ **A** ear
   - ⊗ **B** soft
   - ○ **C** sharp

4. Crows make ___ caws.
   - ⊗ **A** loud
   - ○ **B** fly
   - ○ **C** was

5. Skunks spray ___ smells.
   - ⊗ **A** bad
   - ○ **B** fur
   - ○ **C** run

6. Bees make ___ honey.
   - ○ **A** sting
   - ⊗ **B** sweet
   - ○ **C** buzz

Review

✓ **Choose** the word in ( ) that completes each sentence. **Write** the sentences.

1. This is my (was, <u>warm</u>) jacket.
2. I wrap (<u>thick</u>, put) quilts around me.
3. I drink a mug of (find, <u>hot</u>) chocolate.
4. I put on (<u>fuzzy</u>, wear) socks.
5. (Are, <u>Soft</u>) mittens keep my hands warm.
6. (Wrap, <u>Fresh</u>) bread smells wonderful.

✓ **Write** each sentence. **Underline** the adjective.

7. People like quiet bedrooms.
   People like <u>quiet</u> bedrooms.
8. Jenny's room has gray walls.
   Jenny's room has <u>gray</u> walls.
9. Shiny stars glow above her.
   <u>Shiny</u> stars glow above her.
10. Smooth floors creak and groan.
    <u>Smooth</u> floors creak and groan.
11. Windows let in cold air.
    Windows let in <u>cold</u> air.
12. Branches tap on frosty glass.
    Branches tap on <u>frosty</u> glass.

Grammar **143**

Summarize

Ask children to tell two important things about adjectives.

- Adjectives describe a person, place, animal, or thing.
- Adjectives can tell how something looks, sounds, tastes, feels, or smells.

Grammar-Writing Connection

Show children that if they want to make word pictures, they need to use adjectives. Write the following paragraph on the board.

Ben and Annie went sailing. Ben wore a ___ swimsuit. Annie wore a ___ dress. It was a ___ day. The ___ boat sailed across the ___ water. Ben and Annie had fun.

Have pairs of children rewrite the paragraph, adding adjectives in the blanks to tell how the things look, sound, taste, feel, or smell. Ask volunteers to read aloud their paragraphs with the group.

Use Strong Adjectives

OBJECTIVES

- Identify characteristics of a riddle.
- Write a riddle using strong adjectives.
- Develop criteria for judging a piece of writing.

TEACH

Read aloud the information in the box at the top of the page. Then say: *As I read two sentences, listen for strong adjectives.*

Think Aloud *Sue wore a nice hat.* When I read this sentence, all I can picture is a girl in a hat. *Nice* doesn't tell me anything about the hat. *Sue wore a floppy hat.* Now I get a more vivid picture of Sue's hat. It hangs down around her head.

Ask children to think of other strong adjectives they could use to describe Sue's hat.

Guided Writing

Read items 1–4 in Exercise 1 with children. Suggest that they compare the underlined words in each pair of sentences. Ask volunteers how they chose the stronger adjective.

Independent Writing

Read the directions for Exercise 2. Discuss children's favorite places and how they might describe them. After they have finished writing, ask volunteers to share their descriptions.

 WRITER'S CRAFT

Use Strong Adjectives

Strong adjectives make vivid word pictures for your readers.

Weak Adjective   Sue wore a <u>nice</u> hat.

Strong Adjective Sue wore a <u>floppy</u> hat.

 Look at the underlined adjectives. Which sentence in each pair has a stronger adjective? **Write** the sentence.

1. Aunt June sent me a <u>pretty</u> scarf.
   Aunt June sent me a <u>red-and-gold</u> scarf.
   Aunt June sent me a red-and-gold scarf.
2. They served <u>fruity</u> punch at the party.
   They served <u>good</u> punch at the party.
   They served fruity punch at the party.
3. The plane was late because of <u>bad</u> weather.
   The plane was late because of <u>stormy</u> weather.
   The plane was late because of stormy weather.
4. He grows <u>fine</u> tomatoes in his garden.
   He grows <u>juicy</u> tomatoes in his garden.
   He grows juicy tomatoes in his garden.

 Describe your favorite place. **Use** strong adjectives to make a vivid picture of the place.
Possible answer: My favorite place is my bedroom. The white furniture and the blue walls make the room feel cool and quiet. I like to sit on my comfortable bed and wrap my soft quilt around me.

144 Writing

RESOURCES

Writing Transparency 16

Write a Riddle

Writing Prompt Choose two things that can be compared, such as two seasons. Write two riddles. Give clues that describe the two things.

What Is It?

It has warm days but cool nights. Rain falls in steady showers. Snow melts away. Colorful tulips bloom, and the brown grass becomes green.

Answer: Spring

Its days and nights are cool. The leaves on the trees turn red, orange, and gold. Then they fall to the ground. A strong wind blows the dry leaves into small piles.

Answer: Fall

Riddles describe the seasons but do not name them.

Strong adjectives help readers picture each season.

Short and long sentences add variety to writing.

Writing **145**

Write a Riddle
ANALYZE THE MODEL

Read aloud the model and the callouts to the left of it. Then prepare children to write their own riddles.

PROMPT

Choose two things to compare. Write two riddles that give clues about the two things. Use strong adjectives.

Getting Started Children can do any of the following.

• Use an organizer (pp. TR28–TR32).
• Think of pairs of things that are both alike and different.
• List adjectives they can use to describe each thing.

Editing/Revising Checklist

☑ Did I hint at the two things without naming them?
☑ Did I use strong adjectives in my riddle clues?
☑ Did I use both short and long sentences in my riddles?

Self-Evaluation Distribute copies of p. TR26 for children to fill out.

Scoring Rubric — Write a Riddle

Rubric 4 3 2 1	4	3	2	1
Focus/Ideas	Riddles with strong focus on topic; excellent descriptive details	Riddles with good focus on topic; good descriptive details	Focus of riddles sometimes unclear; needs more descriptive details	Little or no focus in riddles; no descriptive details
Organization/ Paragraphs	Clues in clear, logical order	Clues in mostly logical order	Clues not in logical order	No order
Voice	Lively, imaginative; shows writer's feelings	Mostly lively, imaginative; shows some feelings	Not very lively or imaginative; shows few feelings	Careless, uninterested; shows no feelings
Word Choice	Vivid, clear word pictures; uses strong adjectives	Clear word pictures; some strong adjectives	Vague word pictures; mostly weak adjectives	Dull word pictures; few or no adjectives
Sentences	Clear, complete sentences; good variety	Most sentences clear, complete; some variety	Some unclear or incomplete sentences; little variety	Many unclear or incomplete sentences; no variety
Conventions	Few or no errors	No serious errors	Many errors	Too many errors

Adjectives for Number, Size, and Shape

TEACH

Read aloud the definitions, instruction, and example in the box on p. 146. Then say:

Adjectives for number tell us how many: *four apples, twelve peaches.* Adjectives for size tell us how big or small: *large pears, small cherries.* Adjectives for shape describe the shapes of things: *round orange, square box.*

Write the example sentence from the box on the board.

Think Aloud **Model** *A round pumpkin has large seeds.* I see three adjectives in this sentence. I know that the word *A* is an adjective because it tells me the sentence is about one pumpkin. The word *round* tells about the shape of the pumpkin. The word *large* tells about the size of the seeds. I know that words that tell about number, size, and shape are adjectives, so *round* and *large* are adjectives.

Adjectives for Number, Size, and Shape

Words for number, size, and shape are **adjectives**.

The words **a** and **an** are also adjectives.

A round pumpkin has **large** seeds.

The word **a** describes how many pumpkins—one.

Round describes the shape of the pumpkin. **Large** describes the size of the seeds.

A **Write** the adjective in each sentence. Then **write** *number, size,* or *shape* to tell what it describes.

1. Tina planted ten sunflowers.
   ten; number
2. Sunflowers are tall plants.
   tall; size
3. They have big stalks.
   big; size
4. Seeds grow in large heads.
   large; size
5. Tina took out oval seeds.
   oval; shape
6. She filled five bags with seeds.
   five; number
7. Tina's garden has twenty tulips.
   twenty; number
8. Tulips grow from round bulbs.
   round; shape

146 Grammar

RESOURCES

Daily Fix-It Lesson 17
   See p. TR6.
   See also Daily Fix-It Transparency 17.
Grammar Transparency 17

B **Find** the adjective that completes each sentence.
Use the clue in ( ) for help. **Write** the sentences.

1. My class visited ___ pumpkin patch. (number)
   long   a   huge
   My class visited a pumpkin patch.

2. There were ___ stacks of pumpkins. (size)
   square   colorful   tall
   There were tall stacks of pumpkins.

3. Each child chose ___ pumpkin. (number)
   one   oval   thin
   Each child chose one pumpkin.

4. Maria and Kevin picked ___ pumpkins. (shape)
   seven   orange   round
   Maria and Kevin picked round pumpkins.

5. I liked ___ pumpkins best. (size)
   one   little   new
   I liked little pumpkins best.

C **Choose** an adjective of your own to complete each sentence. **Use** the clue in ( ). **Write** the sentences.
Possible answers:

6. Here are ___ pies. (shape)
   Here are round pies.

7. You can cut a pie into ___ pieces. (number)
   You can cut a pie into six pieces.

8. I like ___ pieces. (size)
   I like big pieces.

9. You need ___ cherries for pie. (size)
   You need small cherries for pie.

10. Use ___ pumpkin for each pie. (number)
    Use one pumpkin for each pie.

Grammar **147**

Guided Practice A

Go through the exercise with children. Point out that there is only one adjective in each sentence. After children find the adjective in a sentence, ask them how they can tell whether the adjective describes number, size, or shape.

TEACHING TIP

Give children additional practice with adjectives.

- Write the following on the board:
  ___ ___ ___ apple
- Ask volunteers to give adjectives that tell about the apple. Remind them that they can use articles.
- Add children's suggested adjectives in a logical order: *a big red apple*.
- Continue with other objects.

Independent Practice B and C

Have children complete the exercises. For Differentiated Instruction and Extra Practice, see p. TR14.

Differentiated Instruction

Strategic Intervention

Say a sentence and have children identify the adjectives in the sentence. For example, *An ant carried a huge crumb.* (An, a, huge) Write the sentence on the board and underline the adjectives and their nouns. (*An ant* carried *a huge crumb.*) Continue with other sentences.

Advanced

Ask children to think about foods they like to eat. Have them write a paragraph about the foods. Tell them they must use adjectives to describe number, size, and shape. Ask volunteers to share what they have written with the group.

ELL

Write nouns (*book, dogs, rug, cups, window*) and adjectives for number, size, and shape (*ten, two, big, tall, round, square*) on index cards, one noun or adjective on a card. Pair children with more proficient English speakers. Have pairs put the adjectives and nouns together in ways that make sense (*ten dogs, round rug*) and then use the phrases to build sentences. (*Ten dogs ran down the street.*) Let pairs read aloud their sentences.

Monitor Progress

Check Grammar

If... children have difficulty identifying adjectives for number, size, and shape,	**then...** show pictures of objects and have children think of number, size, and shape adjectives to describe each one.

Test Preparation

☑ **Write** the letter of the correct answer.

1. This apple had ___ seeds.
- ○ **A** run
- ⊗ **B** six
- ○ **C** go

2. Do ___ apples have more seeds?
- ⊗ **A** large
- ○ **B** chew
- ○ **C** fill

3. Those ___ seeds come from sunflowers.
- ○ **A** fast
- ⊗ **B** oval
- ○ **C** plant

4. The ___ peas on your plate are seeds.
- ⊗ **A** round
- ○ **B** cook
- ○ **C** swim

5. Pieces of corn from ___ cob are seeds.
- ○ **A** cut
- ○ **B** farmer
- ⊗ **C** a

6. You might eat ___ seeds on bread.
- ○ **A** grow
- ○ **B** stick
- ⊗ **C** tiny

148 Grammar

Review

✓ **Choose** the adjective in ( ) that completes each sentence. **Write** the sentences.

1. Here is (<u>an</u>, vine) orange pumpkin.
2. Make a (stir, <u>giant</u>) pot of pumpkin soup.
3. Put the soup into (<u>round</u>, pour) bowls.
4. Eat the soup with (<u>square</u>, spoon) crackers.
5. Roast (pan, <u>eighty</u>) pumpkin seeds.
6. Store the seeds in (wrap, <u>small</u>) bags.

✓ **Write** the sentences. **Underline** the adjective in each sentence.

7. Squashes grow on long vines.
   Squashes grow on <u>long</u> vines.
8. Oval watermelons grow on vines.
   <u>Oval</u> watermelons grow on vines.
9. Thin vines may climb poles.
   <u>Thin</u> vines may climb poles.
10. Vines can crawl up a fence.
    Vines can crawl up <u>a</u> fence.
11. Two vines can twist together.
    <u>Two</u> vines can twist together.
12. Oranges and lemons grow on short trees.
    Oranges and lemons grow on <u>short</u> trees.

Grammar **149**

Summarize

Have children tell what they know about adjectives for number, size, and shape:

- Words for number, size, and shape are adjectives.
- The words *a* and *an* are also adjectives because they tell about the number one.

Grammar-Writing Connection

Write the following recipe on the board without the underscores.

Fruit Salad
<u>Two</u> <u>large</u> apples
<u>Three</u> <u>small</u> kiwis
<u>One</u> <u>big</u> carton of blueberries
<u>One</u> <u>oval</u> cantaloupe
<u>One</u> <u>small</u> lemon
Cut fruit into <u>small</u> pieces and combine in a <u>round</u> bowl. Cut the lemon in <u>two</u> pieces and squeeze lemon over the fruit. Refrigerate.

Have children list the adjectives for number, size, and shape in the recipe. You may wish to have them write their own recipes using adjectives for number, size, and shape. Ask them to share their recipes with the class.

Show, Don't Tell

150 Writing

OBJECTIVES

- Identify characteristics of a food review.
- Write a food review using words that show, don't tell.
- Develop criteria for judging a piece of writing.

TEACH

Read aloud the information in the box at the top of the page. Then say: *As I read two sentences, think about which one shows rather than tells.*

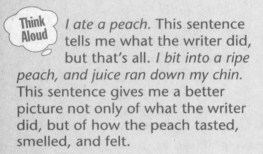

Think Aloud *I ate a peach.* This sentence tells me what the writer did, but that's all. *I bit into a ripe peach, and juice ran down my chin.* This sentence gives me a better picture not only of what the writer did, but of how the peach tasted, smelled, and felt.

Guided Writing

Read items 1–3 in Exercise 1 with children. Have children explain how they would choose words from the box to replace the underlined words in the sentences. Ask volunteers to read aloud their new sentences.

Independent Writing

Read the directions for Exercise 2. Discuss today's weather with children. Brainstorm words they might use in their descriptions. Call on volunteers to read aloud their writing.

Show, Don't Tell

When you write about something, **show—don't tell**— how it looks, sounds, tastes, smells, or feels.

No   I ate a peach.

Yes   I bit into a ripe peach, and juice ran down my chin.

 Choose words from the box to replace the underlined words in each sentence. **Write** the new sentences.

crackles across the sky

crying and shaking

shouted and clapped

1. He was <u>scared</u>.
   He was crying and shaking.
2. Lightning <u>is loud</u>.
   Lightning crackles across the sky.
3. The children <u>made noise</u>.
   The children shouted and clapped.

 What is the weather like today? **Describe** it. **Show, don't tell,** how it looks, sounds, and feels.

150 Writing
Possible answer is on page TR35.

RESOURCES

Writing Transparency 17

Write a Food Review

Writing Prompt Write a review of a food that a relative makes. Describe the food and tell whether you like it or not and why.

Writer states opinion of the pie.

Strong adjectives make a vivid picture of the pie.

Writer shows rather than tells reader about the pie.

Aunt Sue's Pumpkin Pie

Aunt Sue's pumpkin pie is the best! It has a thin, flaky crust. The filling is creamy and smooth. The filling melts in your mouth. Aunt Sue uses cinnamon, ginger, and cloves in the filling. How do I know she has just made pumpkin pie? I can smell the spices in her house! I love this pie.

Writing **151**

Write a Food Review

ANALYZE THE MODEL

Read aloud the model and the callouts to the left of it. Then prepare children to write their own reviews.

PROMPT

Write a review of a food that one of your relatives makes. What is the food like? Do you like it or not? Use words that show, not tell.

Getting Started Children can do any of the following.

- Use an organizer (pp. TR28–TR32).
- Think of a favorite food they like to eat at a family gathering.
- List vivid words to describe the food.

Editing/Revising Checklist

☑ Did I show, not tell, in my food review?

☑ Did I use strong adjectives to make vivid pictures?

☑ Did I use adjectives for numbers, size, and shape correctly?

Self-Evaluation Distribute copies of p. TR26 for children to fill out.

Scoring Rubric — Write a Food Review

Rubric 4 3 2 1	4	3	2	1
Focus/Ideas	Review with clear opinion and good reasons used to persuade	Review with clear opinion and reasons that help persuade	Review with unclear opinion and few reasons that persuade	Review with no opinion or persuasive reasons
Organization/ Paragraphs	Opinion followed by reasons in logical order	Opinion followed by reasons	Order not clear	No order
Voice	Lively; shows writer's feelings	Mostly lively; shows some feelings	Not lively; shows few feelings	Careless; no feelings
Word Choice	Uses persuasive words and words that show, not tell	Some persuasive words and words that show, not tell	Few persuasive words or words that show, not tell	No persuasive words; no attempt to show, not tell
Sentences	Smooth, complete sentences; good variety	Most sentences smooth, complete; some variety	Some choppy or incomplete sentences; little variety	Many choppy or incomplete sentences; no variety
Conventions	Few or no errors	No serious errors	Many errors	Too many errors

Adjectives That Compare

OBJECTIVES

OBJECTIVES

- Recognize adjectives that compare.
- Use adjectives that compare correctly in writing.
- Become familiar with adjectives that compare on standardized tests.

TEACH

Read aloud the instruction and examples in the box on p. 152. Then say:

When an adjective is used to compare two persons, places, animals, or things, -er is added to the adjective: *taller, shorter.* When an adjective is used to compare three or more persons, places, animals, or things, -est is added to the adjective: *tallest, shortest.*

Write on the board the first example sentence from the box. *(The chick is smaller than the hen.)*

Think Aloud **Model** When I read this sentence, I see that the adjective *smaller* ends in -er. This ending tells me that this adjective is comparing two persons, places, animals, or things. What two things are being compared? The chick and the hen.

Write on the board the second example sentence from the box. *(The egg is smallest of the three.)* Together with children, identify the adjective that is used to compare three or more things and the things that are being compared. *(smallest; egg to chick and hen)*

LESSON 18

Adjectives That Compare

Add **-er** to an adjective to compare two persons, places, or things.

Add **-est** to an adjective to compare three or more persons, places, or things.

The chick is **smaller** than the hen.

Smaller compares two things—the chick and the hen.

The egg is **smallest** of the three.

Smallest compares three things—the egg, the chick, and the hen.

A **Write** the sentences. **Circle** adjectives that compare two things. **Underline** adjectives that compare three or more things.

1. Lions are faster than zebras.
   Lions are (faster) than zebras.
2. The cheetah is the fastest animal on land.
   The cheetah is the <u>fastest</u> animal on land.
3. The blue whale is the longest animal of all.
   The blue whale is the <u>longest</u> animal of all.
4. Dolphins are longer than porpoises.
   Dolphins are (longer) than porpoises.

152 Grammar

RESOURCES

Daily Fix-It Lesson 17
   See p. TR6.
   See also Daily Fix-It Transparency 17.
Grammar Transparency 17

B **Choose** the adjective in ( ) that completes each sentence. **Write** the sentences.

1. A lamb is (<u>shorter</u>, shortest) than a calf.
2. A chick is (shorter, <u>shortest</u>) of all.
3. A kitten is (<u>taller</u>, tallest) than a mouse.
4. A cat is (taller, <u>tallest</u>) of the three.
5. A turtle is (slower, <u>slowest</u>) of all.
6. A cow is (<u>slower</u>, slowest) than a rabbit.

C **Add** *-er* or *-est* to the word in ( ) to complete each sentence. **Write** the sentences.

7. This pond is ___ of all the forest ponds. (deep)
   This pond is deepest of all the forest ponds.
8. It is ___ now than last night. (quiet)
   It is quieter now than last night.
9. The water is ___ in summer than in winter. (warm)
   The water is warmer in summer than in winter.
10. That frog is ___ than this fish. (small)
    That frog is smaller than this fish.
11. The turtle has the ___ shell I have ever seen. (round)
    The turtle has the roundest shell I have ever seen.
12. Today is the ___ day of the whole week. (cool)
    Today is the coolest day of the whole week.

Grammar **153**

Guided Practice A

Go through the exercise with children. After they have identified the adjectives that compare, ask them what things are being compared in each sentence.

TEACHING TIP

Show children that -est adjectives are often used to compare one thing to many other things.

- Point to this sentence in Exercise A: *The cheetah is the fastest animal on land.*
- Talk about how the cheetah is being compared to all the other kinds of animals that live on land.
- Continue with this sentence from Exercise A: *The blue whale is the longest animal of all.* (The blue whale is being compared to all other animals on Earth.)

Independent Practice B and C

Have children complete the exercises. For Differentiated Instruction and Extra Practice, see p. TR14.

Differentiated Instruction

Strategic Intervention

Hold up an eraser and a marker and say: *The eraser is smaller than the marker.* Ask children how many things are being compared. (*two*) Write the sentence on the board, pausing to ask children if the adjective *small* should end with *-er* or *-est*. Ask them to explain their answer.

Advanced

Play "What Is It?" Have children choose an object, keeping it secret, and write three sentences about the object using at least one adjective that compares. For example, *It is sometimes taller than a house. It changes colors. It is usually the biggest plant in a yard. What is it?* (*A tree*) Have children read aloud their clues and see if others can guess what the object is.

ELL

To build on the lesson concept, place a nickel and a dime on a table. Ask children to compare the two coins using an adjective that ends with either *-er* or *-est*. Then place a nickel, a dime, and a quarter on the table and ask children to compare these coins using an adjective that ends with either *-er* or *-est*. Continue with other pairs and sets.

Monitor Progress

Check Grammar

If... children have difficulty understanding adjectives that compare,	**then...** go through the test items with them and show how you would eliminate incorrect answers.

Test Preparation

✔ **Write** the letter of the correct answer.

1. Mary's frog is ___ than Todd's snake.
   - ○ **A** green
   - ⊗ **B** greener
   - ○ **C** greenest

2. Dan's parrot is the ___ animal of all.
   - ○ **A** bright
   - ○ **B** brighter
   - ⊗ **C** brightest

3. Mark's shirt is ___ than Lucia's shirt.
   - ○ **A** light
   - ⊗ **B** lighter
   - ○ **C** lightest

4. Ling's shirt is ___ of the three.
   - ○ **A** dark
   - ○ **B** darker
   - ⊗ **C** darkest

5. Sara is the ___ child of all.
   - ○ **A** old
   - ○ **B** older
   - ⊗ **C** oldest

6. Marty is ___ than Jason.
   - ○ **A** young
   - ⊗ **B** younger
   - ○ **C** youngest

Review

✓ **Write** the sentences. **Circle** adjectives that compare two things. **Underline** adjectives that compare three or more things.

1. Our classroom is (colder) than yours.
2. Mei Ling is the (tallest) girl in the class.
3. Juan talks (louder) than Donna.
4. Luis is (smarter) than I am.
5. Who is (kindest) of all the children?

✓ **Add** -er or -est to the word in ( ) to complete each sentence. **Write** the sentences.

6. A frog has (few) legs than a crab.
   A frog has fewer legs than a crab.
7. The tadpole is the (small) animal in the pond.
   The tadpole is the smallest animal in the pond.
8. This pond is (clean) of all.
   This pond is cleanest of all.
9. The grass is (green) here than there.
   The grass is greener here than there.
10. The mud is (soft) than the grass.
    The mud is softer than the grass.

Grammar **155**

REVIEW

Summarize

Have children tell two important things about adjectives that compare.

- Add -er to an adjective to compare two persons, places, animals, or things.
- Add -est to an adjective to compare three or more persons, places, animals, or things.

Grammar-Writing Connection

Have children choose three or more characters from a favorite story or book and write sentences comparing the characters. Remind children to use adjectives that end with -er or -est.

Peter Pan is taller than Wendy.

Tinkerbell is shorter than Wendy.

Tinkerbell is smallest of the three.

Wendy is quick, but Peter Pan is quicker.

Tinkerbell is quickest.

Repetition and Rhyme

TEACH

Read aloud the information in the box at the top of the page. Then say: *Listen as I read and tell me if you hear any repeated or rhyming words.*

Think Aloud *Once there was a frog, frog, frog. Who sat upon a log, log, log.* Is there any repetition? Yes, the words *frog* and *log* are each repeated three times. Is there any rhyme? Yes, the ending sounds of *frog* and *log* are the same.

Guided Writing

Read items 1–3 in Exercises 1 and 2. For items 1–2, have children name the word or words that are repeated. For item 3, ask children how they found the words that rhyme.

Independent Writing

Discuss favorite poems and nursery rhymes with children. Together write several lines from one of the poems and look for repeated words and rhyming words. Then ask children to write a rhyme of their own.

 WRITER'S CRAFT

Repetition and Rhyme

Sometimes a writer repeats a word or a group of words. This is called **repetition**. Sometimes a writer uses words whose ending sounds are the same. This is called **rhyme**.

Once there was a frog, frog, frog,

Who sat upon a log, log, log.

| **Repetition** | *frog* 3 times, *log* 3 times |
| **Rhyme** | fr*og* and l*og* |

 Write the repeated word or words.

1. Cock-a-doodle-do, how are you?

   Cock-a-doodle-do, I'll let you know soon.
   Cock-a-doodle-do

2. The boys were playing ball. The boys were riding bikes. The boys were having fun!
   The boys were

 Write the words that rhyme.

3. Pat saw a cat. The cat saw a rat. The rat saw a bat. The bat saw Pat.
   Pat, cat, rat, bat

156 Writing

RESOURCES

Writing Transparency 18

Write a Song

Writing Prompt Write a song about things you could do when you were a baby or things you can do now. Use a familiar tune, such as "Old MacDonald Had a Farm." Use rhyme.

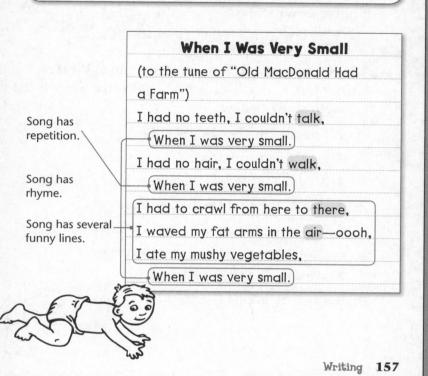

When I Was Very Small

(to the tune of "Old MacDonald Had a Farm")

I had no teeth, I couldn't talk,

When I was very small.

I had no hair, I couldn't walk,

When I was very small.

I had to crawl from here to there,

I waved my fat arms in the air—oooh,

I ate my mushy vegetables,

When I was very small.

Song has repetition.

Song has rhyme.

Song has several funny lines.

Writing **157**

Write a Song
ANALYZE THE MODEL

Read aloud the model and the callouts to the left of it. Then prepare children to write their own songs.

PROMPT

Write a song about you as a baby or about you now. Tell what you could do then or what you can do now. Use repetition and rhyme if you wish.

Getting Started Children can do any of the following.

- Use an organizer (pp. TR28–TR32).
- List things they can do or once did.
- Write rhyming words that they can use in their song.

Editing/Revising Checklist

☑ Did I focus on the topic in my song?

☑ Did I include repeated words or rhyming words?

☑ Did I use adjectives that compare correctly?

Self-Evaluation Distribute copies of p. TR26 for children to fill out.

Scoring Rubric Write a Song

Rubric 4 3 2 1	**4**	**3**	**2**	**1**
Focus/Ideas	Song with strong focus on topic and memorable details	Song with good focus on topic and interesting details	Song with weak focus on topic and few details	Song with no focus and no details
Organization/ Paragraphs	Uses song format	Mostly uses song format	Tries to use song format	No song format
Voice	Lively, imaginative; shows writer's feelings	Fairly lively, imaginative; shows some feelings	Not very lively or imaginative; shows few feelings	Shows no interest, imagination, or feelings
Word Choice	Vivid, well-chosen words; uses repetition and rhyme	Some vivid words; uses repetition or rhyme	Few vivid words; attempts to use rhyme	Dull, overused words; no repetition or rhyme
Sentences	Uses structures appropriate to song	Structures mostly appropriate to song	Some structures not appropriate to song	No attempt to match structures to song
Conventions	Few or no errors	No serious errors	Many errors	Too many errors

Adverbs That Tell *When* and *Where*

TEACH

Read aloud the definition and examples in the box on p. 158. Then say:

What is an adverb? An adverb is a word that tells more about a verb. An adverb can tell when or where.

Write on the board the two example sentences from the box. *(Today our family is moving. I hurry downstairs.)* Point to each sentence as you talk about it.

Think Aloud **Model** As I read the first sentence, I know that the word *today* is an adverb because it tells when. When is our family moving? Today. In the second sentence, the word *downstairs* tells me where. Where am I hurrying? Downstairs. So *downstairs* is an adverb.

LESSON 19

Adverbs That Tell When and Where

> **Adverbs** tell more about a verb. Some adverbs show **when** or **where**.
>
> Today our family is moving.
>   **Today** tells when.
> I hurry **downstairs.**
>   **Downstairs** tells where.

A **Write** the adverb from each sentence. **Write** *when* if the adverb shows when. **Write** *where* if the adverb shows where.

1. I packed my books yesterday.
   yesterday; when
2. Now I pack my toys.
   Now; when
3. My bike must be somewhere.
   somewhere; where
4. The movers set the boxes down.
   down; where
5. The moving van is parked outside.
   outside; where
6. Soon we will get to our new house.
   Soon; when
7. We should arrive tomorrow.
   tomorrow; when
8. I will be happy there.
   there; where

158 Grammar

B Find the adverb to complete each sentence. **Use** the clue in ( ) to help you. **Write** the sentences.

1. ___ I must find my kitten. (when)

   Call   Now   Spotted
   Now I must find my kitten.

2. Her basket is ___. (where)

   one   see   inside
   Her basket is inside.

3. She isn't ___. (where)

   here   can   tell
   She isn't here.

4. I search ___ for my kitten. (where)

   jump   many   everywhere
   I search everywhere for my kitten.

5. ___ I find her asleep in a box. (when)

   Fun   Play   Then
   Then I find her asleep in a box.

C Choose an adverb from the box to complete each sentence. **Use** the clue in ( ). **Write** the sentences.

outside	always	now	today	somewhere

Possible answers:

6. I (when) lose things.
   I always lose things.

7. (When) I lost my rocks.
   Today I lost my rocks.

8. They were (where) in the backyard.
   They were outside in the backyard.

9. I will start looking for them (when).
   I will start looking for them now.

10. My rocks must be (where).
    My rocks must be somewhere.

Grammar **159**

PRACTICE

Guided Practice Ⓐ

Go through the exercise with children. After they have identified the adverb in each sentence, ask them how they decided whether the adverb shows when or where.

TEACHING TIP

- Write this sentence on the board: *Today Margo plays outside.*

- Read the sentence aloud and ask children: *When does Margo play?* (today) *Where does Margo play?* (outside)

- Point out that asking when or where questions helps children identify the adverbs in the sentence.

Independent Practice Ⓑ and Ⓒ

Have children complete the exercises. For Differentiated Instruction and Extra Practice, see p. TR14.

Differentiated Instruction

Strategic Intervention

Write the following sentences on the board:

   ___ I am at home.

   I will go to school ___.

   I walked the dog ___.

Have children fill in the blanks with adverbs that tell when. Suggest that they read the sentence and then ask *When?* to help them think of an adverb that tells when.

Advanced

Ask children to think about a place they would like to visit and write several sentences about the place. Remind them to include adverbs that tell when and where. Invite volunteers to share their writing.

ELL

Create scaffolding by pointing to something in the room and saying: *The (desks) are inside.* Point to something outside and say: *The (trees) are outside.* Ask children: *Where are the desks?* (inside) *Where are the trees?* (outside) Point out that *inside* and *outside* are adverbs that tell where. Continue with sentences using the adverbs *today* and *yesterday* that tell when.

Test Preparation

✔ **Write** the letter of the correct answer.

1. Two kittens are ___.
- ○ **A** for
- ⊗ **B** inside
- ○ **C** purr

2. I will choose a kitten ___.
- ○ **A** paws
- ○ **B** see
- ⊗ **C** today

3. A gray kitten ran ___.
- ⊗ **A** here
- ○ **B** fur
- ○ **C** pretty

4. I reached ___.
- ⊗ **A** down
- ○ **B** few
- ○ **C** want

5. ___ I touched its soft fur.
- ○ **A** Far
- ⊗ **B** Then
- ○ **C** Go

6. ___ the kitten is mine.
- ○ **A** Round
- ○ **B** Like
- ⊗ **C** Now

Review

✔ **Choose** the adverb in ( ) that completes each sentence. **Write** the sentences.

1. Trucks carry things (<u>everywhere</u>, beside).

2. (Around, <u>Yesterday</u>) this truck hauled cars.

3. Vans move people (<u>far</u>, never).

4. This tank truck (near, <u>always</u>) carries milk.

5. (Upstairs, <u>Tomorrow</u>) that truck will haul steel.

✔ **Write** the adverb from each sentence. **Write** *when* if the adverb shows when. **Write** *where* if the adverb shows where.

6. Greg went to a new school today.
   today; when

7. He walked inside.
   inside; where

8. There everyone welcomed him.
   There; where

9. Greg walked upstairs to his classroom.
   upstairs; where

10. His locker was nearby.
   nearby; where

Summarize

Have children tell you what they know about adverbs that tell when and where.

- Adverbs tell more about a verb.
- Some adverbs tell when or where.

Grammar-Writing Connection

Point out that people often use adverbs that tell when and where in their writing. On the board, write the following itinerary, or trip schedule, without underscores:

June 20
<u>Today</u> we leave for the lake.
We will get <u>there</u> <u>tomorrow</u>.

June 21
We will hike <u>outside</u>.
<u>Then</u> we will go swimming.

June 24
<u>Now</u> we leave the lake.
We will be at home <u>soon</u>.

Ask volunteers to come to the board and underline the adverbs that tell when and where.

Sound Words

TEACH

Read aloud the information in the box at the top of the page. Then have children listen as you read.

Think Aloud *Bees buzz by me.* When I say the word *buzz,* it sounds like the sound a bee makes as it flies by. *Buzz* is a sound word.

Have children think of other words that sound like the sounds they name, such as *hiss, roar, plop,* and *sizzle.*

 ## Guided Writing

Read items 1–8 in Exercise 1 with children. After they identify the sound word in each sentence, read the sentences together, exaggerating the sound words.

 ## Independent Writing

Read the directions for Exercise 2. Discuss with children the sights and sounds of a busy street. Brainstorm a list of possible sound words. Ask volunteers to read aloud their descriptions.

Sound Words

Sound words are words that sound like the sounds they name.

Bees <u>buzz</u> by me.

Say the word *buzz.* It sounds like the sound that bees make.

 Write the sound word in each sentence.

1. The soda fizzes in the glass.
   fizzes
2. She shut the screen door with a bang.
   bang
3. A snake hissed in the grass.
   hissed
4. He slurped soup from a mug.
   slurped
5. The lion's roar scared the small child.
   roar
6. The chick cheeps for its mother.
   cheeps
7. The happy kitten purrs.
   purrs
8. We heard the ding-dong of the school bell.
   ding-dong

 Imagine you are standing by a busy street. **Describe** what you hear and see. **Use** as many sound words as you can. Possible answer: Cars honk and beep. Trucks bump and rumble. A bus wheezes to a stop. Above the noise of the traffic, a siren wails.

162 Writing

RESOURCES

Writing Transparency 19

Write a Poem

Writing Prompt Write a poem about moving. Tell how you feel about moving to a new place, home, or school.

Writer uses rhyme to make poem fun to read.

Writer shows feelings and how they change.

Writer uses repetition to make poem lively.

Writer uses sound words to make a vivid picture.

> We are in our new house.
>
> I don't like it at all.
>
> My door doesn't creak,
>
> My floor doesn't squeak,
>
> And the bathroom is way down the hall.
>
> Shh! Wait! Did you hear that?
>
> It's not so bad, after all.
>
> My floor just creaked,
>
> My door just squeaked,
>
> And I can slide—whoosh—down the hall!

Writing **163**

Write a Poem
ANALYZE THE MODEL

Read aloud the model and the callouts to the left of it. Then prepare children to write their own poems.

> **PROMPT**
>
> Write your own poem about moving. Tell about your feelings. Use some sound words if you can.

Getting Started Children can do any of the following.

- Use an organizer (pp. TR28–TR32).
- Think of a time when they went to a new place for the first time.
- Make lists of feeling and sound words.

Editing/Revising Checklist

✓ Did I use sound words in my poem?

✓ Did I tell my feelings about moving?

✓ Did I use adverbs that tell when and where correctly?

Self-Evaluation Distribute copies of p. TR26 for children to fill out.

Scoring Rubric Write a Poem

Rubric 4 3 2 1	4	3	2	1
Focus/Ideas	Poem with clear focus and strong details	Poem with good focus and details	Poem not always focused; few details	Poem with no focus or details
Organization/ Paragraphs	Uses poem structure	Mostly uses poem structure	Tries to use poem structure	No poem structure
Voice	Imaginative; clearly shows writer's feelings	Fairly imaginative; shows writer's feelings	Not very imaginative; shows few feelings	Shows no imagination or feelings
Word Choice	Vivid word pictures; uses rhyme, repetition, and sound words	Good word pictures; uses rhyme and sound words	No word pictures; few rhyming or sound words	Incorrect, dull, or overused words; no rhyme, repetition, or sound words
Sentences	Uses structures appropriate to poem	Structures mostly appropriate to poem	Some structures not appropriate to poem	No attempt to match structures to poem
Conventions	Few or no errors	No serious errors	Many errors	Too many errors

Adverbs That Tell How

OBJECTIVES

- Recognize adverbs that tell how.
- Use adverbs that tell how correctly in writing.
- Become familiar with adverbs on standardized tests.

TEACH

Read aloud the definition and example in the box on p. 164. Then say:

We know that some adverbs tell more about a verb by showing when or where. Other adverbs tell more about a verb by showing how an action is done. These adverbs usually end with *-ly*.

Write on the board the example sentence from the box. *(When Dad looked up, he saw the dark clouds clearly.)*

Think Aloud

Model When I read this sentence, I know that the word *clearly* is an adverb. It tells more about the verb *saw* because it tells how Dad saw the dark clouds. I also know *clearly* is an adverb because it ends with *-ly*.

Adverbs That Tell How

An **adverb** can tell more about a verb by telling **how** an action is done. Adverbs that tell how usually end in **-ly**.

When Dad looked up, he saw the dark clouds **clearly**.

Clearly tells *how* Dad saw the clouds.

A **Write** each sentence. **Underline** the adverb that tells how.

1. We listened <u>carefully</u> to Dad's words.
2. We <u>quickly</u> went to a safe place.
3. We sat <u>quietly</u> in the basement.
4. The wind blew <u>wildly</u>.
5. Thunder boomed <u>loudly</u>.
6. We heard all the noises <u>clearly</u>.
7. <u>Suddenly</u> the basement was dark.
8. We waited <u>silently</u> for the lights.

164 Grammar

RESOURCES

Daily Fix-It Lesson 20
    See p. TR7.
    See also Daily Fix-It Transparency 20.
Grammar Transparency 20

B **Write** the sentence. **Use** the word in ( ) that tells how.

1. The storm ends (<u>quickly</u>, rain).
2. The sun shines (<u>brightly</u>, breeze).
3. Birds (flying, <u>sweetly</u>) sing.
4. The wind blows (always, <u>softly</u>).
5. The streets dry (far, <u>slowly</u>).
6. (<u>Carefully</u>, Late) I open the door.

C **Write** each sentence with an adverb that tells how. **Use** each adverb once. Possible answers:

7. My sister sings <u>softly</u>.
8. The baby cries <u>loudly</u>.
9. The man speaks <u>slowly</u>.

| loudly |
| slowly |
| softly |

10. Her brother walks <u>quickly</u>.
11. That woman dances <u>badly</u>.
12. He climbs <u>carefully</u>.

| carefully |
| quickly |
| badly |

Guided Practice A
Go through the exercise with children. Ask volunteers to tell how they identified the adverb in each sentence.

TEACHING TiP

Point out that an adverb can appear before or after the verb in a sentence.

- Write these sentences on the board.
  I filled the cup <u>carefully</u>.
  I <u>carefully</u> filled the cup.
  <u>Carefully</u> I filled the cup.

- Point out that the adverb *carefully* appears after the verb *filled* in the first sentence and before the verb in the second and third sentences. However, the three sentences have the same meaning.

Independent Practice B and C

Have children complete the exercises. For Differentiated Instruction and Extra Practice, see p. TR14.

Differentiated Instruction

Strategic Intervention
Write these sentences in a row on the board.

  I will sing ___.
  I will play my flute ___.
  I will play my drums ___.
  I will tiptoe ___.

Read aloud the first sentence. Have children ask *How?* and think of an appropriate adverb to put in the blank. Write their suggested adverb(s) under the blank. Read the sentence together. Continue with other sentences.

Advanced
In a four-minute period, have pairs of children think of as many adverbs that tell how as they can and write the adverbs in sentences. One partner might write adverbs while the other partner writes sentences with the adverbs. Then the partners can trade tasks. The pair with the most sentences is the winner.

ELL
Pair English language learners with more proficient English speakers. Give each pair a sheet of paper. Have one partner write three verbs. That child gives the paper to the other partner, who writes an adverb that tells more about each verb.

  walk   slowly
  dance   gracefully
  run   quickly

Have partners trade places and continue with other verbs and adverbs.

Test Preparation

✔ **Write** the letter of the correct answer.

1. I fell ___.
   - ○ **A** tomorrow
   - ⊗ **B** suddenly
   - ○ **C** trip

2. I called ___ for help.
   - ⊗ **A** loudly
   - ○ **B** close
   - ○ **C** phone

3. ___ Dad rushed in.
   - ○ **A** Around
   - ○ **B** Hurry
   - ⊗ **C** Quickly

4. He checked me ___.
   - ○ **A** never
   - ○ **B** looked
   - ⊗ **C** carefully

5. Dad held ice ___ on my foot.
   - ⊗ **A** tightly
   - ○ **B** ahead
   - ○ **C** cube

6. ___ I felt better.
   - ○ **A** Cold
   - ⊗ **B** Slowly
   - ○ **C** Up

166 Grammar

Review

✓ **Write** the sentence that has an adverb.

1. Ms. Ling is a good teacher.

<u>Helen learned quickly.</u>

2. <u>Ms. Ling carefully wrote letters.</u>

Helen printed them.

3. Ms. Ling read a story.

<u>Helen gladly told about it.</u>

4. <u>The teacher smiled proudly at Helen.</u>

Helen thanked her.

✓ **Choose** the adverb that completes each sentence. **Write** the sentences.

5. Snow fell ___ all day.

lightly   kindly   warmly
Snow fell lightly all day.

6. I walked ___ into the snow.

badly   neatly   bravely
I walked bravely into the snow.

7. ___ a rabbit hopped past.

Suddenly   Brightly   Slowly
Suddenly a rabbit hopped past.

8. I ___ slipped on some ice.

freshly   nearly   deeply
I nearly slipped on some ice.

Grammar **167**

Summarize

Ask children how they can identify an adverb that tells how.

- An adverb that tells how shows how an action is done.
- An adverb that tells how usually ends with *-ly*.

Grammar-Writing Connection

Explain to children that by adding adverbs, they can give their readers more information about how actions are done.

No adverb: Mai waved good-bye.

With adverb: Mai <u>sadly</u> waved good-bye.

With adverb: Mai waved good-bye <u>happily</u>.

Focus/Ideas

TEACH

Read aloud the information in the box at the top of the page. Then say: *Listen to what I read. What is the main idea? Do all the sentences focus on the main idea?*

 Think Aloud I needed to buy vegetables for a salad. I went to the store. I bought lettuce and tomatoes. It was hot outside. When I got home, I made a salad.

Have children identify the main idea of the paragraph. *(buying vegetables for a salad)* and the sentence that does not focus on the main idea. *(It was hot outside.)*

 Guided Writing

Read items 1–2 in Exercise 1 with children. Have them identify and read aloud sentences that do not focus on the main idea in each paragraph.

 Independent Writing

Read the directions for Exercise 2. Talk with children about the seasons. When they have finished writing, ask volunteers to read aloud their paragraphs.

Focus/Ideas

A good paragraph has a main idea. The **main idea** is what the paragraph is about. Each sentence in the paragraph should tell about the main idea. When you are writing a paragraph, make every sentence **focus** on your main idea.

 Which two sentences in each paragraph do NOT focus on the main idea? **Write** the sentences.

1. Every summer I go to the beach with my family. Mountains are nice too. I dig in the sand and splash in the water. Where are my hiking shoes? The beach is my favorite place.
   Mountains are nice too. Where are my hiking shoes?

2. Two months ago Travis planted tomato seeds. Last year he planted pumpkin seeds. The tiny tomato seeds grew into large green plants. Soon Travis will pick ripe tomatoes. Tomatoes and carrots are good in salads.
   Last year he planted pumpkin seeds. Tomatoes and carrots are good in salads.

 Write a paragraph about your favorite season. **Make sure** every sentence focuses on the main idea of the paragraph.   Possible answer is on page TR35.

168 Writing

RESOURCES

Writing Transparency 20

Describe the Weather

> **Writing Prompt** Choose a kind of storm. Imagine the storm is happening right now. Write a paragraph about what the storm looks, sounds, and feels like.

Main idea comes in the first sentence.

Vivid words give a clear picture of the hurricane.

All sentences focus on telling about the hurricane.

Weather News

We are in the middle of a hurricane. A hurricane brings heavy rain and strong winds. Rain is pouring down. The wind is blowing very hard. You can't stand or walk outside. Water fills the streets and yards. Before the storm, my dad and I covered the windows. My mom carried food, water, and candles to the second floor. We moved upstairs because we are safer there.

Writing **169**

Describe the Weather

ANALYZE THE MODEL

Read aloud the model and the callouts to the left of it. Then prepare children to write their own weather descriptions.

> **PROMPT**
> Write a description of a kind of storm. Make sure every sentence focuses on the main idea. Use vivid words to describe the storm.

Getting Started Children can do any of the following.

- Use an organizer (pp. TR28-TR32).
- Talk to family members about storms children have experienced.
- Make a list of descriptive words suitable for the storm they choose.

Editing/Revising Checklist

☑ Did I make my main idea clear?

☑ Did I focus all my sentences on the main idea?

☑ Did I use adverbs that tell how correctly?

Self-Evaluation Distribute copies of p. TR26 for children to fill out.

Scoring Rubric — Describe the Weather

Rubric 4 3 2 1	4	3	2	1
Focus/Ideas	Description with excellent details that all focus on topic	Description with good details that all focus on topic	Description with some details that do not focus on topic	Description with few details or details that do not focus on topic
Organization/ Paragraphs	Main idea, then details in clear, logical order	Main idea, then details in mostly logical order	Main idea and details not well organized	No main idea; no order to details
Voice	Imaginative, lively writing; shows how writer feels	Fairly imaginative and lively; shows some feelings	Not very imaginative or lively; shows few feelings	Careless, uninterested; shows no feelings
Word Choice	Vivid, clear word pictures that appeal to senses	Good word pictures; some appeal to senses	Dull word pictures	Incorrect, dull, or overused words
Sentences	Smooth sentences; good variety	Most sentences smooth; some variety	Many choppy or stringy sentences; little variety	Choppy or incomplete sentences; no variety
Conventions	Few or no errors	No serious errors	Many errors	Too many errors

Pronouns

OBJECTIVES

- Recognize pronouns.
- Use pronouns correctly in writing.
- Become familiar with pronouns on standardized tests.

TEACH

Read aloud the definition, instruction, and examples in the box on p. 170. Then say:

We know that nouns are words that name persons, places, animals, or things. The words *he, she, it, we, you,* and *they* are pronouns. Pronouns can take the place of nouns.

Write the first two example sentences from the box *(Rosa is a doctor. She helps people.)* on the board. Point to the pronoun as you talk about it.

Model *Rosa is a doctor. She helps people.* The pronoun *She* in the second sentence refers to Rosa. Instead of using the noun *Rosa* again, the pronoun *she* takes the place of *Rosa.*

Write the last two examples on the board. Have children identify the pronoun in the second sentence *(They)* and tell the nouns that the pronoun replaces. *(Dan, Marie)*

LESSON 21

Pronouns

A **pronoun** is a word that takes the place of a noun or nouns. The words **he, she, it, we, you,** and **they** are pronouns.

Rosa is a doctor. **She** helps people.

She takes the place of the noun **Rosa.**

Dan and **Marie** are nurses. **They** help people.

They replaces the nouns **Dan** and **Marie.**

A **Write** the pronoun that can take the place of the underlined word or words.

1. <u>Animals</u> come to Dr. Soto. They
   They   We   You

2. <u>Alice Johnson</u> helps run the town. She
   It   She   He

3. <u>Jason and I</u> pick up trash. We
   You   We   She

4. <u>Mr. Jones</u> takes food to sick people. He
   She   He   It

5. <u>The fire truck</u> is shiny and new. It
   He   We   It

170 Grammar

RESOURCES

Daily Fix-It Lesson 21
  See p. TR7.
  See also Daily Fix-It Transparency 21.
Grammar Transparency 21

B **Write** the pronoun that can take the place of the underlined word or words. **Use** *he, she, it, we,* or *they.*

1. Sue Krensky talks to the children at school.
   She
2. The children listen to the police officer.
   They
3. Juan and I want to be police officers.
   We
4. Juan asks Officer Krensky many questions.
   He
5. Someday the dream will come true.
   it

C **Read** the pairs of sentences. **Choose** a pronoun to fill in each blank. **Use** *he, she, it, we,* or *they.* **Write** the new sentences.

6. Uncle Ralph is a firefighter.
   ____ knows about fires.
   He knows about fires.
7. This helmet belongs to Uncle Ralph.
   ____ protects his head.
   It protects his head.
8. Hoses are on the fire truck.
   ____ spray water on the fire.
   They spray water on the fire.
9. Beth Mills drives the fire truck.
   ____ has to drive fast.
   She has to drive fast.
10. My sister and I go to the fire station.
    ____ visit Uncle Ralph.
    We visit Uncle Ralph.

Guided Practice **A**

Go through the exercise with children. Ask them to explain how they chose the pronoun to replace the underlined word or words. Have volunteers read aloud the sentences using first the original subjects and then the replacement pronouns.

TEACHING TIP

To help children remember the kinds of nouns that the pronouns can replace, write the chart below on the board.

This pronoun can replace nouns like these.

he	Ed	the man
she	Sue	the girl
it	the cat	the box
we	Joe and I	the boys and I
they	Ed and Sue	the girls

Independent Practice
B and **C**

Have children complete the exercises. For Differentiated Instruction and Extra Practice, see p. TR15.

Differentiated Instruction

Strategic Intervention

Write this paragraph on the board without the underscores.

Harold Jackson had an earache. Harold went to see Dr. Mary Foster. Dr. Mary Foster looked in Harold's ear and said, "Harold's ear is infected. Use these drops. These drops will help."

Have children replace the underlined words with pronouns. *(He, She, It, They)* Read aloud the new paragraph and discuss how the pronouns make the paragraph sound smoother.

Advanced

Challenge children to write stories using at least three of the lesson pronouns. Suggest that they check their writing by underlining the pronouns. Ask volunteers to share their stories with the class.

ELL

Build on the lesson concept by writing sentences such as the following in a row on the board, underlining words as shown.

Annie likes animals.
Annie and I visited the vet.
The dogs licked our hands.
A cat rubbed on my legs.
Ed brought his parrot.

Write *He, They, It, She,* and *We* on self-stick notes, one per note. Give the notes to children and have them place the pronoun under the word or words it replaces.

Monitor Progress

Check Grammar

If... children have difficulty using pronouns,	**then...** write a short paragraph from a familiar book on the board and help children identify pronouns as you read aloud.

Test Preparation

☑ **Mark** the letter of the correct pronoun.

1. <u>Nancy Loo</u> is a weather reporter.
   - ○ **A** We
   - ⊗ **B** She
   - ○ **C** It

2. <u>The weather</u> is important to many people.
   - ⊗ **A** It
   - ○ **B** They
   - ○ **C** We

3. <u>The children</u> invited Ms. Loo to their class.
   - ○ **A** You
   - ⊗ **B** They
   - ○ **C** He

4. <u>Brian</u> asked a question about hail.
   - ○ **A** We
   - ○ **B** It
   - ⊗ **C** He

5. <u>Consuelo and I</u> asked about sleet.
   - ○ **A** You
   - ○ **B** He
   - ⊗ **C** We

6. <u>Ms. Loo</u> told us about cold fronts.
   - ⊗ **A** She
   - ○ **B** We
   - ○ **C** They

Review

✓ **Write** each sentence. **Underline** the pronoun.

1. Will you get a job someday?
Will you get a job someday?

2. She will work on computers.
She will work on computers.

3. We will fix cars.
We will fix cars.

4. They want to work with animals.
They want to work with animals.

5. Maybe he will be a vet.
Maybe he will be a vet.

6. It is a useful job.
It is a useful job.

✓ **Rewrite** each sentence. **Change** the underlined word or words to *he, she, it, we,* or *they*.

7. The fire station is busy today.
It is busy today.

8. Lisa checks the siren.
She checks the siren.

9. Dan and Dave wash the fire truck.
They wash the fire truck.

10. Mario cooks in the kitchen.
He cooks in the kitchen.

11. Maya and I test the air tanks.
We test the air tanks.

12. The air tanks must be full.
They must be full.

Grammar **173**

Summarize

Have children tell you two important things about pronouns.

- A pronoun takes the place of a noun or nouns.
- *He, she, it, we, you,* and *they* are pronouns.

Grammar-Writing Connection

Explain to children that using pronouns in place of nouns will help make their writing less wordy and easier to read.

Wordy: The firefighters were in a hurry. <u>The firefighters</u> grabbed their gear.

Less wordy: The firefighters were in a hurry. <u>They</u> grabbed their gear.

Word Choice

TEACH

Read aloud the information in the box at the top of the page. Then say: *Listen carefully as I read two sentences.*

Think Aloud *He had a nice sweater.* Who is *he?* What does *had* mean? What does *nice* tell about the sweater? This sentence doesn't tell me very much. *Jack wore a blue and red striped sweater.* This sentence is much clearer. Now I know who the sweater belongs to, what he is doing with the sweater, and what the sweater looks like.

 ## Guided Writing

Read items 1–4 in Exercise 1 with children. Remind them to listen for the sentence in each pair that is clearer and livelier. Ask volunteers to tell what words make these sentences more interesting.

 ## Independent Writing

Read the directions for Exercise 2. Talk with children about jobs they think are interesting. After they have completed their writing, ask volunteers to read aloud what they have written.

 WRITER'S CRAFT

Word Choice

Choose words carefully. Use exact nouns, strong verbs, and exciting adjectives. They will make your writing clear and lively.

No He <u>had</u> a <u>nice</u> sweater.

Yes <u>Jack</u> <u>wore</u> a <u>blue and red striped</u> sweater.

 Write the sentence in each pair that sounds more interesting.

1. A person was here.
   <u>A firefighter visited our class.</u>

2. She showed us stuff.
   <u>Ms. Li showed us her helmet and boots.</u>

3. <u>We learned rules for fire safety.</u>
   We learned new things.

4. The firefighter told some stories.
   <u>The firefighter told exciting stories about rescues.</u>

 Write about a job you would like to have. **Choose** your words carefully.

Possible answer: I want to be a police officer. I will protect people and solve crimes. I will drive a squad car and keep the neighborhood safe.

174 Writing

RESOURCES

Writing Transparency 21

Give an Award

Writing Prompt Give an award to a community worker, such as a firefighter, police officer, teacher, or librarian. Tell what the person does. Explain why he or she deserves the award.

Person chosen for the award is introduced in the first sentence.

Writer gives reasons to support her choice.

Careful word choice gives readers a clear picture of the person.

And the Award Goes to . . .

I think we should give an award to Mr. Grant. He is the best teacher I have ever had. He makes learning exciting and interesting. That is important. He wants us to ask questions. Sometimes he answers them, but mostly he helps us find the answers for ourselves. He is always patient, even when we don't understand something the first time. He just explains it another way.

Writing 175

Give an Award
ANALYZE THE MODEL

Read aloud the model and the callouts to the left of it. Then prepare children to give their own awards.

PROMPT

Pick a community worker you think deserves an award. Name the person and tell why he or she should get an award. Choose your words carefully.

Getting Started Children can do any of the following.

- Use an organizer (pp. TR28–TR32).
- Think of people in their community whom they admire.
- Make a list of what they admire most about these people.

Editing/Revising Checklist

☑ Did I choose words that make my writing clear?

☑ Did I include reasons that support my choice?

☑ Did I use pronouns correctly?

Self-Evaluation Distribute copies of p. TR26 for children to fill out.

Scoring Rubric — Give an Award

Rubric 4 3 2 1	4	3	2	1
Focus/Ideas	Award with clearly stated choice and excellent supporting reasons	Award with stated choice and good supporting reasons	Award with unclear choice and few supporting reasons	Award with no stated choice or supporting reasons
Organization/ Paragraphs	Choice followed by reasons in logical order	Choice followed by reasons in mostly logical order	Choice and reasons not in clear order	No order
Voice	Lively, thoughtful; shows writer's feelings	Generally lively, thoughtful; shows some feelings	Not very lively or thoughtful; shows few feelings	Careless, uninterested; shows no feelings
Word Choice	Clear, well-chosen words; good picture of person	Clear words; reasonable picture of person	Vague or general words; picture of person not clear	Dull or incorrect words; no picture of person
Sentences	Smooth sentences; good variety	Most sentences smooth; some variety	Many choppy or stringy sentences; little variety	Choppy or incomplete sentences; no variety
Conventions	Few or no errors	No serious errors	Many errors	Too many errors

Pronouns for One and More Than One

- Recognize pronouns for one and more than one.
- Use pronouns for one and more than one correctly in writing.
- Become familiar with singular and plural pronouns on standardized tests.

TEACH

Read aloud the definitions and examples in the box on p. 176. Then say:

We know that a pronoun can take the place of a noun or nouns. Some pronouns take the place of singular nouns. Other pronouns take the place of plural nouns.

Write the first two example sentences from the box *(Grandma builds things. She uses wood.)* on the board. Point to them.

Think Aloud **Model** When I read these two sentences, I see that the pronoun *She* takes the place of the noun *Grandma* in the second sentence. *Grandma* names one person, and *She* is a pronoun that names only one.

Write the last two example sentences from the box *(Grandma and I worked. We built a birdhouse.)* on the board. Have children identify the pronoun in the second sentence *(We),* tell whether it names one or more than one *(more than one),* and name the nouns it replaces. *(Grandma, I)*

Pronouns for One and More Than One

He, she, and **it** are pronouns that name only one.

We and **they** are pronouns that name more than one.

Grandma builds things. **She** uses wood.

She is a pronoun that names one person— Grandma.

Grandma and I worked. **We** built a birdhouse.

We is a pronoun that names more than one— Grandma and I.

A **Write** the sentences. **Circle** the pronouns that name only one. **Underline** the pronouns that name more than one.

1. On the way home one night, we saw a cat.
   On the way home one night, <u>we</u> saw a cat.
2. It was sitting by the side of the road.
   (It) was sitting by the side of the road.
3. Mom said we should stop.
   Mom said <u>we</u> should stop.
4. She handed Dad a blanket.
   (She) handed Dad a blanket.
5. He wrapped the blanket around the cat.
   (He) wrapped the blanket around the cat.
6. They took the cat to a vet.
   <u>They</u> took the cat to a vet.

176 Grammar

RESOURCES

Daily Fix-It Lesson 22
   See p. TR8.
   See also Daily Fix-It Transparency 22.
Grammar Transparency 22

B **Write** the pronoun in ( ) that can take the place of the underlined word or words.

1. <u>Travis and I</u> visit Grandma and Grandpa. (<u>We</u>, He)

2. <u>Grandma</u> wants a planter box. (They, <u>She</u>)

3. <u>Grandma and I</u> nail boards together. (<u>We</u>, She)

4. <u>Grandpa</u> has a truck. (They, <u>He</u>)

5. <u>The truck</u> is bright red. (They, <u>It</u>)

6. <u>Grandpa and Travis</u> drive to the store. (<u>They</u>, He)

C **Write** a new sentence about the underlined word or words in each sentence. **Use** *he, she, it, we,* or *they* in your sentence.

Example   <u>My sisters and I</u> got a kitten.
                 We were very excited.
                 Possible answers:

7. <u>Kittens</u> are baby cats.
    They can be very cute.

8. <u>Sara</u> wants a name for the kitten.
    She thinks Fluffy is good.

9. <u>Martha and I</u> have another name.
    We want to call the kitten Peanut.

10. <u>Dad</u> doesn't like our names.
    He thinks Squealer is the best name.

Grammar **177**

PRACTICE

Guided Practice Ⓐ

Go through the exercise with children. Point out that each sentence has only one pronoun. After children have found the pronoun, ask them how they can tell whether the pronoun names one or more than one.

TEACHING TIP

Help children distinguish pronouns for one from pronouns for more than one.

• Write in a column on the board: *Susan, The girls, Doug and I, Howard, The dog.*

• Have children make up sentences using the words as subjects: *The girls take a walk.* Write their sentences.

• Ask children how they would replace the words with pronouns. Have them tell if they need a pronoun for one or a pronoun for more than one.

Independent Practice
Ⓑ and Ⓒ

Have children complete the exercises. For Differentiated Instruction and Extra Practice, see p. TR15.

Differentiated Instruction

Strategic Intervention

Write sentences with singular and plural subjects on the board. *(Claire swings the bat. The boys chase the ball.)* Read the sentences together. Then have children come to the board, circle the subjects, and write the pronouns that can replace the nouns. Read the new sentences together.

Advanced

Ask children to write several sentences about animals they are interested in. Challenge them to include pronouns for one and more than one in their sentences. Invite volunteers to share what they have written.

ELL

Pair English language learners with children who understand the concept. Give each pair a magazine picture that shows several people and objects. Ask the pairs to write the lesson pronouns on self-stick notes and then label parts of their picture with the notes. Have them say sentences using first nouns and then pronouns. Model the exercise. *(Two men are talking. They are talking.)*

Suggest that children look carefully at the underlined word or words in each sentence. Point out that they can narrow the answer choices by first deciding whether the noun or nouns require a pronoun for one or more than one.

Monitor Progress

Check Grammar

If... children have difficulty identifying pronouns for one or more than one,	**then...** go through the test items with them and determine the correct answers together.

Test Preparation

✓ **Mark** the letter of the pronoun that can take the place of the underlined word or words.

1. <u>Storms</u> can be loud.
- ○ **A** She
- ○ **B** We
- ⊗ **C** They

2. <u>A high wind</u> can blow down trees.
- ○ **A** They
- ⊗ **B** It
- ○ **C** He

3. <u>Patty and I</u> do not like thunder.
- ○ **A** He
- ○ **B** It
- ⊗ **C** We

4. <u>Dad</u> says lightning can hurt people.
- ⊗ **A** He
- ○ **B** They
- ○ **C** We

5. <u>Ice storms</u> make roads slick.
- ⊗ **A** They
- ○ **B** He
- ○ **C** She

6. <u>Mom</u> loves snow.
- ○ **A** We
- ⊗ **B** She
- ○ **C** They

178 Grammar

Review

✓ **Write** the pronoun in each sentence. **Write** *one* if the pronoun names only one. **Write** *more than one* if the pronoun names more than one.

1. The kitten was outside, and Kevin found it.
   it; one
2. Where did he look?
   he; one
3. We will ask Sara.
   We; more than one
4. She says Kevin looked in the yard.
   She; one
5. Will they keep the kitten?
   they; more than one

✓ **Write** each sentence. **Replace** the underlined word or words. **Use** *he, she, it, we,* or *they.*

6. <u>Animals</u> come in many colors.
   They come in many colors.
7. <u>Calvin</u> has a green lizard.
   He has a green lizard.
8. <u>Louisa</u> bought an orange fish.
   She bought an orange fish.
9. <u>Paul</u> got a blue and red bird.
   He got a blue and red bird.
10. <u>Beth and I</u> found a brown puppy.
    We found a brown puppy.

Grammar **179**

Summarize

Ask children what they know about pronouns for one and more than one.

- Pronouns that name only one are *he, she,* and *it.*
- Pronouns that name more than one are *we* and *they.*

Grammar-Writing Connection

Explain to children that using pronouns makes their writing smoother and less wordy because they avoid repeating nouns.

Wordy: Emily took the dogs for a walk. <u>Emily</u> wanted to walk, but <u>the dogs</u> wanted to run.

Not wordy: Emily took the dogs for a walk. <u>She</u> wanted to walk, but <u>they</u> wanted to run.

Use Persuasive Words

- Identify characteristics of writing reasons.
- Write reasons using persuasive words.
- Develop criteria for judging a piece of writing.

TEACH

Read aloud the information in the box at the top of the page. Then say: *As I read, listen carefully for words that persuade.*

 Think Aloud This is the best meatloaf I've ever tasted. You should make it every day. Everyone needs to try it.

Review with children the persuasive words they heard. Write the words on the board. *(best, should, needs)*

 ## Guided Writing

Read the letter in Exercise 1 with children. Have them tell which persuasive word from the box they would put in each blank. Ask a volunteer to read aloud the completed letter.

 ## Independent Writing

Read the directions for Exercise 2. Discuss trips children might like to take. Point out that they need good reasons and persuasive words. Ask volunteers to read aloud their letters.

 WRITER'S CRAFT

Use Persuasive Words

A writer wants readers to agree with his or her opinion. The writer **uses words** such as *should, need, must, best, worst,* and *most important* **to persuade readers.**

 Use the words from the box to complete the letter. **Write** the letter.

Word Bank
important
best
need
should

Dear Mom,
 I think we **(1)** ___ visit Washington, D.C., this summer. We can see the White House and many other famous buildings. All Americans **(2)** ___ to learn about their nation's capital. Visiting Washington would be the **(3)** ___ trip we could take. Most **(4)** ___, we could do it together!
                              Love,
                              Zoe

1. should 2. need 3. best 4. important

Write a letter to a parent telling about a trip you would like to take. **Give** reasons for the trip. **Use** words that persuade. Possible answer is on page TR36.

180 Writing

RESOURCES

Writing Transparency 22

Write Reasons

Writing Prompt Explain why you should have a pet. Tell the kind of pet you want, and give reasons to support your idea.

Words are used to persuade readers that this is a good idea.

Writer gives reasons to support idea.

Writer saves most important reason for last.

Why We Should Have a Pet

I think we should get a dog. Tad and I study hard and get good grades. We always do our chores. A dog would be the best reward that we could get. Also, we are responsible. We will take care of a dog. Most important, a dog could protect our house when we are away.

Writing **181**

Write Reasons

ANALYZE THE MODEL

Read aloud the model and the callouts to the left of it. Then prepare children to write their own reasons.

PROMPT

Write reasons why you should have a pet. Give reasons that support your idea. Use words to persuade your readers.

Getting Started Children can do any of the following.

- Use an organizer (pp. TR28–TR32).
- Make a list of possible pets and choose the one they like best.
- Write reasons for having the pet and choose the best ones.

Editing/Revising Checklist

☑ Did I give good reasons that support my idea?

☑ Did I use words that will help persuade my readers?

☑ Did I use pronouns correctly?

Self-Evaluation Distribute copies of p. TR26 for children to fill out.

Scoring Rubric — Write Reasons

Rubric 4 3 2 1	4	3	2	1
Focus/Ideas	Clearly stated idea; excellent reasons that persuade	Stated idea; good reasons that persuade	Idea not clearly stated; few reasons that persuade	No clear idea; no reasons that persuade
Organization/ Paragraphs	Reasons in logical order, most important last	Reasons in logical order	Order of reasons not clear	No order
Voice	Thoughtful; shows writer's feelings	Mostly thoughtful; shows some feelings	Not very thoughtful; shows few feelings	Careless, uninterested; shows no feelings
Word Choice	Uses persuasive words	Uses some persuasive words	Uses few persuasive words	No persuasive words
Sentences	Smooth sentences; good variety	Most sentences smooth; some variety	Many choppy or stringy sentences; little variety	Many unclear, incomplete, choppy sentences; no variety
Conventions	Few or no errors	No serious errors	Many errors	Too many errors

Using *I* and *Me*

- Recognize the pronouns *I* and *me*.
- Use *I* and *me* correctly in writing.
- Become familiar with the pronouns *I* and *me* on standardized tests.

TEACH

Read aloud the instruction and examples in the box on p. 182. Then say:

We know that pronouns take the place of nouns. The pronouns *I* and *me* replace a specific noun: your name. *I* replaces your name when it is in the subject of a sentence. *Me* replaces your name when it is used after an action verb.

Write on the board the last two example sentences from the box. *(The dog and I sing together. People give the dog and me special awards.)*

Think Aloud **Model** The subject of the first sentence is *The dog and I.* The pronoun *I* is used in place of the speaker's name. *I* is always used in the subject of a sentence. In the second sentence, *the dog and me* comes after the action verb *give.* The pronoun *me* is used in place of the speaker's name. *Me* is always used after an action verb. In both sentences, the dog is named first and the speaker is named last: *The dog and I, the dog and me.*

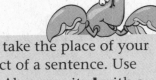

LESSON 23

Using *I* and *Me*

The pronouns **I** and **me** take the place of your name. Use **I** in the subject of a sentence. Use **me** after an action verb. Always write **I** with a capital letter.

   I always wanted a dog. Mom bought **me** one.

When you talk about yourself and another person or thing, name yourself last. The pronouns **I** and **me** take the place of your name.

   The dog and **I** sing together.
People give the dog and **me** special awards.

A Use *I* or *me* to complete each sentence. **Write** the sentences.

1. ___ have a dog named Pepper.
   I have a dog named Pepper.
2. Pepper and ___ are best friends.
   Pepper and I are best friends.
3. Dad teaches Pepper and ___ funny songs.
   Dad teaches Pepper and me funny songs.
4. Singing makes Pepper and ___ happy.
   Singing makes Pepper and me happy.
5. Maybe Pepper and ___ can sing for you.
   Maybe Pepper and I can sing for you.
6. Invite Pepper and ___ to your house.
   Invite Pepper and me to your house.

182 Grammar

RESOURCES

Daily Fix-It Lesson 23
   See p. TR8.
   See also Daily Fix-It Transparency 23.
Grammar Transparency 23

B Find the word or words that complete each sentence. **Write** the sentences.

1. ___ are good pet owners.

   Ali and I   Ali and me   me and Ali
   Ali and I are good pet owners.

2. ___ keep Bingo on a leash in the park.

   me   I   i
   I keep Bingo on a leash in the park.

3. Bingo walks next to ___.

   me and Ali   Ali and I   Ali and me
   Bingo walks next to Ali and me.

4. Ali helps ___ with Bingo's bath.

   I   i   me
   Ali helps me with Bingo's bath.

C Answer each question. **Add** words to finish each sentence. **Use** *I* or *me* in the sentences.
Possible answers:

5. Did you go to the pet store?

   Yes, ___.
   Yes, I went today.

6. Who went with you?

   James ___.
   James went with me.

7. What kind of bird did you see?

   He and ___.
   He and I saw a parrot.

8. What did the bird do?

   The bird ___ James and ___.
   The bird scolded James and me.

Grammar   **183**

PRACTICE

Guided Practice A

Go through the exercise with children. Remind them that *I* is used in the subject of a sentence and *me* is used after an action verb. Ask volunteers to tell how they decided whether to use *I* or *me* in each sentence.

TEACHING TIP

Give children additional practice in using the pronouns *I* and *me*.

- On the board, write other *I* and *me* sentences modeled on those in Exercise A. Leave a blank in place of *I* or *me*.
- Have volunteers take turns coming to the board and writing *I* or *me* to complete each sentence.
- *Ask children to explain why they chose that pronoun.*

Independent Practice B and C

Have children complete the exercises. For Differentiated Instruction and Extra Practice, see p. TR15.

Differentiated Instruction

Strategic Intervention

On the board, write sentences with *I* or *me*. Make some of the sentences incorrect: *Ben and me have a cat. Dale lent Ed and I his bike.* Have children write OK by the correct sentences and revise the sentences that are incorrect by crossing out the incorrect pronoun and writing the correct pronoun above it.

Advanced

Write story starter sentences that use the pronoun *I* or *me* on slips of paper and have each child choose one from a container. Challenge children to use the sentences to begin a short story. Invite volunteers to share their stories with the group. Check their use of the pronouns *I* and *me*.

ELL

Have each child write *I* on one card and *me* on another card. On the board, write sentences with *I* or *me*, leaving out the pronoun: *Mom and ___ went to the store. ___ got a cart. Mom let ___ push.* Read each sentence aloud with children, pausing at the blank. Have them hold up the pronoun that goes in the blank. Read the completed sentence together before going on to the next sentence.

Test Preparation

✓ **Mark** the letter of the correct answer.

1. ___ like baseball.
   - ⊗ **A** I
   - ◯ **B** i
   - ◯ **C** me

2. ___ go to a baseball game.
   - ◯ **A** I and Mom
   - ⊗ **B** Mom and I
   - ◯ **C** Mom and me

3. Mom buys ___ popcorn.
   - ◯ **A** I
   - ⊗ **B** me
   - ◯ **C** he

4. A ball almost hits ___.
   - ◯ **A** Mom and I
   - ◯ **B** me and Mom
   - ⊗ **C** Mom and me

5. ___ jump for the ball.
   - ◯ **A** i
   - ◯ **B** me
   - ⊗ **C** I

6. The ball just misses ___.
   - ⊗ **A** me
   - ◯ **B** I
   - ◯ **C** Mom and I

Review

✓ **Choose** the word in ( ) that completes each sentence. **Write** the sentences.

1. (I, Me) have a dog that does tricks.

2. Sparky can bring (I, me) balls.

3. Jerry and (I, me) hide from Sparky.

4. Sparky finds Jerry and (I, me).

5. Let (I, me) show you his new trick.

✓ **Write** the sentence that uses *I* or *me* correctly. **Underline** *I* or *me*.

6. Rosa and me care for our class hamster.
Rosa and I feed the hamster.
Rosa and I feed the hamster.

7. I bring it fresh water.
The hamster shows Rosa and I its tricks.
I bring it fresh water.

8. Me and Rosa clean out its cage.
Rosa and I do not like that job.
Rosa and I do not like that job.

9. Mr. Davis helps Rosa and I.
He hands me the hamster.
He hands me the hamster.

10. Rosa and me took good care of the pet.
The class thanked Rosa and me.
The class thanked Rosa and me.

Grammar **185**

Summarize

Ask children to tell four important things about using *I* and *me*.

- The pronouns *I* and *me* take the place of your name.
- *I* is always a capital letter.
- Use *I* in the subject of a sentence and *me* after an action verb.
- When you talk about another person or thing and yourself, name yourself last.

Grammar-Writing Connection

Explain that one way to identify the correct pronoun in a group of words such as *Toby and I* or *Dana and me* is to say the sentence with just the pronoun and not the other words in the group.

Toby and (I, me) play chess.

Say: I play chess.
Me play chess.

Ask: Which is correct?
(I play chess.)

Correct: Toby and I play chess.

Toby invited Dana and (I, me).

Say: Toby invited I.
Toby invited me.

Ask: Which is correct?
(Toby invited me.)

Correct: Toby invited Dana and me.

Know Your Audience

OBJECTIVES

- Identify characteristics of rules.
- Write rules that show you know your audience.
- Develop criteria for judging a piece of writing.

TEACH

Read aloud the information in the box at the top of the page. Then say: *Listen as I read two sentences.*

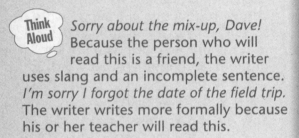

Think Aloud *Sorry about the mix-up, Dave!* Because the person who will read this is a friend, the writer uses slang and an incomplete sentence. *I'm sorry I forgot the date of the field trip.* The writer writes more formally because his or her teacher will read this.

Guided Writing

Read items 1–3 with children. Have them tell the audience each group of sentences is intended for. Have volunteers share how they made their choices.

Independent Writing

Read the directions for Exercise 2. Discuss gifts children have received from older relatives and what they might write. When they are finished, ask volunteers to share their notes.

 WRITER'S CRAFT

Know Your Audience

Before you begin writing, you need to **know your audience.** The audience is the person or people who will read your writing. Write with your audience in mind.

To a Friend	Sorry about the mix-up, Dave!
To a Teacher	I'm sorry I forgot the date of the field trip.

 Write the letter of the audience that matches each group of sentences best.

A Your classmates **B** Your older sister
  C The editor of your local paper

1. Your idea for Mom's gift is OK with
B me. Let's go to the mall on Saturday.

2. Our town will be 125 years old next year.
C We need to plan a special celebration.

3. Ms. Huber's birthday is next Thursday.
A What are we going to give her?

 Write a note to an older relative thanking him or her for a gift. **Think** about your audience.

Possible answer is on page TR36.

186 Writing

RESOURCES

Writing Transparency 23

Write Pet Care Rules

Writing Prompt Write your classmates a set of rules for taking care of a pet. Think about your audience.

Writer uses words and voice that are suitable for the audience.

Rules are put in a numbered list to make them easy to read.

Writer gives reasons to help explain some rules.

Pet Care Rules

1. Your pet must be fed every day. Choose the right food.
2. Your pet needs fresh water every day. Keep the dish in the same place.
3. You should spend time with your pet. Animals get lonely too.
4. Don't let your pet roam outside. Pets need to be safe.
5. It is important to take your pet to a vet every year. Animals need a checkup too.

Writing **187**

Write Pet Care Rules

ANALYZE THE MODEL

Read aloud the model and the callouts to the left of it. Then prepare children to write their own rules.

PROMPT

Write rules for taking care of a pet. Keep in mind for whom you are writing the rules. Organize the rules.

Getting Started Children can do any of the following.

- Use an organizer (pp. TR28–TR32).
- Talk with others about pet care.
- List important things to remember about taking care of pets.

Editing/Revising Checklist

☑ Did I organize my rules in a way that is easy to read?

☑ Did I use words that are suitable for my audience?

☑ Did I use pronouns correctly?

Self-Evaluation Distribute copies of p. TR26 for children to fill out.

Scoring Rubric — Write Pet Care Rules

Rubric 4 3 2 1	4	3	2	1
Focus/Ideas	Clearly stated rules with strong focus on topic	Clear rules with good focus on topic	Rules not always clear or focused on topic	Rules with no clarity or focus
Organization/ Paragraphs	Rules well organized and easy to read	Rules generally organized	Rules somewhat disorganized; hard to read	No organization
Voice	Shows knowledge of and interest in topic	Shows some knowledge of and interest in topic	Interested in topic but lacks knowledge	No knowledge or interest shown
Word Choice	Clear, well-chosen words; suitable for audience	Clear words; mostly suitable for audience	Many words off topic or unsuitable for audience	Most words off topic or unsuitable for audience
Sentences	Complete sentences; good variety	Most sentences complete; some variety	Some incomplete sentences; little variety	Many incomplete sentences; no variety
Conventions	Few or no errors	No serious errors	Many errors	Too many errors

Different Kinds of Pronouns

TEACH

Read aloud the instruction and examples in the box on p. 188. Then say:

We know that the pronoun *I* is used only in the subject of a sentence. So are the pronouns *he, she, we,* and *they.* We know that the pronoun *me* is used only after action verbs in sentences. So are the pronouns *him, her, us,* and *them.* The pronouns *you* and *it* can be used anywhere in a sentence.

Write the first two example sentences from the box (*Calvin has a new bike. He can't ride it.*) on the board.

Model I see that both of these sentences tell me about Calvin and his new bike. However, the first sentence uses nouns (*Calvin* and *bike*) while the second sentence uses pronouns (*He* and *it*) instead of the nouns *Calvin* and *bike. He* is used because it is in the subject of the sentence. *It* can be used anywhere in the sentence.

Write the last two example sentences from the box (*Calvin is riding the bike. Angela helped him.*) on the board. Ask children why the pronoun *him* is used in the second sentence.

LESSON 24

Different Kinds of Pronouns

The pronouns **I, he, she, we,** and **they** are used as subjects of sentences.

The pronouns **me, him, her, us,** and **them** are used after action verbs.

The pronouns **you** and **it** can be used anywhere in a sentence.

Calvin has a new bike. **He** can't ride **it.**

The pronoun **he** is the subject of a sentence.

The pronoun **it** is used after the action verb *ride.*

Calvin is riding the bike. Angela helped **him.**

The pronoun **him** is used after the action verb *helped.*

A **Write** the pronoun in each sentence. **Write** *Subject* or *After action verb* to tell where it is used.

1. Sally helped me ride a bike.
   me; After action verb
2. It got a flat tire.
   It; Subject
3. Dad drove over and found us.
   us; After action verb
4. He took Sally home.
   He; Subject

RESOURCES

Daily Fix-It Lesson 24
   See p. TR8.
   See also Daily Fix-It Transparency 24.
Grammar Transparency 24

B **Choose** the pronoun in ( ) that can take the place of the underlined word or words. **Write** the sentences.

1. <u>Friends</u> help each other. (**They**, Them)
2. Dee gave <u>Morris</u> singing lessons. (he, <u>him</u>)
3. <u>Boris</u> helped Alice skate. (<u>He</u>, Him)
4. Paul read <u>Nancy</u> a story. (she, <u>her</u>)
5. Pablo made <u>Jan and Ray</u> soup. (they, <u>them</u>)
6. How can you help <u>your friends</u>? (we, <u>us</u>)

C **Choose** pronouns from the box to take the place of the underlined words. **Write** the sentences.

it	her	they
we	us	she

7. <u>Jon and I</u> will go exploring.
   We will go exploring.
8. Lisa told <u>Jon and me</u> about a good place.
   Lisa told us about a good place.
9. <u>Lisa</u> said we could explore there.
   She said we could explore there.
10. We asked <u>Lisa</u> where the place is.
    We asked her where the place is.
11. Lisa said <u>the place</u> is the library.
    Lisa said it is the library.
12. <u>Our adventures</u> would be in books.
    They would be in books.

Grammar **189**

Guided Practice A

Go through the exercise with children. After they have found the pronoun in each sentence, ask them how they can tell where the pronoun is used.

TEACHING TIP

Point out that to help them decide what pronoun to use in a sentence, children should look for the verb and see whether the pronoun comes before or after it.

- Write sentences such as those below on the board. Have children find the verbs, see where the pronouns should be, and decide what pronouns to use.

  Mom and (I, me) had a party.
  Dave gave (I, me) a present.

Independent Practice B **and** C

Have children complete the exercises. For Differentiated Instruction and Extra Practice, see p. TR15.

Differentiated Instruction

Strategic Intervention

Write this sentence form on the board:

___ helped ___.

Ask children to suggest pronouns to complete the sentence. (*I helped him. We helped them. She helped us.*) Have children explain why they chose these pronouns. Continue with other sentence forms.

Advanced

Ask children to write about how their friends help them. Remind them to use different kinds of pronouns. Ask volunteers to share their writing with the group. Check their use of pronouns.

ELL

Write the pronouns *I, he, she, we,* and *they* on the board. Have pairs of children think of sentences using each pronoun. Let them write their sentences on the board. Have others circle the pronouns and check that they are correct. Repeat the activity for the pronouns *me, him, her, us,* and *them.*

Monitor Progress

Check Grammar

| **If...** children have difficulty identifying different kinds of pronouns, | **then...** write additional sentences on the board for them to complete with the correct pronouns. |

Test Preparation

✓ **Mark** the letter of the correct answer.

1. My friends and ___ wanted some fun.
   - ○ **A** me
   - ○ **B** they
   - ⊗ **C** I

2. Bess told ___ about finger painting.
   - ○ **A** we
   - ⊗ **B** us
   - ○ **C** it

3. Bess showed ___ and me some pictures.
   - ⊗ **A** them
   - ○ **B** they
   - ○ **C** I

4. ___ had painted each one.
   - ⊗ **A** She
   - ○ **B** Her
   - ○ **C** Him

5. Then ___ all painted pictures.
   - ○ **A** her
   - ⊗ **B** we
   - ○ **C** it

6. Do ___ like finger painting?
   - ○ **A** me
   - ○ **B** it
   - ⊗ **C** you

190 Grammar

Review

✔ **Write** the pronoun that completes each sentence. **Circle** pronouns used as subjects. **Underline** pronouns used after action verbs.

1. (We), Us) have a new clubhouse.
2. Dad helped (we, <u>us</u>) with the work.
3. All my friends like (he, <u>it</u>).
4. (They), Them) bring games and books.

✔ **Find** the pronoun that takes the place of the underlined word or words. **Write** the sentences.

5. <u>Paco and I</u> like cheese.
   Us   We   Her
   We like cheese.
6. Mom gave <u>my sister and me</u> two new cheeses.
   we   they   us
   Mom gave us two new cheeses.
7. My sister liked <u>the two cheeses</u> very much.
   them   they   you
   My sister liked them very much.
8. <u>Paco</u> wanted some cheese too.
   Me   He   Him
   He wanted some cheese too.

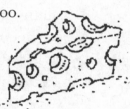

Summarize

Ask children to tell three important things they learned about different kinds of pronouns.

- *I, he, she, we,* and *they* are used in subjects of sentences.
- *Me, him, her, us,* and *them* are used after action verbs.
- *You* and *it* can be used anywhere in a sentence.

Grammar-Writing Connection

Remind children that using pronouns in their writing will make it smoother and less wordy.

Wordy: Oscar and Erica saw James and me at school. <u>Oscar and Erica</u> asked <u>James and me</u> to a party.

Less wordy: Oscar and Erica saw James and me at school. <u>They</u> asked <u>us</u> to a party.

Know Your Purpose

- Identify characteristics of a letter.
- Write a letter showing that you know your purpose for writing.
- Develop criteria for judging a piece of writing.

TEACH

Read aloud the information in the box at the top of the page. Then say: *Listen as I read. Think about the writer's purpose for writing.*

Think Aloud The public library shows a free movie every Thursday. The movie is shown at 7:00 P.M. in the conference room.

Ask children whether the writer's purpose was to persuade, give information, or make someone laugh. *(give information)* Have them explain how they made their choice.

Guided Writing

Read items 1–6 in Exercise 1 with children. Ask them how they chose the most likely purpose for each topic.

Independent Writing

Read the directions for Exercise 2. Discuss with children funny things that have happened to them. Ask how they might make their readers laugh. Have volunteers read aloud their writing.

 WRITER'S CRAFT

Know Your Purpose

Before you write, you need to **know your purpose.** Your purpose may be to persuade someone, to give information, or to make someone laugh.

 Write the letter of the purpose that matches each topic best.

> **A** Persuade someone
> **B** Give information
> **C** Make someone laugh

1. A joke about a cactus and a porcupine C
2. Why we need a bigger playground A
3. How cats see in the dark B
4. Why people should recycle newspapers A
5. A funny story about a pet lizard C
6. Facts about beavers B

 Write about something funny that happened to you. **Remember** that your purpose is to make your reader laugh.   Possible answer is on page TR36.

192   Writing

RESOURCES

Writing Transparency 24

Write a Letter

Writing Prompt Pretend you are Advice Person. Read the letter from "Puzzled." Write a letter giving advice to "Puzzled."

Dear Advice Person,
    My friend borrows my books and toys. Then he never returns them. What should I do?
                                    Puzzled

Writer focuses on purpose of the letter—to give advice about a problem.

Writing follows the correct letter form.

Writer uses pronouns correctly.

Dear Puzzled,

    Speak up! Ask your friend to return all your books and toys. Maybe he just forgot he had them. Then think twice before you let him borrow anything else. If you do, be sure your name is on everything. Make a list of what you lend him.

    You might invite your friend over to your house to play. Then you can keep your toys and books at home.

                                    Advice Person

Writing **193**

Write a Letter
ANALYZE THE MODEL

Read aloud the model and the callouts to the left of it. Then prepare children to write their own letters.

PROMPT

Now pretend you are Advice Person. Write a letter to "Puzzled." Remember that your purpose is to give "Puzzled" advice about a problem.

Getting Started Children can do any of the following.

• Use an organizer (pp. TR28–TR32).
• Think what they would do if they had the same problem as "Puzzled."
• Talk with others about the problem.

Editing/Revising Checklist

☑ Did I use the correct format for a letter?
☑ Did I clearly show my purpose for writing?
☑ Did I use pronouns correctly?

Self-Evaluation Distribute copies of p. TR26 for children to fill out.

Scoring Rubric   Write a Letter

Rubric 4 3 2 1	4	3	2	1
Focus/Ideas	Letter with strong focus on purpose; excellent ideas	Letter with good focus on purpose; good ideas	Letter with weak focus on purpose; few ideas	Letter with no focus on purpose; no ideas
Organization/ Paragraphs	Uses letter format	Mostly uses letter format	Tries to use letter format	No letter format
Voice	Friendly, serious; addresses reader directly	Friendly, mostly serious; addresses reader directly	Not very friendly or serious; forgets to address reader	Uninterested in topic or reader
Word Choice	Clear, well-chosen words; strong verbs	Clear words; some strong verbs	Mostly vague words; few strong verbs	Dull words; no strong verbs
Sentences	Clear, complete sentences; good variety	Complete sentences; some variety	Some incomplete sentences; little variety	Many incomplete sentences; no variety
Conventions	Few or no errors	No serious errors	Many errors	Too many errors

Contractions

TEACH

Read aloud the definition, instruction, and examples in the box on p. 194. Then say:

Sometimes when we speak or write, we put two words together to make a shorter word. One or more letters are left out, and an apostrophe takes their place. This shorter word is called a *contraction.*

Write the first two example sentences from the box *(We will clean up. We'll clean up.)* on the board.

Model When I look at these two sentences, I see that they are almost the same. The first sentence begins with the words *We will.* The second sentence begins with the word *We'll.* This is the contraction formed by putting together the pronoun *we* and the verb *will.* The letters *w* and *i* are left out, and an apostrophe takes their place. *We will* becomes *we'll.*

Write the last two example sentences. *(We were not careful. We weren't careful.)* Have children explain how the verb *were* and the word *not* form the contraction *weren't.*

Contractions

A **contraction** is a short way to put two words together. An **apostrophe (')** takes the place of one or more letters. Contractions can be formed by putting together a pronoun and another word, such as *will, are,* or *is.*

We will clean up. **We'll** clean up.

Many contractions are formed with verbs and the word *not.*

We **were not** careful. We **weren't** careful.

(A) Write the contraction that means the same as the underlined words.

1. I <u>did not</u> spill paint on purpose.
   don't   didn't   doesn't
   didn't
2. Tina <u>could not</u> get out of the way.
   couldn't   can't   shouldn't
   couldn't
3. Now <u>she is</u> covered with paint.
   he's   she'll   she's
   she's
4. Dad <u>is not</u> too mad at us.
   weren't   isn't   wasn't
   isn't

194 Grammar

RESOURCES

Daily Fix-It Lesson 25
   See p. TR9.
   See also Daily Fix-It Transparency 25.
Grammar Transparency 25

B Replace the underlined words with a contraction from the box. **Write** the contraction.

it's	didn't	she's
I'll	don't	we've

1. Tanya's mother said, "<u>Do not</u> go too far."
   Don't
2. Tanya <u>did not</u> listen to her mother.
   didn't
3. Now <u>she is</u> lost in the park.
   she's
4. <u>We have</u> been looking for her.
   We've
5. <u>It is</u> lucky someone found her.
   It's
6. Tanya said, "Next time <u>I will</u> listen, Mom."
   I'll

C Write some rules about how to get along with people. **Use** the contractions below in your rules.
Possible answers are on page TR36.

7. you'll
8. don't
9. shouldn't
10. you're
11. can't
12. I've

Grammar **195**

Guided Practice A

Go through the exercise with children. Let volunteers tell how they chose the contraction for each sentence. Together read aloud each sentence first with the two words and then with the contraction.

TEACHING TiP

Explain to children that we use contractions all the time when we speak. We also use contractions in informal writing, such as a letter to a friend. Only in formal writing, such as a research report, do we avoid using contractions.

Independent Practice B and C

Have children complete the exercises. For Differentiated Instruction and Extra Practice, see p. TR15.

Differentiated Instruction

Strategic Intervention

Ask children questions and have them answer using contractions.

Did you go to the movies? (No, I didn't go.)

Have you been to that theater before? (Yes, I've been there.)

Do you like my cap? (Yes, it's cool.)

Have volunteers write their answers on the board, circle the contractions, and tell what two words make up the contractions.

Advanced

Ask children to write about a time when things didn't go the way they planned. Remind them to use contractions. Have children exchange their papers with a partner. The partners circle the contractions and above them write the two words that mean the same as the contractions.

ELL

On chart paper, write sentences, each containing two words that can be made into a contraction: *We are not going. They will call soon.* Write the matching contractions on cards and give them to children. Read the sentences together and have children tape the correct contraction over the two words that mean the same. Read the sentences with the contractions.

TEST-TAKING TiP

Point out that children are looking for the contraction that can replace the two underlined words in each sentence. Suggest that they compare the two words in the sentence to each answer choice to find the correct contraction.

Monitor Progress

Check Grammar

If... children have difficulty identifying contractions,	**then...** write contractions in one column on the board and the words that form them in a second column and have children match items in the columns.

Test Preparation

✔ **Mark** the letter of the correct answer.

1. <u>We are</u> learning about signs.
   - ○ **A** We'll
   - ⊗ **B** We're
   - ○ **C** They're

2. "<u>Do not</u> walk" is an important sign.
   - ⊗ **A** Don't
   - ○ **B** Doesn't
   - ○ **C** Didn't

3. <u>I will</u> ask which sign is a triangle.
   - ○ **A** You'll
   - ○ **B** They'll
   - ⊗ **C** I'll

4. We <u>did not</u> know a stop sign has eight sides.
   - ○ **A** dosn't
   - ⊗ **B** didn't
   - ○ **C** wouldn't

5. We also learned <u>it is</u> red.
   - ○ **A** she's
   - ○ **B** it'll
   - ⊗ **C** it's

6. To be safe, we <u>should not</u> forget these signs.
   - ⊗ **A** shouldn't
   - ○ **B** couldn't
   - ○ **C** wouldn't

Review

☑ **Find** the contraction in ( ) that means the same as the underlined words. **Write** each sentence. **Use** the contraction.

1. Alex <u>has not</u> cleaned his room. (<u>hasn't</u>, isn't)
2. <u>He is</u> busy watching the baby. (He'll, <u>He's</u>)
3. Linda <u>did not</u> make her bed. (<u>didn't</u>, don't)
4. <u>She will</u> make toast for Mom. (She's, <u>She'll</u>)
5. <u>They are</u> good helpers. (<u>They're</u>, They'll)

☑ **Find** each contraction. **Write** the contraction. **Write** the two words that mean the same as the contraction.

6. We'll have a bake sale.
   We'll; We will
7. The children don't have a sign.
   don't; do not
8. We're sure we will need one.
   We're; We are
9. One girl couldn't find paint.
   couldn't; could not
10. She's still looking now.
    She's; She is

Grammar **197**

Summarize

Ask children to tell what they know about contractions.

- A contraction is a short way to put two words together.
- An apostrophe takes the place of one or more letters.
- A contraction can be formed from a pronoun and a verb or from a verb and the word *not*.

Grammar-Writing Connection

Explain to children that because we use contractions when we speak, dialogue sounds more natural when contractions are used. Using the words that make up the contractions can make dialogue sound stiff and unrealistic.

Too formal: Jack said, "I am afraid I did not find the missing ring."

More natural: Jack said, "I'm afraid I didn't find the missing ring."

Get Your Reader's Attention

TEACH

Read aloud the information in the box at the top of the page. Then say: *Listen as I read a title.*

Think Aloud The title of the article is *How to Get a Free Trip to Hawaii.* That title gets my attention! I would love to go to Hawaii, and a free trip would be great. The title makes me curious. It makes me want to find out how I can get the free trip.

Ask children to think of opening sentences for the same article that will make readers want to read on. Write their suggestions on the board and discuss which sentence is best.

Guided Writing

Read items 1–2 with children. Ask them why they think the title or opening sentence they chose would get a reader's attention.

Independent Writing

Read the directions for the last exercise. Help children recall what it was like to try something for the first time. Ask volunteers to share their titles and opening sentences.

 WRITER'S CRAFT

Get Your Reader's Attention

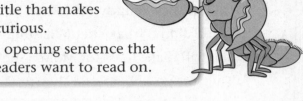

If you want readers to read your writing, you must **get their attention.** Here are two ways:

- Write a title that makes readers curious.
- Write an opening sentence that makes readers want to read on.

 Write the title that is more likely to get a reader's attention.

   1. My First Day at School
      The Day I Was Invisible

 Write the opening sentence that is more likely to get a reader's attention.

   2. Why would anyone camp in a cow pasture?
      We went camping last August.

 Write about trying something for the first time. **Write** a title and an opening sentence to get your reader's attention. Possible answer is on page TR37.

198 Writing

RESOURCES

Writing Transparency 25

Make a Sign

Writing Prompt Think of something important that you want people to do. Make a sign to persuade them that they should do what you say.

Title grabs reader's attention by asking a question.

Strong opening sentences make reader want to read on.

All sentences focus on purpose of the sign—to persuade.

What Do Your Kids Think?

Do you really know? If you don't, there may be a reason. When was the last time you really talked with your kids? Ask them questions and listen to what they say. How will you know what they are thinking if you don't ask and listen?

Writing **199**

Make a Sign
ANALYZE THE MODEL

Read aloud the model and the callouts to the left of it. Then prepare children to make their own signs.

PROMPT

Now make your own sign. What do you want people to do? Why should they do it? Try to persuade readers as well as get their attention.

Getting Started Children can do any of the following.

- Use an organizer (pp. TR28-TR32).
- Make a list of things that are important to them and choose one.
- Write reasons and cross out those that are not persuasive enough.

Editing/Revising Checklist

☑ Did I write a title and/or opening sentence that will get readers' attention?

☑ Did I use contractions correctly?

Self-Evaluation Distribute copies of p. TR26 for children to fill out.

Scoring Rubric | Make a Sign

Rubric 4 3 2 1	4	3	2	1
Focus/Ideas	Sign with strong focus on topic; convincing details	Sign with good focus; mostly convincing details	Sign with unclear focus; few convincing details	Sign with no focus or details
Organization/ Paragraphs	Attention-grabbing title and opening sentence	Good title and opening sentence	Weak title and opening sentence	No title or opening sentence
Voice	Lively, persuasive; clearly shows writer's feelings	Mostly lively, persuasive; shows some feelings	Somewhat lively, not persuasive; shows few feelings	Careless, uninterested; shows no feelings
Word Choice	Uses persuasive words	Uses some persuasive words	Uses few persuasive words	No persuasive words
Sentences	Smooth sentences; good variety	Most sentences smooth; some variety	Many choppy or stringy sentences; little variety	Incomplete sentences; no variety
Conventions	Few or no errors	No serious errors	Many errors	Too many errors

Using Capital Letters

- Recognize capital letters.
- Use capital letters correctly in writing.
- Become familiar with capital letters on standardized tests.

TEACH

Read aloud the instruction and examples in the box on p. 200. Then say:

We know that proper nouns begin with capital letters. Proper nouns are special names for people, places, animals, and things. Other proper nouns are the names of the days of the week, months of the year, holidays, and titles for people. They begin with capital letters too.

Write the example sentences from the box *(The first day of January is New Year's Day. Every year Mr. Lewis has a big party. Coach Landi will order new uniforms.)* on the board.

Think Aloud **Model** In the first sentence, I see that the words *January* and *New Year's Day* begin with capital letters. That is because *January* is the name of a month and *New Year's Day* is the name of a holiday. In the second and third sentences, the words *Mr.* and *Coach* begin with capital letters because they are titles for people.

Using Capital Letters

Days of the week, months of the year, and **holidays** begin with capital letters.

The first day of **January** is **New Year's Day.**

Titles for people begin with capital letters.

Every year **Mr.** Lewis has a big party. **Coach** Landi will order new uniforms.

A **Write** the sentences. **Use** capital letters for the words in ( ).

1. Every (may) our family goes to a baseball game.
2. This is how we spend (memorial day).
3. This holiday is always on a (monday).
4. (dr.) and (mrs.) Carlson bring flags for everyone.
5. Dad packs everything on (sunday).
6. On the (fourth of july), we will go with (officer) Chang to another game.

200 Grammar

RESOURCES

Daily Fix-It Lesson 26
    See p. TR9.
    See also Daily Fix-It Transparency 26.
Grammar Transparency 26

B **Find** the words that need capital letters. **Write** the words correctly. The number in ( ) tells how many capital letters are needed.

1. st. patrick's day is on march 17. (4)
   St. Patrick's Day, March
2. Every year coach Kelly and mrs. O'Malley are in the parade. (2)
   Coach, Mrs.
3. This year the fourth of july is on a friday. (3)
   Fourth of July, Friday
4. The Bartons and ms. Lutz always go to the barbecue at mr. Garcia's house. (2)
   Ms., Mr.
5. Isn't thanksgiving on the fourth thursday in november? (3)
   Thanksgiving, Thursday, November

C **Find** the word in the box that completes each sentence. **Write** the sentences. **Use** capital letters.

november	mr.	saturday	miss	flag day

6. ___ James Thomas was a baseball player.
   Mr. James Thomas was a baseball player.
7. He was born on ___ 16, 1941.
   He was born on November 16, 1941.
8. His favorite holiday is ___.
   His favorite holiday is Flag Day.
9. He married ___ Alice Larkin in 1963.
   He married Miss Alice Larkin in 1963.
10. The wedding was on a ___.
    The wedding was on a Saturday.

Grammar **201**

Guided Practice Ⓐ

Go through the exercise with children. Have them identify the words in parentheses as a day, month, holiday, or title for a person.

TEACHING TIP

Point out to children that while some titles for people are abbreviations (Mr., Mrs., Ms., Dr.), other titles are whole words. (Coach, Officer) Explain that these titles begin with capital letters only if they come before people's names: *Coach Landi, the coach of the football team; Officer Chang, the officer in the squad car.*

Independent Practice
Ⓑ **and** Ⓒ

Have children complete the exercises. For Differentiated Instruction and Extra Practice, see p. TR16.

Differentiated Instruction

Strategic Intervention

Give children copies of birth or marriage announcements from a newspaper. Have them underline words that begin with capital letters. Ask volunteers to tell why the words are capitalized.

Advanced

Have children write an announcement about an upcoming family event. Remind them to use capital letters where appropriate. Ask them to exchange papers and underline the words that begin with capital letters in their partner's work. Have volunteers share their announcements with the class.

ELL

Write the days, months, and major holidays in three columns on the board and highlight the initial capital letters. Read the words together. Ask children to say the days, months, and holidays in their home languages. Ask them if the words begin with capital letters. If possible, have them write the names on the board next to the English names.

Test Preparation

☑ **Mark** the letter of the correct answer.

1. My birthday is on ___ 14.
   - ○ **A** january
   - ⊗ **B** February
   - ○ **C** march

2. I was born on ___.
   - ○ **A** Valentine's day
   - ○ **B** valentine's day
   - ⊗ **C** Valentine's Day

3. My friend ___ has the same birthday.
   - ○ **A** mrs. Loomis
   - ⊗ **B** Miss Loomis
   - ○ **C** ms. Loomis

4. This year our birthdays are on ___.
   - ⊗ **A** Wednesday
   - ○ **B** wednesday
   - ○ **C** wednesDay

5. My sister was born on ___.
   - ⊗ **A** Labor Day
   - ○ **B** Labor day
   - ○ **C** labor Day

6. Her birthday is in ___.
   - ○ **A** october
   - ○ **B** november
   - ⊗ **C** September

Review

✓ **Find** the two words that need capital letters in each sentence. **Write** the sentences.

1. Baseball practice runs from april through august.
   Baseball practice runs from April through August.
2. Our coaches are ms. Lopez and dr. Logan.
   Our coaches are Ms. Lopez and Dr. Logan.
3. tuesday and thursday are our practice days.
   Tuesday and Thursday are our practice days.
4. The first game is saturday, may 10.
   The first game is Saturday, May 10.

✓ **Find** the word in each pair of sentences that is missing a capital letter. **Write** that sentence correctly.

5. Are you going to the game with mrs. Frank?
   The game will be on Friday, August 12.
   Are you going to the game with Mrs. Frank?
6. I finally met Captain Dale last week.
   He will be here until october 30.
   He will be here until October 30.
7. Our town has a parade on Veterans day.
   This year it will be on a Wednesday.
   Our town has a parade on Veterans Day.
8. Was New year's Day always in January?
   No, Mr. Lee said it used to be in March.
   Was New Year's Day always in January?

Grammar **203**

Summarize

Have children tell you what they learned about using capital letters.

- Days of the week, months of the year, and holidays begin with capital letters.
- Titles for people begin with capital letters.

Grammar-Writing Connection

Remind children that using proper nouns can help make their writing clearer and more specific.

Too general: The doctor will be gone until after the holiday.

More specific: Dr. Waxman will be gone until after Labor Day.

Supporting Details

OBJECTIVES

OBJECTIVES

- Identify characteristics of writing facts.
- Write facts using supporting details.
- Develop criteria for judging a piece of writing.

TEACH

Read aloud the information in the box at the top of the page. Then say: *Listen as I read. Think about the main idea and the supporting details.*

Think Aloud Melanie and Jesse went on a trip. First they drove to the West Coast. Then they drove down the coast from Seattle to San Diego. It was a long trip.

Ask children what the main idea of the paragraph is. *(Melanie and Jesse went on a trip.)* Ask them if the other sentences tell supporting details. *(yes)*

Guided Writing

Read the items in Exercise 1 with children. Have them identify the main idea of each paragraph. Ask them how knowing that helps them choose the supporting detail that goes in the paragraph.

Independent Writing

Read the directions for Exercise 2. Brainstorm games, sports, and activities with children. When they have finished writing, ask volunteers to read aloud their paragraphs.

 WRITER'S CRAFT

Supporting Details

The main idea of a paragraph is what the paragraph is about. The **supporting details** tell more about the main idea. Every sentence in the paragraph should tell a supporting detail.

 Read the paragraphs. **Write** the letter of the supporting detail that fits in each paragraph.

> **A** In the winter it was too cold and snowy to play most sports outside.
>
> **B** Often they made patterns of squares, circles, and rings.

1. James Naismith was a gym teacher in Massachusetts. He invented a team sport that his students could play inside. A

2. Settlers in the American colonies brought quilting with them from Europe. They sewed scraps of cloth together. B

 Write a paragraph about a game, sport, or activity. **Use** only details that support your main idea.

Possible answer is on page TR37.

RESOURCES

Writing Transparency 26

Write Facts

Write Facts

Writing Prompt Write facts about a game or sport that you like. You may need to look up facts in books or on the Internet.

All details support the main idea of winning the World Series.

Writer uses capital letters correctly.

An exclamation helps make the paragraph interesting.

Baseball Dream

All baseball fans have one dream. They want their team to win the World Series in October. In the World Series, the best teams from the National League and the American League play each other. The winner is the champion. In 2004 the Boston Red Sox won the World Series. Their fans had been dreaming about this for 86 years! The Red Sox had not won the World Series since 1918.

Writing **205**

Write Facts

ANALYZE THE MODEL

Read aloud the model and the callouts to the left of it. Then prepare children to write their own facts.

PROMPT

Write facts about your favorite game or sport. Look up facts if you need to. Make sure every sentence supports your main idea.

Getting Started Children can do any of the following.

- Use an organizer (pp. TR28–TR32).
- Find books or web sites about their game, sport, or activity.
- Choose facts that they think will interest their readers.

Editing/Revising Checklist

✓ Did I make my main idea clear?
✓ Did I write a supporting detail in every sentence?
✓ Did I use capital letters correctly?

Self-Evaluation Distribute copies of p. TR26 for children to fill out.

Scoring Rubric Facts

Rubric 4 3 2 1	4	3	2	1
Focus/Ideas	Focused paragraph with excellent facts	Generally focused paragraph with good facts	Unfocused paragraph with few relevant facts	Paragraph with no focus or facts
Organization/ Paragraphs	Clear main idea; supporting details in logical order	Main idea stated; supporting details in order	Main idea unclear; supporting details not in order	No main idea or supporting details
Voice	Serious, knowledgeable	Mostly serious, knowledgeable	Not always appropriate for topic	Careless, uninterested
Word Choice	Clear, well-chosen words	Words mostly well chosen	Some words that don't fit topic	Many words that don't fit topic
Sentences	Smooth sentences; good variety	Most sentences smooth; some variety	Many choppy or stringy sentences; little variety	Unclear, incomplete, or choppy; no variety
Conventions	Few or no errors	No serious errors	Many errors	Too many errors

Quotation Marks

- Recognize quotation marks.
- Use quotation marks correctly in writing.
- Become familiar with quotation marks on standardized tests.

TEACH

Read aloud the definition and examples in the box on p. 206. Then say:

When we write what someone says, we put quotation marks at the beginning and end of the person's words. Then we put the speaker's name and a word such as *said* or *asked* outside the quotation marks.

Write the example sentences from the box *(Kim asked, "What is a symbol?" "A symbol is something that stands for something else," Jerome said.)* on the board.

Think Aloud **Model** I see that in the first sentence, the question Kim asks has quotation marks at the beginning and end. Kim's name and the word *asked* are outside the quotation marks because they are not words that Kim said. They tell who is speaking. In the second sentence, quotation marks show the beginning and end of Jerome's statement. Jerome's name and the word *said* are not inside the quotation marks because they are not words that Jerome said.

Quotation Marks

Quotation marks (" ") show the beginning and ending of the words someone says. The speaker's name and words such as **said** or **asked** are not inside the quotation marks.

Kim asked, "What is a symbol?"

"A symbol is something that stands for something else," Jerome said.

A **Write** the sentences. **Add** quotation marks where they are needed.

1. "What is a symbol of our country?" asked Emma.

2. David said, "Our flag is a symbol."

3. "The bald eagle is a symbol too," said Liam.

4. Miki asked, "Why is the bald eagle a symbol?"

5. Sasha said, "The bald eagle is strong and free, and so is the United States."

6. "Let's find out more about the bald eagle," Alan said.

206 Grammar

RESOURCES

Daily Fix-It Lesson 27
See p. TR9.
See also Daily Fix-It Transparency 27.
Grammar Transparency 27

B **Write** the sentences that use quotation marks correctly.

1. "Plan a Fourth of July party, said Laura."

   "Plan a Fourth of July party," said Laura.
   "Plan a Fourth of July party," said Laura.

2. I have some flags," Ted said.

   "I have some flags," Ted said.
   "I have some flags," Ted said.

3. Jim asked, "Do we have plates with stars?"

   "Jim asked, Do we have plates with stars?"
   Jim asked, "Do we have plates with stars?"

4. Get red, white, and blue balloons, "Vi said."

   "Get red, white, and blue balloons," Vi said.
   "Get red, white, and blue balloons," Vi said.

5. "Who is on our list to invite?" asked Ben.

   "Who is on our list to invite? asked Ben."
   "Who is on our list to invite?" asked Ben.

C **Write** each sentence. **Add** quotation marks and a name.

Possible answers:

6. Where do we see flags? asked ___.
   "Where do we see flags?" asked Charles.

7. A flag flies outside our school, said ___.
   "A flag flies outside our school," said Rashid.

8. I see a flag in our classroom! ___ shouted.
   "I see a flag in our classroom!" Matt shouted.

9. ___ stated, The town hall has a flag in front.
   Bella stated, "The town hall has a flag in front."

10. Do cars ever have flags? ___ asked.
    "Do cars ever have flags?" Frank asked.

Grammar **207**

Guided Practice **A**

Go through the exercise with children. Remind them to put quotation marks before and after only the words that are said by the speaker. Ask volunteers to show where they placed the quotation marks.

TEACHING TiP

Explain to children that sets of quotation marks are always used in pairs, with one set at the beginning of quoted words and the other set at the end of the quoted words. Children should always check to see that they have included both opening (beginning) and closing (ending) quotation marks when they write a quotation.

Independent Practice **B** and **C**

Have children complete the exercises. For Differentiated Instruction and Extra Practice, see p. TR16.

Differentiated Instruction

Strategic Intervention

Write these sentence forms on the board.

Mary asked, "___?"

"___," answered Patrick.

Ask children to think of questions for Mary and answers for Patrick. Have volunteers write the quotations inside the quotation marks to complete the sentences. Read aloud the pairs of sentences with children, pointing to the quotation marks.

Advanced

Have pairs of children "interview" each other. Each partner asks the other partner two questions, such as *What is your favorite color? When is your birthday?*, and then writes the questions and answers using quotation marks. (*I asked, "What is your favorite color?" Jamal said, "I like blue."*) Have partners check each other's work.

ELL

Display a picture from a magazine or story that shows people talking to one another. Ask children to suggest things the people might be saying. Write their ideas on the board as sentences with quotations, but omit the quotation marks. Ask volunteers to come to the board and add quotation marks. Read the sentences together.

TEST-TAKING TIP

Tell children to look carefully at the three answer choices in each item. Remind them that quotation marks should appear at the beginning and end of only the words that the person says.

Monitor Progress

Check Grammar

If... children have difficulty understanding how to use quotation marks,	**then...** have them look at quotations in their reading materials and find the quotation marks at the beginning and end of the quotations.

Test Preparation

✓ **Mark** the letter of the sentence with the correct quotation marks.

1. ○ **A** "Who were some presidents? asked Ellie."
   ⊗ **B** "Who were some presidents?" asked Ellie.
   ○ **C** Who were some presidents?" asked Ellie.

2. ○ **A** "Al said, Washington was the first president."
   ○ **B** "Al said," Washington was the first president.
   ⊗ **C** Al said, "Washington was the first president."

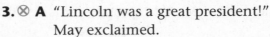

3. ⊗ **A** "Lincoln was a great president!" May exclaimed.
   ○ **B** "Lincoln was a great president! May exclaimed.
   ○ **C** "Lincoln was a great president! May exclaimed."

4. ○ **A** Was John Adams a president? "asked Abigail."
   ⊗ **B** "Was John Adams a president?" asked Abigail.
   ○ **C** "Was John Adams a president? asked Abigail."

5. ⊗ **A** "When was Jimmy Carter president?" asked Bill.
   ○ **B** When was Jimmy Carter president? "asked Bill."
   ○ **C** "When was Jimmy Carter president? asked Bill.

Review

☑ **Write** the sentences. **Add** quotation marks if they are needed. **Write** *C* after the sentences that are correct.

1. "Who can describe our flag? asked Ms. Lee.
   "Who can describe our flag?" asked Ms. Lee.
2. Betsy answered, "Well, there are thirteen stripes."
   C
3. Jerry said, The stripes are red and white.
   Jerry said, "The stripes are red and white."
4. "There are fifty white stars in a blue box," Art added.
   C
5. "The stars are in rows, Ross stated."
   "The stars are in rows," Ross stated.

☑ **Write** the sentences. **Add** quotation marks.

6. Fred asked, Did you know each state has a flag?
   Fred asked, "Did you know each state has a flag?"
7. California's flag has a bear on it, said Mei Ling.
   "California's flag has a bear on it," said Mei Ling.
8. Does Arizona's flag have a sunset? Carol asked.
   "Does Arizona's flag have a sunset?" Carol asked.
9. Jen stated, Vermont's flag has a pine tree and a cow.
   Jen stated, "Vermont's flag has a pine tree and a cow."
10. Does the Texas flag have a lone star? Sam asked.
    "Does the Texas flag have a lone star?" Sam asked.

Grammar **209**

REVIEW

Summarize

Ask children what two important things they learned about quotation marks.

- Quotation marks show the beginning and end of the words someone says.
- The speaker's name and words such as *said* or *asked* are not inside the quotation marks.

Grammar-Writing Connection

Explain to children that good writers know that it is often best to let characters speak for themselves.

Without quotation marks:

Nicholas says he wants to go to the beach, but Charlotte says she wants to go to the pool. Kathryn says she doesn't want to go to either one. She wants to shop. So Nicholas goes to the beach, Charlotte goes to the pool, and Kathryn goes to the mall.

With quotation marks:

"I want to go to the beach," said Nicholas.

"But I want to go to the pool," said Charlotte.

Kathryn said, "I don't want to go to either one. I want to shop."

So Nicholas goes to the beach, Charlotte goes to the pool, and Kathryn goes to the mall.

Discuss with children how the two paragraphs are different and which one is more interesting to read.

Eliminate Wordiness

OBJECTIVES

- Identify characteristics of answering a question.
- Write an answer to a question using no more words than are needed.
- Develop criteria for judging a piece of writing.

TEACH

Read aloud the information in the box at the top of the page. Then say: *As I read, listen for words that can be left out or changed.*

Think Aloud It seems like I'm always late. I have a lot of trouble getting up, and I move around kind of slow in the morning. I think that I need a great big loud alarm clock!

Discuss with children what words should be left out or changed to eliminate wordiness in the paragraph. *(I'm always late. I have trouble getting up, and I move slowly in the morning. I need a big loud alarm clock!)*

Guided Writing

Read items 1–5 in Exercise 1 with children. Ask them which words should be left out or changed in each sentence. Have volunteers read their revised sentences.

Independent Writing

Read the directions in Exercise 2. Discuss parades children have seen. Call on volunteers to read aloud their paragraphs to the group.

 WRITER'S CRAFT

Eliminate Wordiness

Don't use more words than are needed.

- Don't use phrases such as *kind of, I think that,* and *it seems like.*
- Don't use *a lot of.* Use *many* or another word.
- Don't use two words that mean the same thing: ~~great~~ big, tiny ~~little~~.
- Don't use several words when you can use one word: *moved* ~~with great slowness~~, *moved slowly.*

 Rewrite each sentence. **Leave out** or **change** words to eliminate wordiness.

1. The soldiers marched with a great big flag.
   The soldiers marched with a big flag.
2. It seems like the parade took a long time.
   The parade took a long time.
3. That flag has a lot of stars on it.
   That flag has many stars on it.
4. The people cheered with great loudness.
   The people cheered loudly.
5. Lila was kind of excited about the parade.
   Lila was excited about the parade.

 Write a paragraph about a parade you have seen. **Check** to see that you don't use more words than are needed. Possible answer is on page TR37.

210 Writing

RESOURCES

Writing Transparency 27

Answer a Question

Writing Prompt Answer this question: What is something that is important to you? Choose an object or event. Explain why this thing is important.

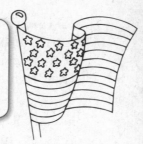

Important thing is named in the opening sentence.

Our Flag

One thing that is important to me is the flag of the United States. Every time I see it, I think about our country. The flag reminds me that Americans are free. I think about all the people who fought and died to protect that freedom. The flag stands for our country. When people around the world see it, they think about our country too.

Choice is supported by reasons.

Writer doesn't use more words than are needed.

Writing **211**

Answer a Question

ANALYZE THE MODEL

Read aloud the model and the callouts to the left of it. Then prepare children to write their own answers to the question.

PROMPT

Now write your answer to the same question. Tell why the object or event is important to you. Don't use more words than are needed.

Getting Started Children can do any of the following.

- Use an organizer (pp. TR28–TR32).
- List objects or events that are important to them.
- Discuss their ideas with friends.

Editing/Revising Checklist

✓ Did I support my choice with reasons?

✓ Did I use only as many words as I needed to?

✓ Did I use quotation marks correctly?

Self-Evaluation Distribute copies of p. TR26 for children to fill out.

Scoring Rubric — Answer a Question

Rubric 4 3 2 1	4	3	2	1
Focus/Ideas	Answer with strong focus on topic; excellent reasons	Answer with good focus on topic; good reasons	Answer not always on topic; few reasons offered	Answer not on topic; no reasons offered
Organization/ Paragraphs	Choice named at beginning; reasons in logical order	Choice named near beginning; reasons in order	Choice not clearly stated; reasons not in order	No choice named; no order
Voice	Serious, persuasive; shows writer's feelings	Mostly serious, persuasive; shows some feelings	Not very serious or persuasive; shows few feelings	Careless, uninterested; shows no feelings
Word Choice	Clear, well-chosen words; not wordy	Words mostly well chosen; generally not wordy	Many vague or general words; sometimes wordy	Dull or incorrect words; often wordy
Sentences	Smooth sentences; good variety	Most sentences smooth; some variety	Many choppy or stringy sentences; little variety	Unclear or incomplete sentences; no variety
Conventions	Few or no errors	No serious errors	Many errors	Too many errors

Using Commas

OBJECTIVES

- Recognize commas.
- Use commas correctly in writing.
- Become familiar with commas on standardized tests.

TEACH

Read aloud the instruction and examples in the box on p. 212. Then say:

We know about punctuation marks such as periods, question marks, exclamation marks, and quotation marks. Commas are another kind of punctuation mark.

Write the examples from the box on the board. Point to each as you talk about it.

Think Aloud **Model** As I look at the addresses, I see a comma between the city and the state: *Little Rock, AR; Niles, Michigan.* In the dates, I see a comma between the date and year *(January 31, 1929)* and between the day and month. *(Tuesday, June 14)* The beginning of a letter has a comma *(Dear Anna,);* so does the ending of a letter. *(Love, Krysta)* In the last example, commas are placed after *Anna* and *Paul* because they are part of three names in a row in the sentence: *Anna, Paul, and Ben.*

LESSON 28

Using Commas

Commas are used in addresses:
1501 Greenwood Ave.
Little Rock, AR 72204
Their home is in Niles, Michigan.

Joe Garcia
411 N. Pine
Taos, NM 93425

Mary Lopez
1501 Greenwood Ave.
Little Rock, AR 72204

Commas are used in dates:
January 31, 1929
Tuesday, June 14

Commas are used to begin and end a letter:
Dear Anna,
Love,
Krysta

Commas are used to separate three or more things in a sentence:
Krysta wrote letters to Anna, Paul, and Beth.

A **Write** the sentences. **Add** commas where needed. The number in ( ) tells how many commas are needed.

1. Grandma lives in Tampa Florida. (1)
Grandma lives in Tampa, Florida.
2. Her birthday party was on June 6 2008. (1)
Her birthday party was on June 6, 2008.
3. She got a hat flowers and cards. (2)
She got a hat, flowers, and cards.
4. We started for home on Sunday June 7. (1)
We started for home on Sunday, June 7.

212 Grammar

RESOURCES

Daily Fix-It Lesson 28
    See p. TR10.
    See also Daily Fix-It Transparency 28.
Grammar Transparency 28

B **Write** the letter. **Add** commas where needed.

1. 124 Maple Street
   124 Maple Street
   Syracuse NY 13210
   Syracuse, NY 13210
2. June 24 2009
   June 24, 2009
3. Dear Jaime
   Dear Jaime,
4. I am at my grandparents' ranch in Colorado. We come here every June. We swim fish and hike. I see my cousins aunts and uncles. It is great. See you soon.

   I am at my grandparents' ranch in Colorado. We come here every June. We swim, fish, and hike. I see my cousins, aunts, and uncles. It is great. See you soon.

5. Your friend
   Your friend,
   Tim
   Tim

C **Write** a letter to a friend about some things you did together. **Add** commas where needed. **Do not write** the words in ( ).

6. (your street) ___

   (your city and state) ___

7. (date) ___ 2 ___

8. (beginning) Dear ___

9. (message) ___

10. (ending)

Possible answers are on page TR37.

(your street) _____
(your city and state) _____
(date) _____
(beginning) _____
      (message) _____
_____
_____
_____
_____
_____
_____
_____

(ending) _____
(your name) _____

Grammar **213**

Guided Practice Ⓐ

Go through the exercise with children. Ask volunteers to tell where they placed commas in the sentences and explain why.

TEACHING TIP

Explain to children that writers use commas to help make clear what they are saying. Review the sentences in Exercise A before commas were added. Discuss with children how adding commas makes the sentences easier to read and understand.

Independent Practice
Ⓑ **and** Ⓒ

Have children complete the exercises. For Differentiated Instruction and Extra Practice, see p. TR16.

Differentiated Instruction

Strategic Intervention

On the board, write sentences and phrases that need commas.

Monday September 30

Leah swam with Jacob Matthew and Ellen.

I live in Park City Utah.

Dear Mom

Love Lisa

Have volunteers go to the board and add commas to the sentences and phrases. Ask them to explain why they added the commas in those places.

Advanced

Have children write a short note to a friend or relative about something they have done recently in school. Remind them to include their address, the date, a beginning, and an ending. Ask volunteers to read aloud their notes. Check their use of commas.

ELL

On the board, write sentences that require commas: *School begins on Monday September 7.* Write commas on self-stick notes. Let children place the commas where they belong in the sentences. Have children tell why they put commas in these places. You might also place the commas incorrectly and let children correct your "mistakes."

Monitor Progress

Check Grammar

If... children have difficulty understanding how to use commas correctly,	**then...** write additional examples on the board and have children practice adding commas.

Test Preparation

✔ **Mark** the letter of the correct answer.

1. ○ **A** Atlanta GA, 30311
   ○ **B** Atlanta, GA, 30311
   ⊗ **C** Atlanta, GA 30311

2. ○ **A** August 31 2008,
   ⊗ **B** August 31, 2008
   ○ **C** August, 31 2008

3. ⊗ **A** Dear Aunt Min,
   ○ **B** Dear, Aunt Min
   ○ **C** Dear Aunt, Min

4. ○ **A** Thanks for the party, gifts and food.
   ○ **B** Thanks for the party, gifts, and, food.
   ⊗ **C** Thanks for the party, gifts, and food.

5. ⊗ **A** I loved the peaches, pie, and chicken.
   ○ **B** I loved, the peaches, pie and chicken.
   ○ **C** I loved the peaches, pie, and, chicken.

6. ○ **A** Your, niece, Paula
   ⊗ **B** Your niece, Paula
   ○ **C** Your, niece Paula

214 Grammar

Review

✓ **Write** the sentences. **Add** commas where needed.

1. Tía will visit on Tuesday March 12.
   Tía will visit on Tuesday, March 12.
2. She lives in Bisbee Arizona.
   She lives in Bisbee, Arizona.
3. I will help Mamá clean, shop, and cook.
   I will help Mamá clean, shop, and cook.
4. Tía will stay until Friday March 15.
   Tía will stay until Friday, March 15.
5. Tía wants to ski skate and sled.
   Tía wants to ski, skate, and sled.

✓ **Write** the letter. **Add** commas where needed.

6. 558 Oak Lane
   558 Oak Lane
   Salina KS 67401
   Salina, KS 67401
7. October 28 2008
   October 28, 2008
8. Dear Luke
   Dear Luke,
9. Today we had a surprise
   party for Mom. I gave her a
   card some beads and a rose.
   We ate sang and danced.

   Today we had a
   surprise party for
   Mom. I gave her a
   card, some beads, and
   a rose. We ate, sang,
   and danced.

10. Your friend
    Your friend,
    Angie
    Angie

Grammar **215**

Summarize

Have children tell you what they know about commas.

- Commas are used in addresses and dates.
- Commas are used to begin and end a letter.
- Commas are used to separate three or more things in a sentence.

Grammar-Writing Connection

Show children how using commas to separate three or more things in a sentence makes the meaning of the sentence clearer.

Without commas: I saw Mary Jackson and Paul last night.

Ask children if the writer means that he or she saw three people (*Mary, Jackson, and Paul*) or two people. (*Mary Jackson and Paul*) They should see that the writer has not made this clear.

With commas: I saw Mary, Jackson, and Paul last night.

Point out that adding commas makes it clear that the writer is talking about three people, not two.

Good Conclusions

OBJECTIVES

- Identify characteristics of a report.
- Write a report with a good conclusion.
- Develop criteria for judging a piece of writing.

TEACH

Read aloud the information in the box at the top of the page. Then say: *As I read the paragraph, listen to the conclusion.*

Think Aloud I learned how to water ski on Deer Lake. At first, it was hard. I fell every time, but I kept trying. Now I can get up on my skis every time.

Ask children why the last sentence is a good conclusion for the paragraph. *(It wraps up the ideas in the paragraph.)*

Guided Writing

Read the items in Exercise 1 with children. Ask them how they decided which of the two conclusions is the better conclusion for each paragraph.

Independent Writing

Read the directions for Exercise 2. Discuss birthday celebrations with children. Ask volunteers to read aloud their paragraphs. Have listeners evaluate the conclusions.

 WRITER'S CRAFT

Good Conclusions

A **good conclusion** wraps up the ideas in a paragraph. It also tries to leave readers with something to think about.

 Write the letter of the stronger conclusion for each paragraph.

1. Our teacher, Ms. Lang, said we could decorate
   A the gym for a costume party. We hung streamers and balloons and gold stars.
   A When people walked in, they cheered and clapped.
   B Everybody liked it.

2. Some people take the same vacation every year.
   A They stay in a cabin by a lake. Often it's the same cabin and the same lake.
   A These people like to be in a familiar place.
   B That sounds boring to me.

 Write a paragraph about a birthday celebration. **Write** a good conclusion. Possible answer: Last year we had a surprise party for my mom. We were waiting for her to arrive. The room was dark, and everyone was hiding and trying to be quiet. The door opened. My dad turned on the lights, and we all jumped up and yelled, "Surprise!" It was my older sister, and we really scared her. Maybe next time she will be on time!

216 Writing

RESOURCES

Writing Transparency 28

Write a Report

Write a Report

Writing Prompt Think of an event that happens every year at your school. Write a report about the event. Tell what happens and why.

First sentence tells what the event is.

First paragraph describes exactly what a food drive is and why it happens.

Writer uses the conclusion to tell why food drives are important.

A School Tradition

Every October and May we have a food drive at Bell School. The students bring cans and boxes of food to school. They put the food into bags. A food bank comes to pick up the bags. The workers give the bags to people who need food.

A food drive helps people who do not have enough to eat. It also reminds us how lucky we are.

Writing **217**

ANALYZE THE MODEL

Read aloud the model and the callouts to the left of it. Then prepare children to write their own reports.

PROMPT

Write your own report about a yearly school event. Remember to tell what happens and why. End your report with a good conclusion.

Getting Started Children can do any of the following.

• Use an organizer (pp. TR28–TR32).
• List school events that interest them.
• Pick an event that they think is important

Editing/Revising Checklist

☑ Did I describe the event clearly?
☑ Did I write a conclusion that wraps up my ideas?
☑ Did I use commas correctly?

Self-Evaluation Distribute copies of p. TR26 for children to fill out.

Scoring Rubric Report

Rubric 4 3 2 1	4	3	2	1
Focus/Ideas	Report with strong focus; excellent supporting details	Report with good focus; good supporting details	Report not always focused; few supporting details	Report with no focus or details
Organization/ Paragraphs	Strong introduction, explanation, conclusion	Good introduction, explanation, conclusion	Weak introduction, explanation, and/or conclusion	No organization
Voice	Serious; shows writer's feelings	Mostly serious; shows some feelings	Not serious enough; shows few feelings	Careless, uninterested; shows no feelings
Word Choice	Uses vivid, specific words	Uses some vivid, specific words	Many vague, general words	Dull or incorrect words
Sentences	Smooth sentences; good variety	Most sentences smooth; some variety	Many stringy or choppy sentences	Confusing, incomplete, or choppy sentences
Conventions	Few or no errors	No serious errors	Many errors	Too many errors

Commas in Compound Sentences

OBJECTIVES

- Recognize commas in compound sentences.
- Use commas correctly when writing compound sentences.
- Become familiar with commas in compound sentences on standardized tests.

TEACH

Read aloud the definition and examples in the box on p. 218. Then say:

We know several ways to use commas. Commas are also used in compound sentences. If two sentences have ideas that go together, they can be combined using a comma and a connecting word such as *and* or *but*. The two sentences become a compound sentence.

Write the first two example sentences from the box (*A cowboy drives the cows to market. His pony helps him.*) on the board.

Think Aloud **Model** When I read these two sentences, I see that the ideas go together. I can make these two sentences into a compound sentence. I put a comma after the first sentence, add the connecting word *and*, and make the *H* in *His* lowercase. Now I have a compound sentence: *A cowboy drives the cows to market, and his pony helps him.*

Commas in Compound Sentences

Sometimes two sentences have ideas that go together. These sentences can be combined using a comma and a connecting word such as **and** or **but**. The combined sentence is called a **compound sentence.**

A cowboy drives the cows to market. His pony helps him.

A cowboy drives the cows to market**, and** his pony helps him.

Cow ponies are small. They are fearless.

Cow ponies are small**, but** they are fearless.

A **Write** each sentence. **Add** a comma where needed. **Circle** the connecting word.

1. Some cowboys rode beside the cows and others rode behind them.
   Some cowboys rode beside the cows, (and) others rode behind them.
2. There were no roads but there were trails.
   There were no roads, (but) there were trails.
3. Cows would get lost and the cowboys would look for them.
   Cows would get lost, (and) the cowboys would look for them.
4. Longhorns could swim but some of the cowboys couldn't.
   Longhorns could swim, (but) some of the cowboys couldn't.

218 Grammar

RESOURCES

Daily Fix-It Lesson 29
See p. TR10.
See also Daily Fix-It Transparency 29.

Grammar Transparency 29

B **Use** the word in ( ) and a comma to combine each pair of sentences. **Write** the new sentence.

1. Every summer we get together.
Grandpa tells us stories. (and)
Every summer we get together, and Grandpa tells us stories.

2. The night is cool. We get warm by the campfire. (but)
The night is cool, but we get warm by the campfire.

3. We huddle together. We don't say a word. (and)
We huddle together, and we don't say a word.

4. Cindy likes the scary stories. I like the funny ones better. (but)
Cindy likes the scary stories, but I like the funny ones better.

5. Grandpa uses different voices. He acts out all the parts. (and)
Grandpa uses different voices, and he acts out all the parts.

6. He often tells the same stories. We like hearing them again. (but)
He often tells the same stories, but we like hearing them again.

C **Complete** the sentences with your ideas. **Add** commas where needed. **Write** the sentences.
Possible answers:

7. Rick wants to be a cowboy but I ___.
Rick wants to be a cowboy, but I want to be a scientist.

8. Cowboys eat beans but I eat ___.
Cowboys eat beans, but I eat pizza.

9. A cowboy likes a hot bath and I ___.
A cowboy likes a hot bath, and I do too.

10. Cowboys work outdoors and I ___.
Cowboys work outdoors, and I like to be outside too.

Grammar **219**

Guided Practice A

Go through the exercise with children. Have volunteers tell where they added the comma in each sentence and what word they circled.

TEACHING TIP

Explain that to combine two sentences to make a compound sentence, the two sentences must have ideas that go together.

- Write these two sentences on the board: *Cowboys work hard. Cow ponies are small.*

- Point out that these two sentences cannot be combined to make a compound sentence because one sentence is about cowboys and the other sentence is about cow ponies. Their ideas do not go together.

Independent Practice B and C

Have children complete the exercises. For Differentiated Instruction and Extra Practice, see p. TR16.

Differentiated Instruction

Strategic Intervention

On the board, write pairs of sentences that can be combined using a comma and the word *and*.

- *Cowboys work hard. Their horses work hard too.*
- *They were hungry. The food tasted good.*
- *The moon came up. A coyote howled.*

Have volunteers come to the board and make compound sentences. Check their work.

Advanced

Ask children to write a short paragraph telling what they know about cowboys. Challenge them to include at least two compound sentences in their paragraphs. Invite volunteers to share what they have written with the group.

ELL

Write these sentences on the board.

The cat meowed, and ___.

I like apples, but ___.

Have children think of sentences that can be added after the connecting words to make compound sentences. Model the process: *The cat meowed, and the dog barked. I like apples, but I don't like pears.* Write each sentence on the board and read it together. Point out the comma and the connecting word.

Monitor Progress

Check Grammar

If... children have difficulty identifying compound sentences,	**then...**write correct and incorrect compound sentences on the board and have children circle the ones that are correct and revise those that are incorrect.

Test Preparation

☑ **Mark** the letter of the correctly written sentence.

1. ○ **A** A chuckwagon was important and, every trail drive had one.
   ○ **B** A chuckwagon was important, and, every trail drive had one.
   ⊗ **C** A chuckwagon was important, and every trail drive had one.

2. ⊗ **A** "Cookie" drove the wagon, and he also made the meals.
   ○ **B** "Cookie" drove the wagon and, he also made the meals.
   ○ **C** "Cookie" drove the wagon, and, he also made the meals.

3. ○ **A** Food was in sacks and drawers but, water was in a barrel.
   ⊗ **B** Food was in sacks and drawers, but water was in a barrel.
   ○ **C** Food was in sacks and drawers, water was in a barrel.

4. ⊗ **A** The beans were tasty, and the biscuits were hot.
   ○ **B** The beans were tasty, the biscuits were hot.
   ○ **C** The beans were tasty, but, the biscuits were hot.

Review

✓ **Write** the sentences. **Underline** the connecting words. **Add** commas where needed.

1. Cowboys get up early and they work hard all day.
   Cowboys get up early, <u>and</u> they work hard all day.
2. Some ranchers raise cattle but others raise sheep.
   Some ranchers raise cattle, <u>but</u> others raise sheep.
3. Cowboys wear bandanas but businessmen wear ties.
   Cowboys wear bandanas, <u>but</u> businessmen wear ties.
4. Cattle have sharp horns and deer have sharp antlers.
   Cattle have sharp horns, <u>and</u> deer have sharp antlers.
5. A cowboy uses a rope but a carpenter uses a hammer.
   A cowboy uses a rope, <u>but</u> a carpenter uses a hammer.

✓ **Use** the word in ( ) and a comma to combine each pair of sentences. **Write** the new sentence.

6. Penny has boots. She needs a hat. (but)
   Penny has boots, but she needs a hat.
7. Jason's belt is brown leather. It has a shiny buckle. (and)
   Jason's belt is brown leather, and it has a shiny buckle.
8. Alex loves her baseball shirt. It is torn. (but)
   Alex loves her baseball shirt, but it is torn.
9. Kiki lost her vest. Her dad found it. (but)
   Kiki lost her vest, but her dad found it.
10. Jay bought a bandana. He wore it today. (and)
    Jay bought a bandana, and he wore it today.

Grammar **221**

Summarize

Have children tell you important things they know about compound sentences.

- If two sentences have ideas that go together, they can be combined into a compound sentence.
- A comma and a connecting word, such as *and* or *but*, are used to make a compound sentence.

Grammar-Writing Connection

Explain that writers use compound sentences to show readers how their ideas go together.

Jason needs a new saddle. Today his dad is getting him one. Jason likes his old saddle. It is coming apart. He is excited about getting a new saddle. He wishes he didn't have to give up the old one.

Point out that if the sentences in this paragraph were made into compound sentences, it would be easier to understand how the ideas go together.

Jason needs a new saddle, and today his dad is getting him one. Jason likes his old saddle, but it is coming apart. He is excited about getting a new saddle, but he wishes he didn't have to give up the old one.

Topic Sentences

OBJECTIVES

- Identify characteristics of a job description.
- Write a job description using a topic sentence.
- Develop criteria for judging a piece of writing.

TEACH

Read aloud the information in the box at the top of the page. Then say: *As I read this paragraph, listen for the topic sentence.*

Park rangers have a great job. They work outside. They take people on nature walks. They watch animals.

Have children identify the topic sentence. *(Park rangers have a great job.)* Ask them how they knew.

Guided Writing

Read the items in Exercise 1 with children. Ask them how they decided which topic sentence belongs to each paragraph.

Independent Writing

Read the directions in Exercise 2. Talk about jobs children know about. Point out that their topic sentence will likely name the job. Ask volunteers to read aloud their paragraphs.

 WRITER'S CRAFT

Topic Sentences

A **topic sentence** tells the main idea of a paragraph. The topic sentence is often the first sentence of the paragraph.

 Write the letter of the topic sentence that should begin each paragraph.

> **A** Chefs are cooks and leaders.
> **B** Cowhands today are like cowhands long ago.

1. __B__ They work on ranches and take care of cattle. They rope cows and ride horses. They work in all kinds of weather.

2. __A__ At fancy restaurants, they plan menus and cook food. They also check the work of the other cooks.

 Write a paragraph about a job that someone you know has. **Begin** with a topic sentence that tells the main idea of the paragraph. Possible answer: My brother has a job at a plant nursery. He works after school and on weekends. Mostly he waters and sprays the plants. He also carries them out to the customers' cars. Sometimes he puts new plants in pots.

222 Writing

RESOURCES

Writing Transparency 29

Write a Job Description

Writing Prompt Write a description of a job. Tell what the job is and what kind of person would be good at this job.

Main idea is stated in topic sentence at beginning of paragraph.

All other sentences give details that support the main idea.

Strong conclusion leaves readers with something to think about.

A Pilot's Job

Pilots have a very important job. They fly airplanes filled with people. The people depend on pilots to get them safely from one place to another. Pilots need to be calm, smart, and brave. They must take care of any problems, and they can't make any mistakes. A mistake could hurt people.

Writing **223**

Write a Job Description

ANALYZE THE MODEL

Read aloud the model and the callouts to the left of it. Then prepare children to write their own job descriptions.

PROMPT

Now write a description of a job. Tell your main idea in a topic sentence. Give details that support the main idea.

Getting Started Children can do any of the following.

- Use an organizer (pp. TR28–TR32).
- Make a list of jobs that interest them.
- Jot down details about each job to see how much they know about it.

Editing/Revising Checklist

- ☑ Did I write a topic sentence that tells my main idea?
- ☑ Did I end with a strong conclusion?
- ☑ Did I include compound sentences and write them correctly?

Self-Evaluation Distribute copies of p. TR26 for children to fill out.

Scoring Rubric — Job Description

Rubric 4 3 2 1	4	3	2	1
Focus/Ideas	Description with strong focus on job; excellent details	Description with good focus on job; good details	Description with weak focus on job; few details	Description with no focus on job or details
Organization/ Paragraphs	Clear topic sentence, then supporting details in logical order	Clear topic sentence, then supporting details mostly in order	Unclear topic sentence; supporting details not in order	No topic sentence; no supporting details; no order
Voice	Lively; interested in topic and reader	Generally lively; some interest in topic and reader	Not very lively or interested in topic or reader	Careless; uninterested in topic or reader
Word Choice	Vivid, specific word picture of job	Good, generally specific word picture of job	Vague or dull word picture of job	Unclear, dull, or incorrect words; no word picture
Sentences	Smooth sentences; good variety	Sentences mostly smooth; some variety	Some choppy or stringy sentences; little variety	Unclear, choppy sentences; no variety
Conventions	Few or no errors	No serious errors	Many errors	Too many errors

The Paragraph

- Recognize paragraphs.
- Use paragraphs correctly in writing.
- Become familiar with paragraphs on standardized tests.

TEACH

Read aloud the definition and example in the box on p. 224. Then say:

How can we tell if a group of sentences is a paragraph? Look for these five things: (1) The sentences are about the same idea. (2) The sentences are in an order that makes sense. (3) One sentence gives the main idea. (4) The other sentences give details about the main idea. (5) The first sentence is indented.

Write the example paragraph from the box on the board. Point out each part as you model how to recognize a paragraph.

Model When I read this group of sentences, I see that all the sentences are about the same idea—the piñata at Carmen's birthday party. The sentences are in an order that makes sense. The first sentence gives the main idea while the other sentences give details about it. The first sentence is indented. So I know that this group of sentences is a paragraph.

The Paragraph

A **paragraph** is a group of sentences about the same idea. The sentences are in an order that makes sense. One sentence gives the main idea. The other sentences give details about the main idea. The first sentence of a paragraph is indented.

Carmen has a piñata at her birthday party. It is shaped like a horse. It has paper streamers for its mane and tail. The piñata is beautiful.

A **Write** the sentences. **Write** *1, 2, 3, 4,* or *5* after each sentence to show the correct order for a paragraph.

1. The piñata breaks, and treats fall out.
   5
2. She misses the piñata the first time.
   2
3. This time she hits the piñata!
   4
4. Carmen swings a stick at the piñata.
   1
5. Carmen swings the stick again.
   3

RESOURCES

Daily Fix-It Lesson 30
See p. TR10.
See also Daily Fix-It Transparency 30.
Grammar Transparency 30

B Write the sentences in the correct order to make a paragraph. **Indent** the first sentence. **Underline** the main idea sentence.

1. Grandma showed me how to dance.

2. The next week I practiced for many hours.

3. At last I was ready for the talent show.

4. Then I tried the dance as she watched.

5. First I watched her do the dance steps.

Grandma showed me how to dance. First I watched her do the dance steps. Then I tried the dance as she watched. The next week I practiced for many hours. At last I was ready for the talent show.

C Decide which sentence does not belong. **Write** the other sentences in the correct order to make a paragraph. **Indent** the first sentence.

6. Afterwards, we always have a meal with our friends.

7. Our whole family likes going to the talent show.

8. I have two dance costumes.

Leave out this sentence.

9. First we look around for seats.

10. Then we sit and watch the show.

Answer is on page TR38.

Grammar **225**

PRACTICE

Guided Practice A

Go through the exercise with children. Together read the sentences in the correct order. Let volunteers tell how they figured out the correct order of the sentences to make a paragraph.

TEACHING TIP

Explain that a writer indents the first sentence of every paragraph so that readers will know that the writer is beginning a new paragraph—and a new idea. Paragraphs are an important part of organizing writing.

Independent Practice B and C

Have children complete the exercises. For Differentiated Instruction and Extra Practice, see p. TR16.

Differentiated Instruction

Strategic Intervention

Give each child a copy of the Expository Writing model in the box on p. 42. Have children identify the sentence that gives the main idea. *(the first one)* Discuss how the other sentences give details about the main idea. Ask children what else tells them that this is a paragraph. *(sentences in an order that makes sense; indented first sentence)*

Advanced

Ask children to write a paragraph about a party they have attended. Remind them of the five things that make a group of sentences into a paragraph. Then have children exchange papers with a partner and check each other's writing using the information on p. 224.

ELL

Pair ELL children with children who have mastered the concept. Display a picture that has a clear main idea *(The children have fun at the party.)* and details. *(One girl blows bubbles. The boys play tag.)* Ask partners to write on paper one sentence that tells the main idea of the picture and two sentences that tell supporting details. Let pairs take turns reading aloud their paragraphs.

Monitor Progress

Check Grammar

If... children have difficulty identifying features of paragraphs,	then... review paragraphs from familiar stories and discuss with children what makes these groups of sentences paragraphs.

Test Preparation

✓ **Read** the paragraph. **Mark** the letter of the correct answer to each question.

Sun and Moon race in the sky every day. Sun climbs high and later dips out of sight. Sun peeks out early in the morning. When it is dark, Moon comes after Sun. Then it starts to rain. But Moon never catches up.

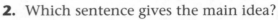

1. What was done to the first sentence?
   - ○ **A** It was kept long.
   - ○ **B** It had quotation marks added.
   - ⊗ **C** It was indented.

2. Which sentence gives the main idea?
   - ⊗ **A** Sun and Moon race in the sky every day.
   - ○ **B** But Moon never catches up.
   - ○ **C** Then it starts to rain.

3. Which sentence does not belong?
   - ○ **A** When it is dark, Moon comes after Sun.
   - ⊗ **B** Then it starts to rain.
   - ○ **C** Sun climbs high and later dips out of sight.

4. Which sentence is out of order?
   - ⊗ **A** Sun peeks out early in the morning.
   - ○ **B** When it is dark, Moon comes after Sun.
   - ○ **C** But Moon never catches up.

226 Grammar

Review

✔ **Write** the sentences in the correct order to make a paragraph. **Indent** the first sentence. **Underline** the main idea sentence.

1. We celebrate Thanksgiving with relatives.

2. Their son, my cousin Al, comes with them.

3. When the last person gets there, we eat.

4. First my aunt and uncle arrive.

5. Soon afterwards, Grandpa drives over.

We celebrate Thanksgiving with relatives. First my aunt and uncle arrive. Their son, my cousin Al, comes with them. Soon afterwards, Grandpa drives over. When the last person gets there, we eat.

✔ **Decide** which sentence does not belong. **Write** the other sentences in the correct order to make a paragraph. **Indent** the first sentence.

6. Grandpa makes wonderful things.

7. Next week he plans to make a drum.

8. Tomorrow he will build a wagon.

9. ~~Grandma is a good painter.~~

10. Right now he is making a wooden yo-yo.

Answer is on page TR38.

Grammar **227**

Summarize

Have children explain what a paragraph is and how they can recognize one.

- A paragraph is a group of sentences about the same idea.
- The sentences in a paragraph are in an order that makes sense.
- One sentence in a paragraph gives the main idea.
- The other sentences in the paragraph give details about the main idea.
- The first sentence of a paragraph is indented.

Grammar-Writing Connection

Explain to children that a sentence that tells the main idea of a paragraph helps readers better understand what the paragraph is about. Otherwise, they might get confused trying to guess the main idea.

No main idea given:
It was red and shiny and he loved to ride it. His friends wanted one too. He let them try it.

What is the writer is talking about? It is hard to tell without a sentence that tells the main idea.

Main idea given:
Jake loved his new scooter. It was red and shiny and he loved to ride it. His friends wanted one too. He let them try it.

Good Paragraphs

- Identify characteristics of a description of a tradition.
- Write a description of a tradition with good paragraphs.
- Develop criteria for judging a piece of writing.

TEACH

Read aloud the information in the box at the top of the page. Then say: *Listen as I read.*

Think Aloud She said my teeth were healthy. I went to the dentist for the first time. She gave me a new toothbrush.

Write the sentences on the board. Ask children what needs to be done to make them into a good paragraph. *(put second sentence first; indent first sentence)*

 Guided Writing

Read the directions and sentences in Exercise 1 with children. Tell them to decide which sentence does not belong before they put the other sentences in order. Ask a volunteer to read aloud the final paragraph.

 Independent Writing

Read the directions for Exercise 2. Talk with children about family traditions. After they write their paragraphs, check to see that they wrote the paragraphs correctly.

 WRITER'S CRAFT

Good Paragraphs

- In a good **paragraph**, all the sentences tell about the same idea.
- One sentence gives the main idea, and the other sentences give details about it.
- The sentences are in an order that makes sense.
- The first sentence is indented.

 Read the sentences below. **Decide** which sentence does not tell about the same idea. **Write** the other sentences in the correct order to make a paragraph. **Indent** the first sentence.

She cuts out large red paper hearts.

Every year Mom and I make valentines.

I get many valentines from my friends.

We write messages on the hearts.

Then we give our valentines to our friends.

Sentence to leave out: I get many valentines from my friends.
Every year Mom and I make valentines. She cuts out large red paper hearts.
We write messages on the hearts. Then we give our valentines to our friends.

Write a paragraph about something your family does on a holiday or other special occasion.

Possible answer is on page TR38.

228 Writing

RESOURCES

Writing Transparency 30

Describe a Tradition

Writing Prompt Write about the things you do to celebrate Thanksgiving at school and at home.

All sentences in each paragraph tell about the same idea.

First sentence in each paragraph is indented.

Writer uses the conclusion to summarize ideas.

Thanksgiving

At school we learn about the first Thanksgiving. The Pilgrims wanted to celebrate a good harvest. They invited the Indians to dinner.

On Thanksgiving Day we celebrate too. We eat turkey, sweet potatoes, cranberry sauce, green beans, and pumpkin pie. Many relatives come to our house. I get to play with my four cousins. We play football or watch it on television.

History, food, family, and football are all part of our Thanksgiving.

Writing **229**

Describe a Tradition

ANALYZE THE MODEL

Read aloud the model and the callouts to the left of it. Then prepare children to write their own descriptions of a tradition.

PROMPT

Write a description of how you celebrate Thanksgiving. Remember all the things you need to do to write good paragraphs.

Getting Started Children can do any of the following.

- Use an organizer (pp. TR28–TR32).
- Talk to family members about the holiday and jot down notes.
- Make a list of what they want to write about.

Editing/Revising Checklist

☑ Did I give the main idea and supporting details?

☑ Did I put my paragraphs in an order that makes sense?

☑ Did I indent the first sentence of each paragraph?

Self-Evaluation Distribute copies of p. TR26 for children to fill out.

Scoring Rubric Description of a Tradition

Rubric 4 3 2 1	4	3	2	1
Focus/Ideas	Description with strong focus on topic; excellent details	Description with good focus on topic; good details	Description not always focused on topic; few details	Description with no focus on topic or details
Organization/ Paragraphs	Correct paragraphs in logical order	Correct paragraphs in mostly logical order	Some incorrect paragraphs; some out of order	No paragraphs
Voice	Lively, interested; shows writer's feelings	Mostly lively, interested; shows some feelings	Not very lively or interested; shows few feelings	Careless, uninterested; shows no feelings
Word Choice	Vivid, clear words	Clear words	Mostly vague words	Dull, repetitive, or incorrect words
Sentences	Smooth sentences; good variety	Most sentences smooth; some variety	Some choppy or stringy sentences; little variety	Many unclear, incomplete, or choppy sentences; no variety
Conventions	Few or no errors	No serious errors	Many errors	Too many errors

Taking Tests

Follow these tips when writing for a test:

Before Writing

- Read the prompt carefully. Think about what it asks you to do.
- Write down key words. For example, here is a prompt:

    Write a <u>thank-you letter</u> to a <u>friend</u>.

    The key words tell you to write a letter to thank a friend. You will use the letter form and thank someone in a friendly voice.
- Use a graphic organizer to plan your composition.

During Writing

- Keep the prompt in mind to stay on the topic.
- Follow your graphic organizer. Stay focused.
- Write a good beginning. You might ask readers a question or give an interesting fact.
- Support your main idea.
- Write a strong ending. You might add a final comment of your own or give your reader a command.

After Writing

- Check grammar, punctuation, and spelling.
- Are there places that need more details or clearer information?

Taking Tests **231**

Writing a Story About Me

A **test** may ask you to write a story about yourself. It should have a beginning, middle, and end.

Understand the prompt. A prompt for a story about yourself could look like this:

Write about a time you were surprised. Tell how you felt. Your story should have a beginning, middle, and end.

Key phrases are *you were surprised, how you felt,* and *beginning, middle, and end.*

Find a good topic. Choose something that you remember well. Make sure you can tell about the beginning, middle, and end of the story.

Organize your ideas. Make a list of details. Then put them in order. Tell how you felt.

My Birthday Surprise	
Nobody talked to me.	Felt sad
Doorbell rang	Friends came over.

Write a good beginning. Tell the reader what you're writing about in your first sentence.

Develop and elaborate ideas. Use the details in your list. Use words that show your feelings.

Write a strong ending. Tell how the event ends.

Check your work. Make changes if you need to.

See how the personal story below follows the prompt.

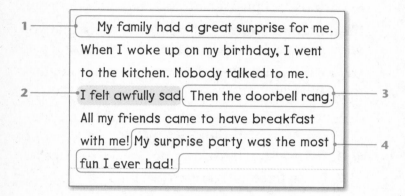

1. My family had a great surprise for me. When I woke up on my birthday, I went to the kitchen. Nobody talked to me.
2. I felt awfully sad. Then the doorbell rang. 3
All my friends came to have breakfast with me! My surprise party was the most 4
fun I ever had!

1. The first sentence organizes the entire piece.

2. The writer tells how he or she felt.

3. Events are in order; clue word *then* is used.

4. The ending sentence wraps up the story.

Writing a How-to Report

When you write directions for going somewhere or making something, include all the information your readers need. Close your eyes and picture the steps you will need to do. That will help you put the steps in order. For example, imagine that you are writing steps for how to make a new home for your goldfish. The step to fill the bowl with water comes before the step to add food to the water.

Writing a How-To Report

A **test** may ask you to write a how-to report. Include all the steps. Use order words such as *first* and *then*.

Understand the prompt. Read the prompt again. Here is a prompt for a how-to report:

Write directions for a craft project you do in school.

Key words and phrases are *directions* and *craft project*.

Find a good topic. Choose something that you know how to do well. Give clear directions and steps.

Organize your ideas. List your steps and put them in order.

Making a Journal
1. You need two pieces of cardboard and some paper.
2. Punch three holes in each piece.
3. Put the paper between the cardboard.
4. Tie the pieces together and decorate the cover.

Write a good beginning. Explain what you are writing about in your first sentence.

Develop and elaborate ideas. Add details so readers know exactly what to do.

Write a strong ending. Tell what you think.

Check your work. Make any changes.

See how the how-to report below follows the prompt.

1 → Did you know that you can make your own journal? You will need two pieces of cardboard and some sheets of blank paper. First, carefully punch three ← 3
holes in each piece of cardboard and
2 < paper. Then slide the paper between the cardboard pieces. Last, tie all the pieces together and decorate the cover.
This is a great place to write all your ideas. ← 4

1. Product and materials are given first.

2. Order words tell when to do each step.

3. Adjectives and adverbs give information.

4. The ending wraps up the ideas in the report.

Taking Tests **235**

Writing a Compare/Contrast Essay

A diagram can help you organize a compare and contrast essay. Choose two subjects, such as seasons, places, or people, that are both alike and different. Then list their likenesses and the differences. After you fill in your diagram, it will be easier to write your essay. Start with an introduction that tells readers what you are comparing. Then you might write a paragraph that tells how your subjects are like each other and a paragraph that tells how they are different. End by summing up your ideas.

Writing a Compare/Contrast Paragraph

A **test** may ask you to write a compare/contrast paragraph. Tell how things are the same and different.

Understand the prompt.   A prompt that asks you to write a compare/contrast paragraph could look like this:

Write about something you did in the past that you still do now. Tell how what you did has changed and how it has stayed the same.

Key phrases are *did in the past* and *do now*.

Find a good topic.   Think of things you do.

Organize your ideas.   Make a diagram.

Write a good beginning.   A good opening sentence will make your reader want to read more.

Things I Read

Past   Now

Both

funny picture books   make me laugh   funny stories

236   Taking Tests

Develop and elaborate ideas. Use the details from your diagram to talk about then and now.

Write a strong ending. Sum up your ideas.

Check your work. Make changes as needed.

See how the paragraph below tells how the topic is the same and different.

1 — I read different things today than I did when I was younger. In the past, I looked at picture books because I couldn't read words yet. The funny pictures made me laugh. Now that I am older, I can read magazines and books. These have funny stories. I still like to laugh when I read, but now I just read different things. — 2 — 3

1. The first sentence states the main idea.

2. The writer tells when something happened.

3. The ending tells what is alike and different.

Writing a Descriptive Paragraph

When you describe something, think about all the things that make it special —the color, the smell, the taste, the way it is used, or the way it feels. You might make a web with your subject in the middle and connecting lines to words that tell about your subject. Avoid words such as *nice*. Instead, use vivid words such as *wobbly, icy, pointed,* and *sharp* that give readers clear pictures.

Writing a Descriptive Paragraph

A **test** may ask you to write a description. Use exciting words that make readers use their senses.

Understand the prompt. A prompt for a description could look like this:

Write a description of an animal that is special to you. Help readers use their senses to picture this animal.

Key words are *description, animal,* and *senses.*

Find a good topic. Choose an animal you know well, such as a zoo animal or a pet.

Organize your ideas. Make an idea web.

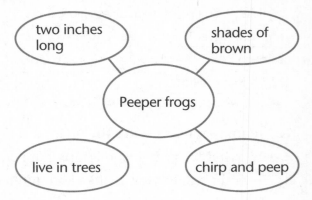

Write a good beginning.   Set up your topic.

Develop ideas.   Paint word pictures.

Write a strong ending.   Address your readers.

Check your work.   Have you used the best words?

See how the description below answers the prompt.

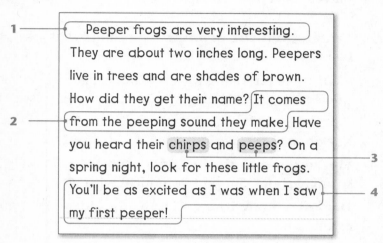

1. Peeper frogs are very interesting.

They are about two inches long. Peepers live in trees and are shades of brown. How did they get their name? It comes from the peeping sound they make. Have you heard their chirps and peeps? On a spring night, look for these little frogs. You'll be as excited as I was when I saw my first peeper!

1. The first sentence states the topic clearly.

2. This is an important detail.

3. Specific nouns add to the word picture.

4. The strong ending shows the writer's feelings.

Taking Tests   **239**

Writing a Persuasive Letter

Before you write a persuasive letter—one in which you try to get someone to do something—think about why you want what you're asking. Be sure that you have good reasons. Then choose words such as *please, try, should,* and *most important* that make your reasons clear and convincing. Also keep in mind who will get your letter. How can you get this person to do what you want? For example, if your brother hates sports, you may have a hard time convincing him to go to a soccer game. On the other hand, if your brother likes music, you could mention that the band will be playing at half-time or that CDs will be given to ten randomly selected people attending the soccer game.

WRITING FOR TESTS

Writing a Persuasive Letter

A **test** may ask you to write a persuasive letter. Support your ideas with examples, facts, and reasons. Use words such as *should* and *most important*. Follow the tips below.

Understand the prompt. A prompt that asks you to write a persuasive letter could look like this:

> Write a letter asking for something special. Persuade your reader. Try to get the reader to see your side.

Key phrases are *letter, persuade,* and *your side.*

Find a good topic. Choose a subject that you feel strongly about. Support your ideas with facts.

Organize your ideas. List reasons for your argument.

Getting a New Bike
My old bike is too small.
I worked and saved money.
I have enough money to buy a new bike.
A new bike will be safer.

Write a good beginning. Tell the reader what you want in the first sentence.

Develop and elaborate ideas. Use facts to support your argument. Use words such as *should* or *best*.

Write a strong ending. Sum up your reasons.

Check your work. Make any necessary changes.

See how the persuasive letter below follows the prompt.

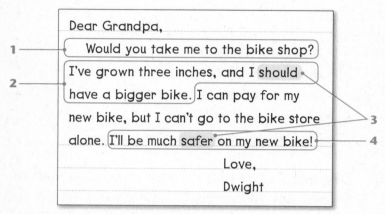

Dear Grandpa,

1 — Would you take me to the bike shop?

2 — I've grown three inches, and I should have a bigger bike. I can pay for my new bike, but I can't go to the bike store alone. I'll be much safer on my new bike!

3

4

Love,

Dwight

1. First sentence states argument.

2. Facts and reasons support argument.

3. Words such as *should* and *safer* are persuasive.

4. Ending sentence gives strongest reason.

Taking Tests **241**

TEST TIP

Writing a Summary

You may be asked to write a summary of information you find in a chart. You will need to put together this information into sentences and paragraphs. Read the information in the chart carefully so that you can summarize it correctly. Your summary should include the important facts from the chart, but it should not sound like a list of facts. Begin and end your summary in a way that gets your reader's attention.

Writing a Summary

Some **tests** may ask you to write a summary from a list of facts, a time line, or a chart. You will need to read the information carefully and use it in your own sentences. Follow the tips below.

Long-Necked Dinosaurs

- About fifty feet long
- Huge size helped protect them
- Didn't eat other dinosaurs
- Ate plants and tree leaves
- Died out about 64 million years ago

Organize your ideas.   How will you present the facts? Think about which facts you want to use first and which you will use at the end of your summary.

Write a good beginning.   Write an interesting beginning sentence that makes your readers want to keep reading. Think of a topic sentence that presents the main idea clearly.

242   Taking Tests

Develop and elaborate ideas. Make sure the details support your main idea.

Write a strong ending. Write sentences that pull the information together.

Check your work. Make any necessary changes.

See how the report below summarizes information.

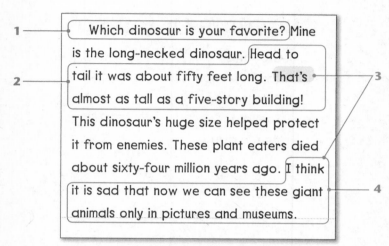

1. Which dinosaur is your favorite? Mine is the long-necked dinosaur. Head to tail it was about fifty feet long. That's almost as tall as a five-story building! This dinosaur's huge size helped protect it from enemies. These plant eaters died about sixty-four million years ago. I think it is sad that now we can see these giant animals only in pictures and museums.

1. The first sentence grabs the reader's attention.

2. The writer paints a picture for the reader.

3. Pronouns and contractions are correct.

4. The last sentence shows the writer's feelings.

Grammar Patrol

Grammar Patrol

adjective   An **adjective** describes a person, place, animal, or thing. An adjective can tell how something looks, sounds, tastes, feels, or smells.

> I love **warm** cookies.
> (**Warm** describes the way the cookies feel.)

- Words for number, size, and shape are adjectives. The words **a** and **an** are also adjectives. Use **a** before a word that begins with a consonant sound. Use **an** before a word with a vowel sound.

> My sister wrote **a** letter.
> Dad gave her **an** envelope.

> (The word **a** describes how many letters—one. The word **an** describes how many envelopes–one.)

> My sister wrote a **long** letter.
> (**Long** describes the size of the letter.)

- Add **–er** to an adjective to **compare** two persons, places, or things.

> Mark is tall**er** than I am.

- Add **–est** to an adjective to **compare** three or more persons, places, or things.

> Sarah is the tall**est** girl in the class.

adverb An **adverb** tells more about a verb.

- Some adverbs tell **when**.

  We're going to the museum **tomorrow.**

- Some adverbs tell **where**.

  We waited **inside.**

- Some adverbs tell **how.** Many adverbs that tell **how** end in **–ly.**

  I ate the ice cream **quickly.**

contraction A contraction is a short way to put two words together. An apostrophe (**'**) takes the place of one or more letters.

- Contractions can be formed by putting together a pronoun and another word, such as **will, are,** or **is.**

  I will see the movie tomorrow.
  I'll see the movie tomorrow.

- Many contractions are formed with verbs and the word **not.**

   I **did not** bring my music.
   I **didn't** bring my music.

noun   A **noun** names a person, place, animal, or thing.

   My **brother** takes **lunch** to **school.**
      (person)   (thing)   (place)

- To make most nouns **plural**, add **-s.**

   pencil + s = pencils   horse + s = horses

- Some nouns add **–es** to form the **plural**. These nouns end in **ss, x, ch,** or **sh.**

   class + es = classes   lunch + es = lunches
   fox + es = foxes   bush + es = bushes

- Some nouns change their spelling to form the **plural**.

Singular	Plural
child	children
man	men
woman	women
foot	feet
tooth	teeth
goose	geese
mouse	mice

- **Proper nouns** are special names for people, places, animals, and things. They begin with capital letters. **Days of the week, months of the year,** and **holidays** also begin with capital letters. Titles for people begin with capital letters. Many titles end with a period **(.)**.

  Heather Frank plays in the band.
  Ms. Young is the director.
  The first concert is at **Jones School** on **Sunday, March** 20.

- **Possessive nouns** show ownership. Many nouns add an **apostrophe** and **s ('s)** to show ownership.

  The trunk of the elephant is very long.
  The elephant**'s** trunk is very long.

- Many **plural possessive nouns** add only an **apostrophe (')** to show ownership.

  The girls**'** shoes are new.

pronoun A **pronoun** takes the place of a noun.

- **He, she,** and **it** are pronouns that name only one. **We** and **they** are pronouns that name more than one.

    David likes games.
    He likes board games.

    David and Chris play chess.
    They play chess.

- The pronouns **I** and **me** take the place of your name. Use **I** in the subject of a sentence. Use **me** after an action verb. Always write **I** with a capital letter.

    I walk to school. Scott walks with **me.**

    When you talk about yourself and another person, name yourself last. The pronouns **I** and **me** take the place of your name.

    Jane and **I** play after school.
    My mom drives Jane and **me** home.

Grammar Patrol **249**

The pronouns **I, he, she, we** and **they** are used as subjects of sentences. The pronouns **me, him, her, us,** and **them** are used after action verbs. The pronouns **you** and **it** can be used anywhere in a sentence.

Ned bakes a cake. **He** frosts **it.**
Paul sees Jill. He waves to **her.**

- The pronoun **me** is used in the telling part of a sentence.

They waited for **me.**

sentence   A sentence tells a complete idea. It begins with a capital letter.

My grandmother makes good cookies.

- A **telling sentence**, or **statement**, ends with a **period (.)**.

Tim played the violin quietly**.**

- An **asking sentence**, or **question**, ends with a **question mark (?)**.

Are you coming over**?**

- A **command** gives an order. It ends with a period **(.)**.

Wash your hands**.**

- An **exclamation** shows strong feeling. It ends with an exclamation mark **(!)**.

    What a beautiful day it is**!**

- A sentence has two parts. It has a **subject** and a **predicate.**

    The girl sings a song.

    The girl   names who the sentence is about (subject)

    sings a song.   tells what the girl does (predicate)

- The words in a sentence must be in an order that makes sense.

    By ate We campfire. The hot dogs   is not a sentence

    We ate hot dogs by the campfire.   is a sentence

- The meaning of a sentence changes if the word order changes.

    The **bag** is in the **box**.

    The **box** is in the **bag**.

    Is the **box** in the **bag**?

- A **compound sentence** has two simple sentences joined by the word **and, but,** or **or**. Use a comma in a compound sentence before the word **and, but,** or **or**.

verb A word that tells what someone or something does is a verb.

JoAnn **reads.**   Jeff **rides** his bike.

- A verb can tell what one person, animal, or thing does. Add **–s** to show what is being done now.

  The rabbit **hops.**

- Do not add **–s** to a verb that tells what two or more people, animals, or things do now.

  Tim and Tom **clean** their room.

- Verbs can tell what happens **now,** what happened in the **past,** or what will happen in the **future.**

  Today Margie **bakes** bread.
  (The verb **bakes** tells about now. It ends with **–s.**)

  Yesterday Margie **baked** bread.
  (The verb **baked** tells about the past. It ends with **–ed.**)

  Tomorrow Margie **will bake** bread.
  (The verb **will bake** tells about the future. It begins with **will.**)

- The verbs **am**, **is**, **are**, **was**, and **were** do not show action. They show what someone or something is or was.

   The baby **is tired.**   Greg **was angry.**

The verbs **am**, **is**, and **are** tell about now.

   I **am** a nurse.   Jose **is** a nurse.   Jo and Dan **are** nurses.

The verbs **was** and **were** tell about the past.

   I **was** thirsty.   He **was** thirsty.   We **were** thirsty.

Use **am**, **is**, and **was** to tell about one person, place, or thing. Use **are** and **were** to tell about more than one person, place, or thing.

Capitalization

sentence   A sentence begins with a capital letter.

The woman is tall.

names for people, places, and pets   The names of people, places, and pets begin with capital letters.

Beth **C**ane and her bird **M**illy live in **D**enver.

titles for people   Titles for people begin with capital letters. Most titles end with a period.

Mr. Lee ate dinner with **Dr.** Sanchez and **Ms.** Fields.

days of the week   The names of the days of the week begin with capital letters.

Our game is on **S**aturday.

months and holidays   The names of months and holidays begin with capital letters.

I know that **M**artin **L**uther **K**ing, **J**r., **D**ay is in **J**anuary.

using I   The pronoun **I** is always used in the subject of a sentence. Always write **I** with a capital letter. Always name yourself last.

Liz and **I** looked for shells.

Punctuation

period Use a period **(.)** at the end of a sentence.

    Robbie plays catch with his dad**.**

- Use a period at the end of a command.

    Stay on the sidewalk**.**

- Most titles for people end with a period.

    Mr**.** Lee ate lunch with Dr**.** King and Ms**.** Bell.

question mark Use a question mark **(?)** at the end of a question.

    Where is your brother**?**

exclamation mark Use an exclamation mark **(!)** at the end of an exclamation.

    What a day we had**!**

quotation marks Quotation marks show the beginning and ending of the words someone says. The speaker's name and words such as **said** or **asked** are not inside the quotation marks.

    "Let's go to the zoo," said Marla.
    Brian asked, "What is your favorite animal?"

apostrophe Use an apostrophe **(')** to take the place of one or more letters in a contraction. A contraction is a short way to put two words together.

Grammar Patrol **255**

is + not = isn't　　　**we + will = we'll**

- Use an apostrophe (') and **s** to show ownership.

  The trunk of an elephant can hold water.
  The elephant**'s** trunk can hold water.

commas

- Commas (**,**) are used in addresses:
  Durham, NC

- Commas are used in dates:
  August 23, 1957　　Saturday, April 12

- Commas are used to begin and end a letter:
  Dear Aunt May,
  Love,
  　　Josh

- Commas are used to separate three things in a sentence.
  Kate ate cereal, toast, and a banana.

- Use a comma before the word **and** or **but** in a compound sentence.
  Liam plays the trumpet, **and** he plays soccer.
  Jack goes to the movies, **but** Lisa stays home.

Frequently Misspelled Words

For many writers, some words are difficult to spell.
You can use this list to check your spelling.

a lot	eat	into	party	thought
about	end	is	people	through
again	every	it's	play	to
all	everybody	knew	presents	too
always	family	know	pretty	took
and	favorite	like	put	tried
another	find	little	really	two
are	first	live	said	under
as	for	look	saw	upon
away	found	love	scared	use
baseball	friend	make	school	very
be	from	many	see	want
beautiful	get	more	so	was
because	girl	my	some	watch
before	give	new	sometimes	we
birthday	go	nice	special	went
brother	going	night	started	were
but	good	not	swimming	what
by	Halloween	now	thank	when
came	has	of	that	where
caught	have	on	that's	who
Christmas	heard	once	the	whole
come	her	one	their	will
could	here	or	them	with
didn't	him	other	then	would
different	his	our	there	you
do	home	out	there's	your
does	house	outside	these	
don't	how	over	they	
down	I	part	they're	

D'Nealian™ Alphabet

a b c d e f g h i
j k l m n o p q r s t
u v w x y z

A B C D E F G
H I J K L M N O
P Q R S T U V
W X Y Z . , ' ?

1 2 3 4 5 6
7 8 9 10

Manuscript Alphabet

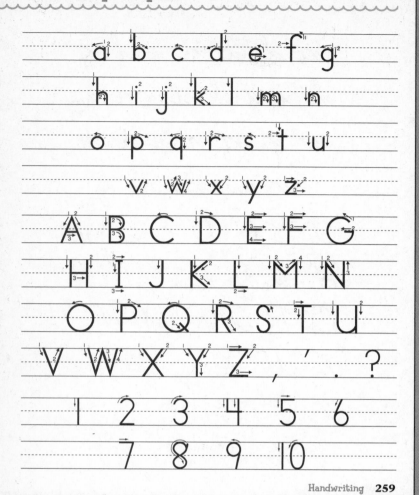

Cursive Alphabet

Index

Describing words. *See* Adjectives.

Descriptive writing. *See* Writing.

E

End marks, 50–53, 68–71, 74–77, 78, 120

Exclamation mark, 74–77

Exclamations. *See* Sentences.

Expository writing. *See* Writing, *types of.*

F

Focus/Ideas. *See* Writing.

Frequently misspelled words, 257

Future tense. *See* Verbs.

H

Handwriting, 258–260

Holidays, 86–89

I

I, 182–185, 188–191

L

Letters, 193, 212–215, 240–241

M

Main idea, 2–3, 168, 204, 222, 224–227

Mechanics. *See* Punctuation.

Months of year, 86–89, 200–203

N

Narrative writing. *See* Writing, *types of.*

Nouns, 80–83, 247–248
plural, 92–95, 116–119
that change spelling, 98–101, 116–119
possessive
plural, 104–107
singular, 104–107
proper, 86–89
days of week, 86–89
holidays, 86–89
months of year, 86–89
titles for people, 86–89
singular, 92–95, 116–119

O

Organization/Paragraphs. *See* Writing.

Index **263**

DAILY FIX-IT 1

1. We will lits what we might see
   We will list what we might see.
2. iris wanted a friend
   Iris wanted a friend.

3. played tag Iris and Walter
   Iris and Walter played tag.
4. Then rode a pony they
   Then they rode a pony.

5. Iris was sd and lonely
   Iris was sad and lonely.
6. wanted she a friend
   She wanted a friend.

7. will go on a field trip
   We will go on a field trip.
8. will go with us Mrs. Brody
   Mrs. Brody will go with us.

9. We helped clean up the mes
   We helped clean up the mess.
10. picked up she the pieces
    She picked up the pieces.

Unit 1 Iris and Walter   Daily Fix-It **1**

© Pearson Education

DAILY FIX-IT 2

1. we will fly into spac.
   We will fly into space.
2. it will be lots of fun
   It will be lots of fun.

3. was hom.
   The astronaut was home.
4. she was gone a long time?
   She was gone a long time.

5. it is a fine day to fly into space
   It is a fine day to fly into space.
6. are in the sky no clouds
   No clouds are in the sky.

7. was late for the soccer game
   He was late for the soccer game.
8. they missed the first goal
   They missed the first goal.

9. That space suit is not my siz
   That space suit is not my size.
10. my friend it will fit
    It will fit my friend.

Unit 1 Exploring Space   Daily Fix-It **2**

© Pearson Education

DAILY FIX-IT 3

1. we saw a bird's nesst in a tree.
   We saw a bird's nest in a tree.
2. went on a camping trip
   We went on a camping trip.

3. A nice breeze
   A nice breeze fanned our faces.
4. my dad and I
   My dad and I went hiking.

5. The strap on my backpack.
   The strap on my backpack broke.
6. That stem of water
   That stream of water was cold.

7. Jen's bike
   Jen's bike had a flat tire.
8. she and Jim
   She and Jim walked home.

9. Henry and Mudge
   Henry and Mudge went camping.
10. the cooking does Henry's mother
    Henry's mother does the cooking.

Unit 1 Henry and Mudge   Daily Fix-It **3**

© Pearson Education

DAILY FIX-IT

1. talked about the desert
   We talked about the desert.

2. when can we go
   When can we go?

3. did you enjoy the desert
   Did you enjoy the desert?

4. I was really exited?
   I was really excited!

5. smiled at the mule
   He smiled at the mule.

6. did you find some cactus jelly
   Did you find some cactus jelly?

7. wear did you drop it.
   Where did you drop it?

8. I lost it in the dessert?
   I lost it in the desert.

9. The desert
   The desert is hot and dry.

10. did you enjoy your walk
    Did you enjoy your walk?

Unit 1   A Walk in the Desert   Daily Fix-It   **4**

DAILY FIX-IT

1. do you really believe that story
   Do you really believe that story?

2. An animal can't
   An animal can't really talk.

3. what time does the game start
   What time does the game start?

4. get that ball
   Get that ball!

5. Does an amt bite icth.
   Does an amt bite itch?

6. oh, it stings too
   Oh, it stings too!

7. take me to see the anteater
   Take me to see the anteater.

8. It has such a strange shap
   It has such a strange shape!

9. look for ants near trees
   Look for ants near trees.

10. watch out, they bite
    Watch out, they bite!

Unit 1   The Strongest One   Daily Fix-It   **5**

DAILY FIX-IT

1. thst dog is smart
   That dog is smart.

2. it's exciteing to see it work hard.
   It's exciting to see it work hard.

3. did you see the dog
   Did you see the dog?

4. he used his nos to find the toy.
   He used his nose to find the toy.

5. The dog has a jub?
   The dog has a job.

6. he is berave.
   He is brave.

7. I want two see the dog pla.
   I want to see the dog play.

8. he is naping on the porch.
   He is napping on the porch.

9. what a good dog he is
   What a good dog he is!

10. will I see him later
    Will I see him later?

Unit 2   Tara and Tiree   Daily Fix-It   **6**

Daily Fix-It **9**

1. The donkey didnt have any food
   The donkey didn't have any food.

2. He mised his lunchs.
   He missed his lunches.

3. He at good food on the farm.
   He ate good food on the farm.

4. But he was'nt at the farm now
   But he wasn't at the farm now.

5. He red a dog storie.
   He read a dog story.

6. He new other storys too.
   He knew other stories too.

7. The donkey blue the hurn.
   The donkey blew the horn.

8. The dog stated to hum a tun.
   The dog started to hum a tune.

9. donkey humed with Dog.
   Donkey hummed with Dog.

10. what fun they had.
    What fun they had!

Unit 2 Bremen Town Musicians

Daily Fix-It **8**

1. Two turtle talked to hur.
   Two turtles talked to her.

2. She askked about his family?
   She asked about his family.

3. They were siting in the dert.
   They were sitting in the dirt.

4. turtle took a purse
   Turtle took a purse.

5. he was nammed Beaver.
   He was named Beaver.

6. Turtle gav him a mint?
   Turtle gave him a mint.

7. His kids hade a new hom.
   His kids had a new home.

8. he asked if she wanted it?
   He asked if she wanted it.

9. They walked to the dame.
   They walked to the dam.

10. turtle likked it very much.
    Turtle liked it very much.

Unit 2 Turtle's Race

Daily Fix-It **7**

1. we want to play baseball
   We want to play baseball.

2. its a fun game.
   It's a fun game.

3. Whos going to play.
   Who's going to play?

4. When will we stat.
   When will we start?

5. I'm made that it is raining.
   I'm mad that it is raining.

6. I hop it does not last long
   I hope it does not last long.

7. it didnt rain much.
   It didn't rain much.

8. Can john be on my team.
   Can John be on my team?

9. I hit the ball had
   I hit the ball hard.

10. What a fun gam this is
    What a fun game this is!

Unit 2 Ronald Morgan

Daily Fix-Its **TR3**

DAILY FIX-IT

1. The dog had pant on his tal.
   The dog had paint on his tail.
2. He wanted to wash it awae.
   He wanted to wash it away.

3. The dog asked the cat for help?
   The dog asked the cat for help.
4. the cat told the dog to wat.
   The cat told the dog to wait.

5. The cat find the sop.
   The cat found the soap.
6. Sh'es a smart cat.
   She's a smart cat.

7. she washed the dogs tail.
   She washed the dog's tail.
8. That mad him happy
   That made him happy.

9. It wasn't' long befoe they left.
   It wasn't long before they left.
10. What fune thay had.
    What fun they had!

DAILY FIX-IT

1. carl think of a idea.
   Carl thinks of an idea.
2. then he make a meel.
   Then he makes meal.

3. we will ete soup for lunch.
   We will eat soup for lunch.
4. We lik a lot of chease on it.
   We like a lot of cheese on it.

5. Science project are not eisy.
   Science projects are not easy.
6. It heps to read about them frist.
   It helps to read about them first.

7. My teme made an robot?
   My team made a robot.
8. It teeth and eihgt wheels!
   It has teeth and eight wheels!

9. Hour project was reallly gude.
   Our project was really good.
10. I fill we shood have won.
    I feel we should have won.

DAILY FIX-IT

1. Could the bowl flote?
   Could the boat float?
2. Where can I find a boal.
   Where can I find a bowl?

3. Did Alan finds the mailbox.
   Did Alan find the mailbox?
4. Jo mail some letters she write.
   Jo mails some letters she wrote.

5. I got the leter a week agaw.
   I got the letter a week ago.
6. I opened itt right away?
   I opened it right away.

7. Shee likes to visit her Grandma.
   She likes to visit her grandma.
8. She show her noo things.
   She shows her new things.

9. Sally likes writting leters.
   Sally likes writing letters.
10. Brad never write bak.
    Brad never writes back.

13

1. Hir purse is durty.
   Her purse is dirty.
2. The tirtle ca'nt run fast.
   The turtle can't run fast.
3. Last week end I sent a leter.
   Last weekend I sent a letter.
4. My mom red a story at bed time.
   My mom read a story at bedtime.
5. He saw a toy in the drive way.
   He saw a toy in the driveway.
6. Some one played a trick on Her.
   Someone played a trick on her.
7. I fish in the pond yesserday.
   I fished in the pond yesterday.
8. I will fished agen tomorrow.
   I will fish again tomorrow.
9. I want to do some thing fur Bill.
   I want to do something for Bill.
10. Do you had any ideas.
    Do you have any ideas?

Unit 3   Anansi Goes Fishing   Daily Fix-It

14

1. Their is a speider in a web.
   There is a spider in a web.
2. Did you friten it
   Did you frighten it?
3. A small childe look at the sky.
   A small child looked at the sky.
4. Tomorrow the day be brite.
   Tomorrow the day will be bright.
5. I wants to finde the right seeds.
   I want to find the right seeds.
6. Me sister wi'll plant them.
   My sister will plant them.
7. Hour yard has a birdbath
   Our yard has a birdbath.
8. Now Birds stopped to drink.
   Now birds stop to drink.
9. I helped Mom made a mail box.
   I helped Mom make a mailbox.
10. Now Her mail stayed dry.
    Now her mail stays dry.

Unit 3   Rosa and Blanca   Daily Fix-It

15

1. He am the hapiest dog.
   He is the happiest dog.
2. Where is their a place too sit?
   Where is there a place to sit?
3. It are smallest than that.
   It is smaller than that.
4. Plants that row of seeds straighterer.
   Plant that row of seeds straighter.
5. I am happyest when I are busy.
   I am happiest when I am busy.
6. Then I finich my work sooner.
   Then I finish my work sooner.
7. He are a plant dotcor.
   He is a plant doctor.
8. I am knot too good withplants.
   I am not too good with plants.
9. The science lab was hoter this weak.
   The science lab was hotter this week.
10. My plant are the smallest one
    My plant is the smallest one.

Unit 3   A Weed Is a Flower   Daily Fix-It

DAILY FIX-IT

1. Jill rod a purple bike
   Jill rode a purple bike.

2. Rick put tap on his ankel.
   Rick put tape on his ankle.

3. I ate a puple grape
   I ate a purple grape.

4. Did you blow a buble?
   Did you blow a bubble?

5. ann made an aple pie.
   Ann made an apple pie.

6. do you like pie.
   Do you like pie?

7. Tom has a bunndle of books?
   Tom has a bundle of books.

8. i am able to write my nam.
   I am able to write my name.

9. Can jim play a buggle?
   Can Jim play a bugle?

10. the show made Me giggle.
    The show made me giggle.

DAILY FIX-IT

1. Mike stod on a huge rok.
   Mike stood on a huge rock.

2. put your cap on the hook
   Put your cap on the hook.

3. Dad cut to pieces of wod.
   Dad cut two pieces of wood.

4. my birthday is in july.
   My birthday is in July.

5. The cok made a pumpkin pie
   The cook made a pumpkin pie.

6. Do you like puding.
   Do you like pudding?

7. Did You put away your game.
   Did you put away your game?

8. brad shok my hand.
   Brad shook my hand.

9. The wogon is ful of pumpkins?
   The wogon is full of pumpkins.

10. The strong wind shok My car.
    The strong wind shook my car.

DAILY FIX-IT

1. the bride wore a white goun.
   The bride wore a white gown.

2. Dan rode a bus dontown
   Dan rode a bus downtown.

3. A grey mose ran up the clock
   A grey mouse ran up the clock.

4. Did you here that sound.
   Did you hear that sound?

5. The frog jumped on the grund
   The frog jumped on the ground.

6. Did max water the flouers?
   Did Max water the flowers?

7. Jed is tallest than lynn.
   Jed is taller than Lynn.

8. The birds flue soth.
   The birds flew south.

9. Mom bought a pound of aples
   Mom bought a pound of apples.

10. Did bill find the crown.
    Did Bill find the crown?

DAILY FIX-IT

1. I witsh i saw the fire truck.
   I wish I saw the fire truck.

2. Those trucks is red
   Those trucks are red.

3. The cherful boy worked quicklie.
   The cheerful boy worked quickly.

4. where is the fire!
   Where is the fire?

5. Fire Fighters use many rules.
   Firefighters use many tools.

6. They carries walkie-talkies
   They carry walkie-talkies.

7. Bill and i went skating
   Bill and I went skating.

8. We am not very gracefull.
   We are not very graceful.

9. Wee have weekly fire drils.
   We have weekly fire drills.

10. I thnk it is great idea.
    I think it is a great idea.

Unit 5   Firefighter!

DAILY FIX-IT

1. Dee wore a blew sweater
   Dee wore a blue sweater.

2. Who drue this picture.
   Who drew this picture?

3. we walk two the park.
   We walk to the park.

4. Did tom drink his juice.
   Did Tom drink his juice?

5. Sam is marys nephew.
   Sam is Mary's nephew.

6. A fact can be prove
   A fact can be proved.

7. The wind blue down a tree?
   The wind blew down a tree.

8. Did pam go home today
   Did Pam go home today?

9. Who spill grape joose on the rug?
   Who spilled grape juice on the rug?

10. Jed filled to bottle with water.
    Jed filled two bottles with water.

Unit 4   Helen Keller

DAILY FIX-IT

1. I wipd my hands on the cloh.
   I wiped my hands on the cloth.

2. the childrin yelled with joy.
   The children yelled with joy.

3. The coboy ride his horse fast.
   The cowboy rode his horse fast.

4. Did jill enjoy the show.
   Did Jill enjoy the show?

5. Did you here that noise.
   Did you hear that noise?

6. A wave destroy my sandcastle
   A wave destroyed my sandcastle.

7. a good friend is loial.
   A good friend is loyal.

8. Did dee make that sound.
   Did Dee make that sound?

9. Sam collect baseball cards
   Sam collects baseball cards.

10. Did your team win the gam.
    Did your team win the game?

Unit 4   I Like Where I Am

DAILY FIX-IT — 22

1. she will un lock the doors.
   She will unlock the doors.

2. She well unpack her groceries?
   She will unpack her groceries.

3. the movie was a reerun.
   The movie was a rerun.

4. She will unplug the Light.
   She will unplug the light.

5. Jamal herd a cat out side.
   Jamal heard a cat outside.

6. He unlocked the dor
   He unlocked the door.

7. Mom get a new bed for hour cat.
   Mom got a new bed for our cat.

8. The ole one was unsaif.
   The old one was unsafe.

9. The cat disappeared in the gras.
   The cat disappeared in the grass.

10. They was afraid of dog.
    It was afraid of the dog.

Unit 5 One Dark Night

© Pearson Education

Daily Fix-It **22**

DAILY FIX-IT — 23

1. the rong date is on the sign
   The wrong date is on the sign.

2. The lam scared the wren away?
   The lamb scared the wren away.

3. she will com the lamb's wool.
   She will comb the lamb's wool.

4. Then the nat bit the ren.
   The gnat bit the wren.

5. The sine said? "Training for dogs."
   The sign said, "Training for dogs."

6. What should i teach my dog.
   What should I teach my dog?

7. My cat chewwed my soks.
   My cat chewed my socks.

8. I wish me knew why?
   I wish I knew why.

9. My dog listen to Me.
   My dog listens to me.

10. Then I and Dad comb his hare.
    Then Dad and I comb his hair.

Unit 5 Bad Dog, Dodger!

© Pearson Education

Daily Fix-It **23**

DAILY FIX-IT — 24

1. It was her fawlt?
   It was her fault.

2. In august they will wak to school.
   In August they will walk to school.

3. I will rite a sine.
   I will write a sign.

4. He laffed on the fone.
   He laughed on the phone.

5. Her didn't play to day.
   She didn't play today.

6. She has an rough coufh.
   She has a rough cough.

7. Jamie and Marge has work too do.
   Jamie and Marge have work to do.

8. Will They work togeter?
   Will they work together?

9. My phriend call me on the phone.
   My friend called me on the phone.

10. Her made me lauff.
    She made me laugh.

Unit 5 Horace and Morris

© Pearson Education

Daily Fix-It **24**

DAILY FIX-IT

25

1. I have a foto of a dolfin.
   I have a photo of a dolphin.
2. it was tuff to take a picture.
   It was tough to take a picture.

3. It was a rough hike to the clif?
   It was a rough hike to the cliff.
4. The fone sounded phunny.
   The phone sounded funny.

5. bill played a joke on her.
   Bill played a joke on her.
6. She would'nt talk to he all day.
   She wouldn't talk to him all day.

7. The auto accident was he's fawlt.
   The auto accident was his fault.
8. He did n't read those sign.
   He didn't read the sign.

9. I useed chawk to draw a sign.
   I used chalk to draw a sign.
10. They goed the write way.
    They went the right way.

DAILY FIX-IT

26

1. i want to be an atlete.
   I want to be an athlete.
2. they're watching ken play
   They're watching Ken play.

3. The croud chears for me.
   The crowd cheers for me.
4. I raned Around the basis.
   I ran around the bases.

5. I thruw the ball to left feild.
   I threw the ball to left field.
6. the crowd cheerd for him.
   The crowd cheered for him.

7. We shou'ldve wun the game.
   We should've won the game.
8. We wouldv'e if w'ed scored!
   We would've if we'd scored!

9. We chear as Joe runs the baises.
   We cheer as Joe runs the bases.
10. Center feald is not home playte.
    Center field is not home plate.

DAILY FIX-IT

27

1. Hour flag has stars and strips.
   Our flag has stars and stripes.
2. We will cook diner for thanksgiving.
   We will cook dinner for Thanksgiving.

3. the flag stands for freedum.
   The flag stands for freedom.
4. Our fleg has stars and stripes.
   Our flag has stars and stripes.

5. some of the strippes are white.
   Some of the stripes are white.
6. People move to america
   People move to America.

7. america's birthday is July 4th.
   America's birthday is July 4th.
8. i painted sturs and stripes.
   I painted stars and stripes.

9. Our flagg has fifty stars?
   Our flag has fifty stars.
10. this is my eighth Birthday.
    This is my eighth birthday.

DAILY FIX-IT

28

1. My favorit aunt collects baskets?
   My favorite aunt collects baskets.
2. Where are we meeting? she asked.
   "Where are we meeting?" she asked.

3. Jordan collects baseball cards
   Jordan collects baseball cards.
4. My favrite aunt salls flowers.
   My favorite aunt sells flowers.

5. Aunt sue cullects dolls.
   Aunt Sue collects dolls.
6. Is that your favorite basket.
   Is that your favorite basket?

7. my aunt gave me a presint.
   My aunt gave me a present.
8. i gave hir my piggy bank.
   I gave her my piggy bank.

9. that was my favurite present.
   That was my favorite present.
10. i use a basket to collekt.
    I use a basket to collect.

Unit 6 Birthday Basket for Tia   Daily Fix-It **28**

© Pearson Education

DAILY FIX-IT

29

1. A hurd wandered the trails?
   A herd wandered the trails.
2. "We will visit dr. Hino today, Mom said.
   "We will visit Dr. Hino today," Mom said.

3. Were sitting by the camfire.
   We're sitting by the campfire.
4. The Cowboy rode the tails.
   The cowboy rode the trails.

5. How many cattel are in the herd.
   How many cattle are in the herd?
6. The Cowboy gallupped.
   The cowboy galloped.

7. We built a camp fire?
   We built a campfire.
8. did you see the herd of cattle.
   Did you see the herd of cattle?

9. Fore couboys sat around.
   Four cowboys sat around.
10. The horses gallopped away
    The horses galloped away.

Unit 6 Cowboys   Daily Fix-It **29**

© Pearson Education

DAILY FIX-IT

30

1. May i borrow your bell.
   May I borrow your bell?
2. It is february," Matt said.
   "It is February," Matt said.

3. Id like to borrw your drum.
   I'd like to borrow your drum.
4. Shake the sivler jingel bell.
   Shake the silver jingle bell.

5. The drumms were clatterin.
   The drums were clattering.
6. are the jingle bells silver?
   Are the jingle bells silver?

7. My voise craked last night.
   My voice cracked last night.
8. He playing the drom loudly.
   He played the drum loudly.

9. I cant hear your voise.
   I can't hear your voice.
10. May i borro your silver ring?
    May I borrow your silver ring?

Unit 6 Jingle Dancer   Daily Fix-It **30**

© Pearson Education

Differentiated Instruction and Extra Practice

LESSON 1 **Sentences**

Find the sentence. Write the sentence.

1. <u>Max is my dog.</u>   my dog
2. to the park   <u>We go to the park.</u>
3. <u>The squirrels see Max.</u>   the squirrels
4. <u>He barks at them.</u>   barks at them.
5. up the trees   <u>They run up the trees.</u>

LESSON 2 **Subjects**

Write each sentence. Underline the subject.

1. <u>A rocket</u> roars into the sky.
2. <u>The next stop</u> is the space station.
3. <u>Two astronauts</u> live there.
4. <u>They</u> need the supplies on the rocket.
5. <u>Food and water</u> are the most important things.

LESSON 3 **Predicates**

Write each sentence. Underline the predicate.

1. My grandpa <u>is a park ranger</u>.
2. Larry and I <u>visited him last summer</u>.
3. Rangers <u>take people on hikes</u>.
4. We <u>went on a hike with Grandpa</u>.
5. He <u>walks very fast</u>!

LESSON 4 **Statements and Questions**

Read each sentence. Write *S* if the sentence is a statement.
Write *Q* if the sentence is a question.

1. A desert is a dry place. S
2. Are deserts always hot? Q
3. Some deserts are cold. S
4. Do cactuses grow in cold deserts? Q
5. Cactuses grow only in hot deserts. S

LESSON 5 **Commands and Exclamations**

Write each sentence. Write *C* if the sentence is a command. Write *E* if it is an exclamation.

1. Buy a ticket to Paris. C
2. Pack a suitcase for a week. C
3. Please call a cab. C
4. This is so exciting! E
5. Wow, what a wonderful trip this will be! E

LESSON 6 Nouns

Write the noun in each sentence. Write *person, place, animal,* or *thing* to tell what the noun names.

1. The <u>lake</u> is big and blue. place
2. A <u>boat</u> sails by. thing
3. The <u>girl</u> is swimming. person
4. Her <u>dog</u> runs up and down. animal
5. The <u>sun</u> shines brightly. thing

LESSON 7 Proper Nouns

Write the two proper nouns in each sentence.

1. <u>Gwen Otis</u> is the pitcher for the <u>Lincoln Lions</u>.
2. Their first game is on <u>April</u> 18 with the <u>Harris Hawks</u>.
3. Their last game is in <u>October</u>, just after <u>Columbus Day</u>.
4. The players practice every <u>Tuesday</u> and <u>Thursday</u>.
5. Their coach, <u>Mr. Novak</u>, says they can win the <u>Central Division</u>.

LESSON 8 Singular and Plural Nouns

Add *-s* or *-es* to each singular noun. Write the plural noun.

1. fox foxes
2. cap caps
3. wagon wagons
4. gas gases
5. rabbit rabbits
6. star starts
7. peach peaches
8. dress dresses
9. kite kites
10. bush bushes

LESSON 9 Plural Nouns That Change Spelling

Choose the correct noun in ( ) to complete each sentence. Write the sentences.

1. Why do (<u>wolves</u>, wolfs) howl at night?
2. Do all (gooses, <u>geese</u>) fly south for the winter?
3. How many (<u>teeth</u>, tooths) do sharks have?
4. Why do (mouses, <u>mice</u>) have long, thin tails?
5. What kind of (<u>feet</u>, foots) do deer have?

LESSON 10 Possessive Nouns

Write the possessive noun in ( ) to complete each sentence.

1. What colors are a (<u>turkey's</u>, turkeys') feathers?
2. Most (turkey's, <u>turkeys'</u>) feathers are not colorful.
3. Are all (rabbit's, <u>rabbits'</u>) tails white?
4. That (<u>rabbit's</u>, rabbits') tail is brown.
5. Many (animal's, <u>animals'</u>) colors are a surprise.

LESSON 11   Verbs

Write the verb in each sentence.

1. Jen <u>helps</u> her mother with dinner.
2. She <u>sets</u> dishes on the table.
3. Mom <u>cooks</u> a stew on the stove.
4. She <u>pours</u> milk into glasses.
5. Jen and Mom <u>eat</u> dinner together.

LESSON 12   Verbs with Singular and Plural Nouns

Write the verb in ( ) that completes each sentence.

1. Clyde and Shona (finds, <u>find</u>) old magazines.
2. Shona (<u>looks</u>, look) for pictures of plants.
3. Clyde (<u>wants</u>, want) pictures of animals.
4. Dad (<u>cuts</u>, cut) out the pictures for them.
5. The children (pastes, <u>paste</u>) the pictures on paper.

LESSON 13   Verbs for Present, Past, and Future

Write the verb in each sentence. Write *N* if the verb tells about now. Write *P* if the verb tells about the past. Write *F* if the verb tells about the future.

1. Yesterday Rosa <u>cooked</u> ham and beans. **P**
2. Today Mom <u>heats</u> soup for lunch. **N**
3. Tomorrow the children <u>will want</u> sandwiches. **F**
4. Last week Dad <u>picked</u> fresh strawberries. **P**
5. Next week I <u>will bake</u> a pumpkin pie. **F**

LESSON 14   More About Verbs

Write the sentences. Use the verb in ( ) that completes the sentence.

1. Last year Jaime (walks, <u>walked</u>) to school.
2. Now he (<u>rides</u>, will ride) the bus.
3. In the future, he (<u>will drive</u>, drives) a car.
4. Yesterday Celia (waits, <u>waited</u>) for her mom.
5. Today Mom (picked, <u>picks</u>) Celia up at 3.

LESSON 15   *Am, Is, Are, Was,* and *Were*

Write the verb in ( ) that completes each sentence.

1. Alexander Graham Bell ___ an inventor. (<u>was</u>, were)
2. The telephone ___ one of his inventions. (<u>is</u>, are)
3. I ___ in a science museum. (<u>am</u>, is)
4. Many inventions ___ on display here. (is, <u>are</u>)
5. Some inventors' ideas ___ strange. (was, <u>were</u>)

LESSON 16 Adjectives and Our Senses

Write the adjective in each sentence that tells how something looks, sounds, tastes, feels, or smells.

1. Dad slices <u>juicy</u> peaches.
2. He sprinkles <u>brown</u> sugar on them.
3. The peaches cook in a <u>hot</u> pan.
4. Dad spreads them on <u>crisp</u> waffles.
5. I spoon up the <u>sweet</u> juice.

LESSON 17 Adjectives for Number, Size, and Shape

Write the adjective in each sentence. Then write *number, size,* or *shape* to tell what it describes.

1. First draw <u>four</u> pumpkins on paper. number
2. Next give them <u>two</u> eyes like triangles. number
3. Then make <u>large</u> mouths from side to side. size
4. Put <u>square</u> teeth inside them. shape
5. Finally, draw <u>long</u> lines from top to bottom. size

LESSON 18 Adjectives That Compare

Write the sentences. Circle adjectives that compare two things. Underline adjectives that compare three or more things.

1. The oak tree is (taller) than the pear tree.
2. Redwoods are the <u>tallest</u> trees of all.
3. Zinnias are (shorter) than sunflowers.
4. Violets are (smaller) than pansies.
5. Tea roses are <u>smallest</u> of all the roses.

LESSON 19 Adverbs That Tell When and Where

Write the adverb from each sentence. Write *when* if the adverb shows when. Write *where* if the adverb shows where.

1. The cab is waiting <u>outside</u>. where
2. <u>Soon</u> the plane will leave. when
3. Mom looks <u>everywhere</u> for Jim. where
4. He is <u>always</u> late. when
5. <u>Now</u> Mom and Jim must hurry. when

LESSON 20 Adverbs That Tell How

Write each sentence. Underline the adverb that tells how.

1. We were walking home <u>slowly</u>.
2. <u>Suddenly</u> the sky grew dark.
3. Lightning flashed <u>brightly</u>.
4. Rain fell <u>loudly</u>.
5. We ran <u>quickly</u> to Carla's house.

LESSON 21   **Pronouns**

Write the pronoun that can take the place of the underlined word or words.

1. Emma Hill is a vet in town.
    <u>She</u>   He   It

2. Ali and I help with the animals.
    They   <u>We</u>   You

3. Steve Fox is a firefighter.
    It   She   <u>He</u>

4. Fire trucks rush to a fire.
    <u>They</u>   You   We

5. A siren warns people.
    He   They   <u>It</u>

LESSON 22   **Pronouns for One and More Than One**

Write the sentences. Circle the pronouns that name only one.
Underline the pronouns that name more than one.

1. Every Saturday <u>we</u> visit Aunt Sophie and Uncle Bob.
2. <u>They</u> live in an apartment on Seventh Street.
3. (She) tells family stories.
4. (He) bakes a chicken pot pie.
5. (It) is always warm and delicious.

LESSON 23   **Using *I* and *Me***

Use *I* or *me* to complete each sentence. Write the sentences.

1. My dog Gloria and ___ are in a talent show.   I
2. Mom helps Gloria and ___ get ready.   me
3. Gloria and ___ perform our tricks for her.   I
4. Mom gives Gloria and ___ good advice.   me
5. Maybe Gloria and ___ will win a prize!   I

LESSON 24   **Different Kinds of Pronouns**

Write the pronoun in each sentence. Write *Subject* or *After action verb* to tell where it is used.

1. Paul tells <u>me</u> funny stories.   After action verb
2. <u>He</u> also knows many silly jokes.   Subject
3. Alison invited <u>him</u> to a party.   After action verb
4. <u>We</u> laughed at the stories and jokes.   Subject
5. <u>I</u> was happy for Paul.   Subject

LESSON 25   **Contractions**

Write the contraction that means the same as the underlined words.

1. Alex <u>does not</u> return his books on time.
    don't   didn't   <u>doesn't</u>

2. Susan <u>was not</u> quiet in the library.
    <u>wasn't</u>   weren't   wouldn't

3. They <u>are not</u> following the rules.
    <u>aren't</u>   can't   isn't

4. <u>She is</u> annoying other people.
    She'll   <u>She's</u>   He'll

5. <u>He will</u> pay a fine for every book.
    He's   <u>He'll</u>   She'll

LESSON 26 Using Capital Letters

Write the sentences. Use capital letters for the words in ( ).

1. Every year we have a party on (valentine's day).
2. The holiday is on (february) 14.
3. Next year the party will be on a (wednesday).
4. We always invite (mr.) and (mrs.) Chase.
5. The Kleins and (coach) Davis will come too.

LESSON 27 Quotation Marks

Write the sentences. Add quotation marks where they are needed.

1. "The bald eagle is a symbol of our country," said Ahmed.
2. Rebecca asked, "What animal would you choose?"
3. Jorge exclaimed, "The grizzly bear would be a great symbol!"
4. "Who picked the eagle?" asked Claire.
5. "The founders of our country chose it," replied Ms. Kupnik.

LESSON 28 Using Commas

Write the sentences. Add commas where needed. The number in ( ) tells how many commas are needed.

1. Grandpa was born on June 18, 1950. (1)
2. He has lived in Germany, England, and Japan. (2)
3. Now he lives in San Jose, California. (1)
4. He will arrive in Michigan on Thursday, December 20. (1)
5. Mom, Dad, Theresa, and I are counting the days. (3)

LESSON 29 Commas in Compound Sentences

Write each sentence. Add a comma where needed. Circle the connecting word.

1. Henry likes cowboy movies, (but) I don't.
2. I love space movies, (but) Henry doesn't.
3. Henry reads history books, (and) I read science fiction.
4. I look to the future, (and) Henry looks to the past.
5. We are different (but) we are still friends.

LESSON 30 The Paragraph

Write the sentences. Write *1*, *2*, *3*, *4*, or *5* after each sentence to show the correct order for a paragraph.

1. We eat every bit of Dad's wonderful turkey. 5
2. He puts his delicious stuffing inside the turkey. 2
3. Dad sets the golden brown turkey on the table. 4
4. Dad always makes our Thanksgiving turkey. 1
5. The stuffed turkey cooks in the oven for six hours. 3

Strategies and Activities
for Developing Writing Traits

Focus/Ideas

Stay on Topic Remind children that when they write about a topic, all their sentences should be about that topic. Write the paragraph below on the board. Ask children which sentence does not belong in the paragraph (*third sentence*) and why it does not belong. (*not on topic of egg hatching*)

> The hen lays an egg. Then she sits on the egg to keep it warm. *The rooster crows loudly.* The egg starts to hatch. A baby chick is trying to break out of the egg.

Good Reasons Ask children to write the name of an activity they like. Then have them list at least three reasons why they like that activity. Ask volunteers to read aloud their activities and reasons. Talk about which reasons are persuasive, which are not, and why.

> I like swimming because
> * it is good exercise. *(good)*
> * it is a year-round activity. *(good)*
> * I just do. *(not good)*

Group Story Help children create a group story. On chart paper, write a sentence that provides the idea for the story: *Flora is on her way to Uncle Bud's house.* Have each child add a sentence that elaborates on the idea. When all children have contributed, read aloud the whole story. Have children check to see that each sentence belongs in the story.

Organization

Steps in a Process Have pairs or small groups of children give oral reports about how to make or do something, such as a craft, recipe, game, or other simple activity. One partner can explain each step in order while the other partner demonstrates the step. Or partners can alternate explaining and demonstrating the steps.

Story of My Life Have children write important events in their lives in order from birth to today. They may have to ask parents or other family members for help so that they will have as many details as possible. Suggest that children organize the details on a time line. When they write their story, encourage them to use time-order words, such as *next, then,* and *later,* and dates to show the order of events.

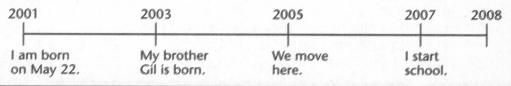

2001	2003	2005	2007	2008
I am born on May 22.	My brother Gil is born.	We move here.	I start school.	

Voice

Listen for Voice Read aloud paragraphs from works with very different voices, such as a humorous story and a science textbook. Ask children what the voice is in each work. If necessary, prompt them with questions: *Does the writer think the topic is funny? serious?* Have children match each work with the word that best describes its voice.

Add Voice On the board, write sentences with a weak voice, such as those below. Read aloud each sentence and ask children if they can tell how the writer feels about the topic. Have them help you rewrite the sentences so that each shows the writer's feelings.

I got a puppy.	*I love my new puppy!*
I went to a party.	*That was the most amazing party ever!*
It snowed.	*I rushed out and danced in the new snow.*
Jake can run.	*I wish I could run as fast as Jake.*

Word Choice

Signal Words Tell children that they can use certain words as signals to help their readers. Here are some signal words and what they can be used to do:

- To show time order: *first, next, then, last*
- To compare: *and, both, too*
- To contrast: *but, unlike*
- To persuade: *must, should, need, important, best, worst*

Have children look for these words in several passages and explain why each author used them.

Vivid Adjectives Remind children that vivid adjectives can make their writing lively and interesting. Write the sentences below on the board. Ask children to improve the sentences by changing the dull adjectives to vivid adjectives.

She is wearing a pretty scarf. *(red, colorful, long)*
I bought a nice sweater. *(warm, orange, fluffy)*
Can you suggest a good movie? *(funny, serious, scary)*
They complained about the bad road. *(rough, slick, narrow)*

Strong Verbs Each step in a how-to report tells about an action. Explain to children that using strong action verbs in the steps gives readers a clearer picture of what to do. Have children replace the weak verb Put in the sentences below with one of these strong verbs: *Glue, Sprinkle, Poke, Spread.*

Put one hole in each cup of dirt. *(Poke)*
Put the ends of the paper strip together. *(Glue)*
Put the newspaper on the table. *(Spread)*
Put glitter on the cardboard. *(Sprinkle)*

Sentences

Different Beginnings Tell children that together you will write a description of the classroom. Write a sentence on the board: *Our room has two windows.* Each child will add a sentence to the description, but each new sentence must begin with a different word: *The floor has green carpeting. Three walls are painted blue.* As you write each sentence, circle the beginning word.

Combine Sentences Have children combine pairs of short sentences using *and* or *but*. Remind them to add a comma to the compound sentence.

> Joe was on time. I was late. *(Joe was on time, but I was late.)*
> I broke a shoelace. I missed the bus. *(I broke a shoelace, and I missed the bus.)*

Point out that only short sentences with ideas that go together can be combined.

Conventions

Why Conventions? Show children that conventions are more than rules. They help make writing clear. Write the sentences below on the board.

> *Jenna Taylor Brad Logan and Kim ate grilled beef tacos cheese rolls roasted corn soup and lemonade at the fair.*
>
> *Jenna Taylor, Brad Logan, and Kim ate grilled beef tacos, cheese rolls, roasted corn soup, and lemonade at the fair.*
>
> *Jenna, Taylor, Brad, Logan, and Kim ate grilled beef, tacos, cheese, rolls, roasted corn, soup, and lemonade at the fair.*

Read each sentence aloud and ask children how many people went to the fair and how many different foods they ate. Point out that changing the punctuation changes the meaning of the sentence.

Use a Checklist Explain to children that a checklist can help them look for errors in their writing. Make a list of appropriate questions about spelling, capitalization, and punctuation, such as those below. Distribute copies of the list to children.

- Does every sentence have a subject and a verb?
- Have I used correct verbs with singular and plural nouns?
- Are all words spelled correctly?

Proofread Your Work Remind children that they should check their writing for errors in spelling, capitalization, and punctuation. Here are a few strategies they can use when they proofread.

- Read their work aloud. Sometimes it is easier to hear errors.
- Read their work several times. Look for one kind of error—spelling, punctuation, capitalization—each time.
- Place a ruler or an index card under each line of text.

Prompts

Narrative Writing

Think of a time when you helped someone. What did you do? How did you feel? Write a story that tells what happened.

Key Features
Story About Me

- Focuses on one incident or event in the storyteller's life
- Uses I, me, and my
- Has a beginning, middle, and end
- Gives details that make the event vivid

Descriptive Writing

Describe the kind of weather you like best. Tell what it looks, sounds, smells, and feels like. Use exact nouns, vivid adjectives, and strong verbs.

Key Features
Description

- Creates a word picture of the person, place, or thing
- Uses words that appeal to the senses
- Elaborates with strong details

Persuasive Writing

You want to do an activity with a friend. Write a letter to your friend. Persuade him or her to do this activity with you. Give at least three good reasons.

Key Features
Persuasive Letter

- Is written in correct letter format
- Uses persuasive words such as *must* or *best*
- Uses reasons, facts, and examples to make a point
- Often organizes facts in order of importance

Expository Writing

Think of something you do every day, such as get dressed or brush your teeth. Write a report that tells the steps for doing this task.

Key Features
How-to Report

- Explains a task fully
- Uses words such as first to show the order of the steps
- Gives necessary information and details
- Has clear sentences to guide readers

Choose two animals you might see at a zoo, such as a lion and an elephant. Write about how these two animals are alike and different.

Key Features
Compare/Contrast Essay

- Compares and contrasts two things
- Uses transition words and details to show likenesses and differences
- Follows a pattern of organization
- Has a clear topic sentence

Narrative Writing Rubric

Rubric	6	5	4	3	2	1
Focus/Ideas	Excellent, focused narrative; many details	Good, focused narrative; sufficient details	Focused narrative; adequate details	Fairly focused narrative; several details	Often unfocused narrative; needs more details	Narrative with no development, focus, or details
Organization/ Paragraphs	Clear sequence of events with time-order words	Mostly clear sequence with some time-order words	Generally clear sequence with one or two time-order words	Fairly clear sequence with some lapses	Confused sequence of events	Incoherent or nonexistent sequence
Voice	Sincere, engaging, and unique voice	Generally sincere and engaging	Pleasant voice but not compelling or unique	Sincere but not engaging or original	No clear, original voice	Uninvolved or indifferent voice
Word Choice	Many vivid descriptive words that show instead of tell	Some vivid words that show instead of tell	Several vivid words that show instead of tell	Tries to use one or two vivid words that show instead of tell	Few vivid words that show instead of tell	No attempt to show instead of tell
Sentences	Clear and varied sentences.	Mostly clear sentences with some variety	Generally clear sentences; tries for variety	Some sentences unclear; needs more variety	Many sentences unclear; little or no variety	Incoherent or short, choppy sentences
Conventions	Few, if any, errors	Several minor errors	Some errors	Several major errors	Many errors	Numerous errors

Rubric	5	4	3	2	1
Focus/Ideas	Excellent, focused narrative; many details	Good, focused narrative; sufficient details	Focused narrative; adequate details	Often unfocused narrative; needs more details	Narrative with no development, focus, or details
Organization/ Paragraphs	Clear sequence of events with time-order words	Mostly clear sequence with some time-order words	Generally clear sequence with one or two time-order words	Confused sequence of events	Incoherent or nonexistent sequence
Voice	Sincere, engaging, and unique voice	Generally sincere and engaging	Pleasant voice but not compelling or unique	No clear, original voice	Uninvolved or indifferent voice
Word Choice	Many vivid descriptive words that show instead of tell	Some vivid words that show instead of tell	Several vivid words that show instead of tell	Few vivid words that show instead of tell	No attempt to show instead of tell
Sentences	Clear, varied sentences	Mostly clear sentences with some variety	Generally clear sentences with some variety	Some sentences unclear; little or no variety	Incoherent or short, choppy sentences
Conventions	Few, if any, errors	Several minor errors	Some errors	Many errors	Numerous errors

Rubric	4	3	2	1
Focus/Ideas	Excellent, focused narrative; many details	Good, focused narrative; sufficient details	Often unfocused narrative; needs more details	Narrative with no development, focus, or details
Organization/ Paragraphs	Clear sequence of events with time-order words	Reasonably clear sequence with one or two lapses	Confused sequence of events	Incoherent or nonexistent sequence
Voice	Sincere, engaging, and unique voice	Generally sincere and engaging	No clear, original voice	Uninvolved or indifferent voice
Word Choice	Many vivid descriptive words that show instead of tell	Some vivid words that show instead of tell	Few vivid words that show instead of tell	No attempt to show instead of tell
Sentences	Clear, varied sentences	Generally clear sentences with some variety	Some sentences unclear; little or no variety	Incoherent or short, choppy sentences
Conventions	Few, if any, errors	Several minor errors	Many errors	Numerous errors

Descriptive Writing Rubric

Rubric	6	5	4	3	2	1
Focus/Ideas	Excellent, focused description; many strong, vivid details	Good, focused description; some good, vivid details	Description focused; some good details	Description generally focused; some details	Description not always focused; needs more vivid details	Description not focused; no vivid details
Organization/ Paragraphs	Topic introduced at beginning; details in sequence	Topic introduced at beginning; details mostly in sequence	Topic stated; details generally in order	Topic not stated at beginning; some details out of order	Topic not introduced at beginning; details confused	Topic not introduced; no order to details
Voice	Clearly shows feelings about topic	Shows some feelings about topic	Shows interest in topic	Tries to show interest in topic	Shows few or no feelings about topic	Not involved with topic
Word Choice	Many vivid sensory words and strong verbs	Some vivid sensory words and strong verbs	Several sensory words or strong verbs	One or two sensory words or strong verbs	Few sensory words or strong verbs	No sensory words or strong verbs
Sentences	Smooth sentences; different kinds	Most sentences smooth; some different kinds	Sentences generally smooth; some variety	Several stringy or choppy sentences; little variety	Many stringy or choppy sentences	Confusing, incomplete, or choppy sentences
Conventions	Few or no errors	No serious errors	Some errors	Some serious errors	Many errors	Many serious errors

Rubric	5	4	3	2	1
Focus/Ideas	Excellent, focused description; many strong, vivid details	Good, focused description; some good, vivid details	Description focused; some good details	Description not always focused; needs more vivid details	Description not focused; no vivid details
Organization/ Paragraphs	Topic introduced at beginning; details in sequence	Topic introduced at beginning; details mostly in sequence	Topic stated; details generally in order	Topic not introduced at beginning; details confused	Topic not introduced; no order to details
Voice	Clearly shows feelings about topic	Shows some feelings about topic	Shows interest in topic	Shows few or no feelings about topic	Not involved with topic
Word Choice	Many vivid sensory words and strong verbs	Some vivid sensory words and strong verbs	Several sensory words or strong verbs	Few sensory words or strong verbs	No sensory words or strong verbs
Sentences	Smooth sentences; different kinds	Most sentences smooth; some different kinds	Sentences generally smooth; some variety	Many stringy or choppy sentences	Confusing, incomplete, or choppy sentences
Conventions	Few or no errors	No serious errors	Some errors	Many errors	Many serious errors

Rubric	4	3	2	1
Focus/Ideas	Excellent, focused description; many strong, vivid details	Good, focused description; some good, vivid details	Description not always focused; needs more vivid details	Description not focused; no vivid details
Organization/ Paragraphs	Topic introduced at beginning; details in sequence	Topic introduced at beginning; details mostly in sequence	Topic not introduced at beginning; details confused	Topic not introduced; no order to details
Voice	Clearly shows feelings about topic	Shows some feelings about topic	Shows few or no feelings about topic	Not involved with topic
Word Choice	Many vivid sensory words and strong verbs	Some vivid sensory words and strong verbs	Few sensory words or strong verbs	No sensory words or strong verbs
Sentences	Smooth sentences; different kinds	Most sentences smooth; some different kinds	Many stringy or choppy sentences	Confusing, incomplete, or choppy sentences
Conventions	Few or no errors	No serious errors	Many errors	Many serious errors

Persuasive Writing Rubric

Rubric	6	5	4	3	2	1
Focus/Ideas	Well-focused argument with clear, well-developed details	Focused argument with clear details	Generally focused argument; details with some support	Argument with few lapses in focus; details attempted	Argument lacking focus; unclear details	Argument with no focus; no clear details
Organization/ Paragraphs	Excellent organization and supporting reasons	Good organization and supporting reasons	Adequate organization and supporting reasons	Some organization and support attempted	Not very organized; few supporting reasons	No organization or supporting reasons
Voice	Convincing, compelling voice	Clear, usually convincing voice	Pleasant but not compelling voice	Sincere but not fully engaged writer	Unconvincing voice	No distinct voice
Word Choice	Uses strong persuasive words well	Uses many persuasive words	Some persuasive words	Words with little persuasive power	Few persuasive words	No persuasive words
Sentences	Correct sentences; varied lengths	Correct, usually varied sentences	Correct sentences; some variety	Overly simple sentences; no variety	Some sentences incorrect	Incorrect sentences; run-ons
Conventions	Few, if any, errors	Several minor errors	Few serious errors	Some errors that confuse	Many errors	Numerous errors

Rubric	5	4	3	2	1
Focus/Ideas	Well-focused argument with clear, well-developed details	Generally focused argument with clear details	Argument with few lapses in focus; generally clear details	Argument lacking focus; unclear details	Argument with no focus; no clear details
Organization/ Paragraphs	Excellent organization and supporting reasons	Good organization and supporting reasons	Adequate organization and supporting reasons	Not very organized; few supporting reasons	No organization or supporting reasons
Voice	Convincing, compelling voice	Clear, usually convincing voice	Pleasant but not compelling voice	Unconvincing voice	No distinct voice
Word Choice	Uses strong persuasive words well	Uses many persuasive words	Some persuasive words	Few persuasive words	No persuasive words
Sentences	Correct sentences; varied lengths	Correct, usually varied sentences	Correct sentences with some variety	Some sentences incorrect	Incorrect sentences; run-ons
Conventions	Few, if any, errors	Several minor errors	Few confusing errors	Many errors	Numerous errors

Rubric	4	3	2	1
Focus/Ideas	Well-focused argument with clear, well-developed details	Generally focused argument with clear details	Argument lacking focus; unclear details	Argument with no focus; no clear details
Organization/ Paragraphs	Excellent organization and supporting reasons	Good organization and supporting reasons	Not very organized; few supporting reasons	No organization or supporting reasons
Voice	Convincing, compelling voice	Clear, usually convincing voice	Unconvincing voice	No distinct voice
Word Choice	Uses strong persuasive words well	Uses many persuasive words	Few persuasive words	No persuasive words
Sentences	Correct sentences; varied lengths	Correct, usually varied sentences	Some sentences incorrect	Incorrect sentences; run-ons
Conventions	Few, if any, errors	Several minor errors	Many errors	Numerous errors

Expository Writing Rubric

Rubric	6	5	4	3	2	1
Focus/Ideas	Exposition with strong focus on topic	Exposition with good focus on topic	Exposition generally focused	Exposition sometimes unfocused	Exposition with weak focus	Exposition with no focus
Organization/ Paragraphs	Strong topic sentences; many supporting details	Good topic sentences; enough supporting details	Adequate topic sentences; some supporting details	Some weak topic sentences; needs more supporting details	Missing some topic sentences and details	No topic sentences; few supporting details
Voice	Strongly interested, informed voice	Interested, informed voice	Voice generally interested, informed	Voice somewhat interested	Vaguely interested voice	Uninterested or uninformed voice
Word Choice	Many vivid, precise words used effectively	Vivid, precise words used well	Some vivid, precise words	One or two vivid, precise words	Few vivid, precise words	No vivid, precise words
Sentences	Clear and varied sentences	Mostly clear sentences; good variety	Generally clear sentences; some variety	Sentences not always clear; needs more variety	Some unclear sentences; little variety	Incoherent sentences; no variety
Conventions	Few, if any, errors	Several minor errors	Some errors	A few errors	Several errors	Numerous errors

Rubric	5	4	3	2	1
Focus/Ideas	Exposition with strong focus on topic	Exposition with good focus on topic	Exposition generally focused	Exposition with weak focus	Exposition with no focus
Organization/ Paragraphs	Strong topic sentences; many supporting details	Good topic sentences; enough supporting details	Adequate topic sentences; some supporting details	Missing some topic sentences and details	No topic sentences; few supporting details
Voice	Strongly interested, informed voice	Interested, informed voice	Voice generally interested, informed	Vaguely interested voice	Uninterested or uninformed voice
Word Choice	Many vivid, precise words used effectively	Vivid, precise words used well	Some vivid, precise words	Few vivid, precise words	No vivid, precise words
Sentences	Clear, varied sentences	Mostly clear sentences; good variety	Generally clear sentences; some variety	Some unclear sentences; little variety	Incoherent sentences; no variety
Conventions	Few, if any, errors	Several minor errors	Some errors	Several errors	Numerous errors

Rubric	4	3	2	1
Focus/Ideas	Exposition with strong focus on topic	Exposition generally focused on topic	Exposition that needs sharper focus	Exposition with no focus
Organization/ Paragraphs	Strong topic sentences; many supporting details	Good topic sentences; some supporting details	Missing some topic sentences and details	No topic sentences; few supporting details
Voice	Strongly interested, informed voice	Interested, informed voice	Vaguely interested voice	Uninterested or uninformed voice
Word Choice	Many vivid, precise words	Some vivid, precise words	Few vivid, precise words	No vivid, precise words
Sentences	Clear, varied sentences	Mostly clear sentences; some variety	Some unclear sentences; little variety	Incoherent sentences; no variety
Conventions	Few, if any, errors	Several minor errors	Several errors	Numerous errors

Self-Evaluation Guide

Name _____

Name of Writing Product _____

Directions Review your final draft. Then rate yourself on a scale from 4 to 1 (4 is the highest) on each writing trait. After you fill out the chart, answer the questions.

Writing Traits	4	3	2	1
Focus/Ideas				
Organization/Paragraphs				
Voice				
Word Choice				
Sentences				
Conventions				

1. What is the best part of this piece of writing? Why do you think so?

_____

_____

_____

_____

2. Write one thing you would change about this piece of writing if you had the chance to write it again.

_____

_____

_____

Self-Evaluation Guide

Name _____

Name of Writing Product _____

Directions Review your final draft. Then rate yourself on each writing feature. After you fill out the chart, answer the questions.

Features

	4	3	2	1
Focus				
Organization				
Support and Elaboration				
Style				

	2	1	0
Conventions			

1. What is the strongest part? Why do you think it is good?

_____

_____

_____

_____

_____

2. What would you change about this piece of writing if you had the chance to write it again? Elaborate on one change you would make.

_____

_____

_____

_____

_____

Title

Characters

Problem

Beginning _____
_____
_____

Middle _____
_____
_____

End _____
_____
_____

Solution

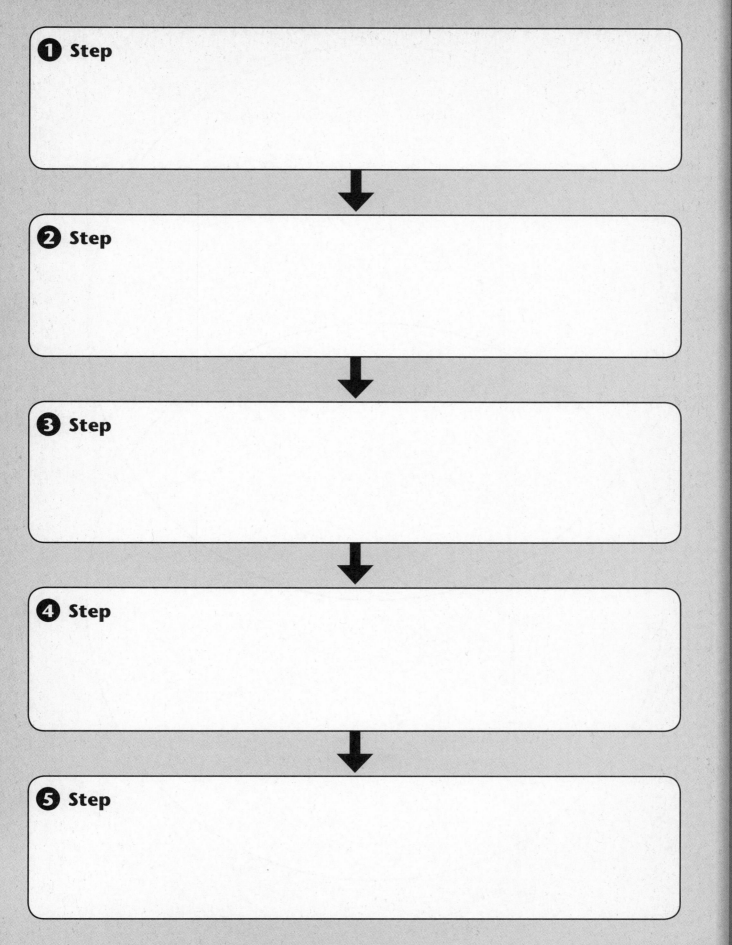

1 Step

2 Step

3 Step

4 Step

5 Step

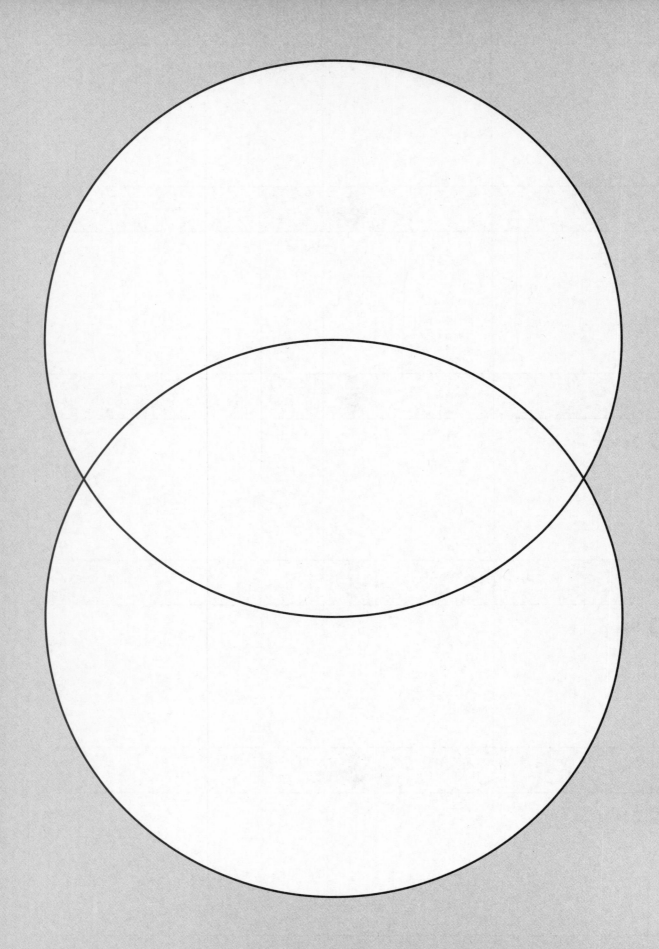

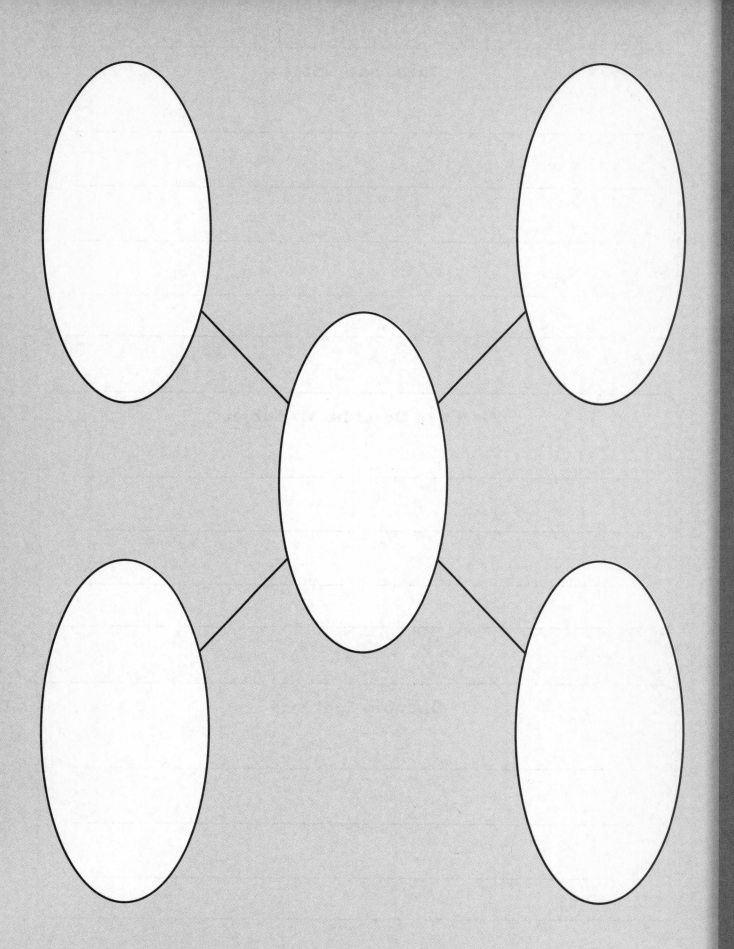

Ideas and Notes

_____

_____

_____

_____

Words to Describe My Subject

_____   _____

_____   _____

_____   _____

Opening Sentence

_____

_____

_____

Answer Key

Page 7 Possible answer

Anyone can learn to swing in the playground. First, sit in the swing and get comfortable. Second, push off from the ground with your feet. Then pump your legs back and forth. Pump in rhythm as you go back and forth. Finally, stop pumping when you are ready to stop.

Page 11 Possible answer

When I do chores, I make more work for everyone. Do you think dusting is easy? Well, when I do it, things somehow fall and break. Helping to cook is no better. Who knew the tomato sauce would spray all over the walls? Now my parents are afraid to ask me to do anything. But that's not so bad, is it?

Page 15 Possible answer

The tulip is a colorful sign of spring. The flower is shaped like a little cup made out of soft petals. It looks perky and cheerful on its long, skinny stem.

Page 19 Answers

Exercise B

4. Each year the family goes to the beach.

5. In June the seashore gets very crowded.

6. This summer the dog will come too.

Exercise C

Last Sunday my family visited the dinosaur museum. We took the train downtown, and then we took a bus to the museum. The dinosaur displays were awesome!

Page 23 Possible answer

On a rainy day, it is fun to watch a video. You can sit on the couch with your friends. While you watch, you can eat popcorn.

Page 54 Possible answer

I had to play "Tulips" for a recital. My heart was pounding when I walked to the piano. Then I took a deep breath and started. The next thing I knew I was done.

Page 60 Possible answer

A bright full moon rose in the sky. The dark shadows on its surface looked like a person's face. The strange eyes were looking right at me!

Page 66 Possible answer

We planted a garden in the backyard last summer. Dad dug up the hard ground. Mom made little holes and dropped several seeds into each one. I covered the tiny seeds with a layer of dirt. Janet watered the seeds with the hose.

Page 90 Possible answer

When you bake cookies with your mom or dad, do these things. Be sure the oven is hot enough. Use a teaspoon to scoop up a ball of dough. Put the balls of dough on a cookie sheet. Check the cookies as they bake.

Page 96 Possible answer

First, go to soccer practice on Saturday morning.
Next, buy a birthday present for Mom at the mall.
Then, send an e-mail to Beth about our science project.
Later, practice the piano before my lesson on Monday.

Page 102 Possible answer

Aunt Celia and Uncle Tito both came from Mexico. They both live at my house. Aunt Celia is a tall, thin woman. Uncle Tito is a short, round man. Uncle Tito tells great stories. Aunt Celia is a good listener.

Page 108 Possible answer

Hey, Krista,

Let's go see a movie on Sunday. *Ghouls' Night Out* is playing at the Cineplex East. The first show is at 4:00 P.M. I'll meet you outside the theater at 3:45.

Denise

Page 126 Possible answer

Last Saturday I went to my friend Ben's house. Guess how many video games he has. On Sunday I visited Grandma Mary. I love her banana muffins!

Page 150 Possible answer

The hot sun shines in a clear blue sky. The air smells warm and dusty. The flowers are wilting. Bees buzz around them.

Page 168 Possible answer

My favorite season is summer. The days are long and hot. I can go to the pool, ride my bike, or play outside. My cousins visit us, or we go to see them. Best of all, there is no school!

Page 180 Possible answer

Dear Dad,

I think we should go to Florida for spring break. We need a break from winter! Florida would be the best place to go for warm, sunny weather. Also, we could visit Aunt Zelda.

Your son,
Josh

Page 186 Possible answer

Dear Uncle George,

Thank you for the gift card. I plan to use it to buy books about animals in Africa. They are my favorite kind of book. I hope I see you soon.

Love,
Audra

Page 192 Possible answer

I saw a black button on the floor. I leaned down to pick it up. Then I discovered that it wasn't a button. It was a big, black beetle! I screamed, dropped it, and ran away. Who knows where the beetle went?

Page 195 Possible answers

7. You'll never make friends if you talk too much.

8. Don't try to act smarter than other people.

9. You shouldn't borrow things without asking.

10. If you're angry with your friends, politely tell them why.

11. You can't break your promises.

12. I've followed these rules, and I do fine!

Page 198 Possible answer

A Long Way Out

I was out in the ocean two miles from shore. Why? My family was snorkeling near a reef. It was my first time. I was scared, but I forgot about that when I saw the hundreds of colorful fish.

Page 204 Possible answer

Tag is an easy game to play. One player is chosen to be "it." "It" chases the other players. They run away. When "it" touches another player, that person becomes "it."

Page 210 Possible answer

On Thanksgiving Day a wonderful parade takes place in New York City. We watch it every year on TV. Huge balloons, marching bands, and floats pass by. Someday I want to go to New York and see this parade.

Page 213 Possible answers

6. 125 Easton Lane
   Boca Raton, FL 33432

7. May 15, 2010

8. Dear Koshi,

9. The picnic was fun. I liked swinging, running, and playing games with you. I liked meeting your mom, dad, and brothers. Write me back.

10. Your friend,
    Louisa

Page 225 Possible answer

Our whole family likes going to the talent show. First we look around for seats. Then we sit and watch the show. Afterwards, we always have a meal with our friends.

Page 227 Answer

Grandpa makes wonderful things. Right now he is making a wooden yo-yo. Tomorrow he will build a wagon. Next week he plans to make a drum.

Page 228 Possible answer

On St. Patrick's Day my dad fixes a dinner of corned beef, boiled potatoes, and cabbage. Dad makes his own corned beef. When it is cooking, you can smell it all over the house. You can also hear Dad singing "Danny Boy."